MOMENTS

The Life and Career of a Texas Newsman

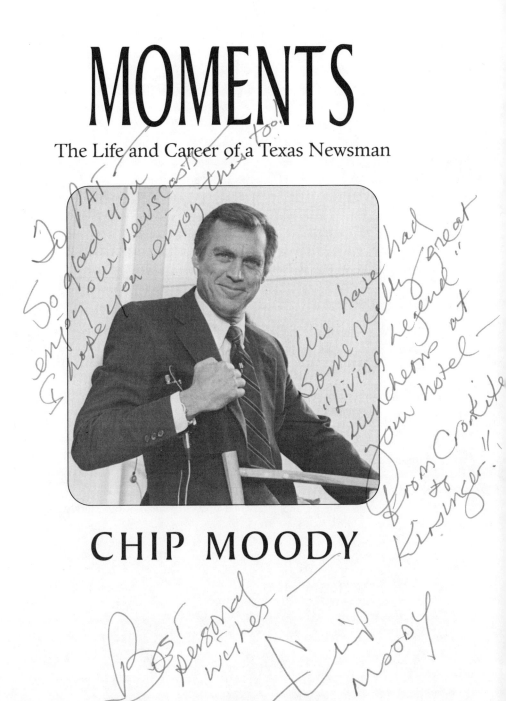

CHIP MOODY

To PAT —
So glad you
enjoy our newscasts too!
I hope you enjoy these too!

We have had
some really great
"Living Legend"
luncheons at
your hotel —
from Cronkite
to Kissinger!!

Best
Personal
wishes —

Chip Moody

DEC 1997

TAYLOR PUBLISHING COMPANY
Dallas, Texas

Published by Taylor Publishing Company
1550 West Mockingbird Lane
Dallas, Texas 75235

Library of Congress Cataloging-in-Publication Data

Moody, Chip.
    Moments : the life and career of a Texas newsman / Chip Moody.
      p.   cm.
    ISBN 0-87833-895-0
    1. Moody, Chip.   2. Television journalists—Texas—Biography.
  I. Title.
PN4874.M5815M66   1995
070'.92—dc20
[B]   95-35286
                                    CIP

Published in the United States of America

10   9   8   7   6   5   4

This book has been printed on acid-free recycled paper.

I would like to acknowledge the special place in my life held by my wonderful parents, Bob and Darlene Moody, my loving wife Vikki, and my two children, Trae and Tiffin, who have all supported and loved me through thick and thin.

But I also want to include in this dedication people who are wrestling with a serious illness—especially those who are confined to a hospital. I've been there, and over the years, thousands and thousands of TV viewers have written me get-well cards and letters. It has been a humbling experience to hear from so many people I have never met in person. As much as I would like to, it has been virtually impossible to respond to all of these well-wishers.

So this book is to return that favor in a small way to all those who wrote me, and to send my best wishes to those fighting illness and pain. Chin up . . . and do your best to be optimistic!

Credits

Written, Directed, and Produced by Chip Moody

Executive Producer	Ed Danko
Publishing Producer	Lynn Brooks
Managing Editor	Jayne Noble
Senior Editor	Holly McGuire
Sales Director	Jim Green
Art Director	Carol Trammel
Publicity Director	Anita Edson

Foreword Written and Produced by Tracy Rowlett

Table of Contents

A Dedication to William Bonney

Poetry assignment by Chip Moody, 10th grade, 1963

He came in one day, all dressed in black . . .
A tall, lean figure in his dark, dusty hat.
He rode tall and easy, his gun at his side . . .
You could tell at a glance from him you'd keep wide.

There were 19 notches upon that gun,
For there wasn't a fight he hadn't won.
He'd won fights in Texas, he'd won fights in Dodge,
He'd won fights wherever he chose to lodge.
This man was a killer, while merely a boy . . .
His hands were quick, his gun their toy.

Into the town rode Ranger Dale Long, a straight strong
build on his pony gray . . .
And Ranger Long knew that this was the day.
A day of death, or a day to smile,
Now both these men would "walk the mile."

High noon was the time for both to meet . . .
And both walked slowly onto the street.
With silence and hate reigning high,
Two lonely vultures roamed the sky.

It was over in a second, this duel between men . . .
And out strode the kid, with notches twice ten.
Although at infamy he did bid . . .
This is dedicated to "Billy the Kid."

Preface

OVER THE YEARS, MANY FRIENDS AND acquaintances have encouraged me to tell the story about my fight against cancer. I've thought about doing that on and off for a long time. But then I decided I really didn't want to make a long story about this big fight against cancer, about how I was one of the lucky ones who came through the treatment. Although I thought my story might make a very hopeful and uplifting book and could perhaps give other patients insight into what they are facing, I figured there were already a number of books like that out there and that my story was not that unique.

But since I am in the public eye, I was urged to write my story. And since I wanted to do something for patients who are now fighting illness or who have friends or relatives who did not live through their experience with cancer, I thought a book might be somewhat encouraging. When I decided to write this book, one very young girl by the name of Megan Mills came to mind—she was a cancer victim who didn't make it. I was one of the lucky ones, and that's why I dedicated this effort to people, like her, who didn't win the battle. Maybe this is one more way I can help kids like Megan. That's also the reason I've been raising money for cancer research for children over the years with the American Cancer Society, the Leukemia Society, the Children's Cancer Fund of Dallas, Children's Medical Center in Dallas, and MD Anderson Cancer Center in Houston.

But instead of just telling the cancer story, I thought I could also include a lot of the different anecdotes that people may find interesting—stories from my everyday life and about people I have met through

1

the years. I'm hoping to do a couple of things here: entertain you with private aspects of my life (and maybe provoke some chuckles), and at the same time raise some money for seriously ill children.

Under the umbrella of the Children's Medical Center, I am honored to have a fund and endowment created in my name for the specific purpose of helping deserving patients and their families. So, our efforts now are channeled into the The Chip Moody Child Care Fund and Endowment for the Children's Medical Center—with a direct impact on the lives of these individuals. Part of the proceeds from this book are dedicated to this fund and the patients who benefit from it.

When Augustus McCrae, in Larry McMurtry's *Lonesome Dove*, was on his deathbed, he told his buddy Captain Call that it had been "one hell of a party, one hell of a ride." Well, I'm hopefully a long time from my deathbed, and in my forty-eight years, this has indeed been "one hell of a ride," mostly due to the interesting experiences I've had. If the Good Lord agrees, I'm a long way off from folding my cards and cashing in my chips!

Chip
Moody

Foreword

―――――

Tracy Rowlett

W<small>HEN</small> I <small>WAS FIRST ASKED TO WRITE</small>
the foreword for this book, I must admit to several conflicting reactions.
First, of course, I was flattered. Chip and I have been competitors and
friends for many years, but neither has ever asked the other for honest
comment or anything bordering on introspection. To be so honest
invites criticism, an item we probably don't deal with all that well anyway, but especially from a peer, and particularly from each other.

Then, there's the problem with how far to go. Just how much should
I say about Chip in my efforts to be honest and insightful? We have
known each other too long not to know a few secrets, things usually left
better unsaid, unless one is commenting for posterity and casting all personal caution to the breezes. Is this a kiss and tell book? I wondered.

But most importantly, I risked exposing something vulnerable in me.
There is often a sharp edge to the humor Chip and I share, a bite to our
jokes that are meant to keep us humble and aware of our many short-
comings as well as those of the business we are in. To speak honestly
about Chip in these few paragraphs would be to drop my guard so that I
might let you—and him—know how I really feel. It's risky.

Thus exposed, here we go:

*Chip and I are at Las Colinas—Marvin Hamlisch is entertaining a gathering
of well-heeled North Texans for a charity event. At the last minute, Chip is
asked to introduce Marvin. He grabs at his pockets for writing materials and
begins to scribble some notes. When the time comes, Chip steps on stage and
reads his hastily crafted Hamlisch introduction. The crowd laughs and giggles
throughout the introduction and after it is over, Chip crows to me about his*

success. "That's not what they were reacting to," I told him. "They were amused at your choice of a writing tablet." *Chip had written his notes for the impromptu, off-the-cuff introduction on the backs of many pictures—all of himself. He carries them around in his coat so he can sign them and hand them out to his fans. As he read the Hamlisch introduction, the audience saw picture after picture of Chip.*

Chip Moody is an anchorman. Whatever else he may be, he is first and always a television personality. More than anyone I know in this business, Chip enjoys the trappings of the job. He loves meeting the public and pressing the flesh and never have I heard him complain (as the rest of us do) about the times when one must surrender some privacy. There is nothing Chip loves more than being recognized and praised and enjoyed. So, while others might shrink from the obvious ego display associated with carrying and signing photographs, there is no such false modesty in Chip.

Now, if it all stopped with just ego, it would not be something worth mentioning, since everyone I know in communications has tremendous ego. But it is the gregarious nature of Chip's personality that makes this display so downright seductive. Darned if I haven't found myself in awe of just how genuine it all is. Chip really likes people. It's not a front. And it just naturally follows that Chip likes Chip. And, with Chip, it's okay. If some of that ego creeps into this book, as I'm sure it will, just remember that Chip Moody loves the spotlight and his is brighter than most. But he is never insincere or mean-spirited or so self-centered that he can't react to others.

Since only an incomplete wall separates my small office cubicle from Chip's, I hear his telephone ring and I hear his cheery salutation: "Chip Moody here..." But soon his voice becomes somber and controlled. He listens and speaks earnestly and with compassion. It's another call from either someone suffering from cancer, or a loved one of a cancer patient. Chip doesn't hurry the conversation, but lets the caller run through a laundry list of feelings. Chip knows. He's been there. He's been afraid, too. He wants to help and does, more by listening than by giving advice, although, when asked, he can do that, too.

I don't know what I would do if told I had cancer. It seems to me that none of us can truly know just how bravely we might face our own mortality until such a time comes. Being the multi-faceted killer it is, cancer now strikes one in three Americans, we are told. Clearly most of us will feel its devastation at some time in our lives, either as victims or relatives of victims. Chip has been both. Even at this writing, as Chip's Hodgkin's disease is in remission—as are the cancers of his father, sister, and a brother—Chip has just learned that his mother has a medium-sized cancerous tumor in one lung.

Bravery isn't always heroic. Sometimes it is just a matter of facing what life deals us and doing the best we can to rise above our own fears. I know Chip has had his dark moments because he has told me about them, about those times when he has been terribly afraid and felt isolated and alone, about waking in the middle of the night, sweating, realizing he had been shouting in his sleep. But those things are never cowardice, not in my eyes. They are only an understandably human reaction to horrific events. I think it is that knowledge of the fearful that gives Chip his compassion and the ability to share knowingly with others just heading down that darkest of paths.

I have also seen Chip's courage up close and I am always amazed and impressed. I have visited Chip in the hospital when he's been tubed and raw from surgery, still smiling, bigger than life, optimistic and, at worst, sort of bored with it all. He rarely complains or feels sorry for himself.

It's 1979 and I'm in the hospital. After starting the 6 p.m. news one evening, I suddenly choke on air, coughing uncontrollably and am forced to leave the set. A friend drives me to the hospital, where my blood pressure is checked and is soaring. My doctor is called and I'm admitted for observation and tests. I hate hospitals and am depressed, refusing to take calls. It's only when my health is restored and I'm back at work that I learn that one of my most consistent callers and well-wishers was Chip, who at the time was a competing anchor working at Channel 5.

This happened before the onset of Chip's Hodgkin's disease. We knew each other, but not well, and in terms of our battle for ratings we saw each other as professional enemies. It was my first insight into the personal side of someone with whom I had been warring since 1974.

It didn't take cancer to give Chip his ability to reach out to others, but his illness did define Chip for others. He became a hero for many, someone who has either challenged and defeated their greatest fear—or, for those who never knew his Hodgkin's disease was in remission, someone who still battled on bravely. To many, he was and is inspirational.

Each time Chip is off the air, whether on vacation or ill with things unrelated to cancer, the station hears from his fans wanting to know where and how he is, a few even accusing station management of a cover-up, a deliberate effort to deceive them of the truly serious nature of his illness. While allegations of a macabre conspiracy are untrue, such claims do underscore the concern many viewers have for Chip.

He is more than just a news reader to his followers. Chip is a role model and champion for some. He has been able to reach through the medium and touch viewers in ways that matter most to them. For some, Chip is more important than the stories he reads. He is a member of the family. So this book should be an illumination. It should not be an epitaph.

It is the year 2015, and computer users and high-definition TV viewers all over the Southwest still dial up WFAA-TV for the latest news. This night the anchor shows his greatest concern as he reassures his audience that Chip Moody is just off once again, and will be back soon, better than ever. Then, as something of an afterthought, he adds, "Oh, and by the way, for those of you who might remember former anchor Tracy Rowlett . . . (an old picture is shown behind the anchor, who is much cheerier now) . . . he died today."

Indeed, Chip Moody may outlive us all. His tenacity and his willingness to fight back against illness are traits we can all learn from. It is my hope—and I'm sure the hope of most of you reading this—that Chip Moody remains in his seat behind the anchor desk at Channel 8 for a long time to come.

I

CAREER MOMENTS

1

From the Cockpit...

WE WERE AT 14 THOUSAND FEET AND headed straight down. It was just a small speeding dot racing over the patchwork-covered farmland. The single-engine, dull gray jet below us had a red star on its tail, and its pilot was determined to shoot us down. It was diving fast and turning right.

Navy Lt. Commander Cecil Ewell and I had rolled our much bigger F-4 Phantom onto its back, pulled the stick back and to the right . . . we began picking up speed only as the green and brown fields below us began looking a lot bigger and a lot closer.

We tried to position ourselves behind the smaller, more maneuverable fighter we wanted to shoot down. Some fighter pilots call it "splashing" the other guy.

The G-suit I was wearing reacted automatically to the heavy aerodynamic forces I was subjected to, inflating quickly around my abdomen and thighs. Despite the reduced flow of blood to my head, my mind and body were still able to function, even as I was pushed hard down in the cockpit's seat. The altimeter was spinning counterclockwise, and another gauge showed we were rushing past Mach .8—more than 600 miles an hour.

Our adversary knew we were gaining. As we accelerated down through five thousand feet, the pilot in the single-engine plane quickly rolled and banked left, nose up, desperately trying to gain altitude.

That was the pilot's mistake, his moment of hesitation. We chopped the throttle back in our F-4 and pulled hard on the stick, making a 6-G

9

turn to the left and cutting the distance and the angle between our heavy twin-engine fighter and our enemy.

For a few seconds that gray jet was lined up dead center in the gun sight (the "pipper" as most pilots call it) mounted on the glare shield of our McDonnell Douglas F-4. This was the "kill zone." Physically flying the heavy jet became a combination of trained reflexes, feeling, and coordinating the stick and throttle to make the plane fol-

Lt. Commander (USNR) Cecil Ewell and me after dogfight training in a F-4 Phantom jet.

low what your brain processed as vital information. It seemed as if we were engaged in an almost unconscious series of movements and reflexes; man and machine became one.

I heard Cecil holler, "Guns, guns, guns!" At that moment, the enemy plane became a casualty of war.

I realized I hadn't even taken a breath since we went inverted and headed downward. The olive-drab oxygen mask was pressed firmly over my nose and mouth— just waiting to give me air. During the wild gyrations and tension of the dogfight, I had simply quit inhaling. As the Phantom entered a more relaxed left turn, the G-forces were reduced and the sausage-like balloons of the G-suit began deflating. I decided I could start breathing again.

The cool, clean oxygen (which has a noticeable odor compared to the air we breathe on the ground) filled my lungs, and I could smell it pushing into my sinuses. The clean odor of oxygen stayed with me for some time after the mission.

A dogfight at 600 miles an hour doesn't last long. Many times the encounter is measured in seconds—ten, fifteen, maybe twenty. If by that time you haven't scored a kill, there's a good chance the other guy did and you are dead.

Had the bullets during my mission been real, the smaller jet would have started shedding chunks of aluminum. Fuel, hydraulic fluid, and smoke would have been pouring from the body of the plane. Then it would have blown up.

With our "victory" under our belt, Cecil, who was nicknamed "Fossil" because of his prematurely graying hair, keyed his microphone and called to the second F-4 fighter with whom we had started the mission at the Dallas Naval Air Station. That pilot, too, had found his hands full trying to evade or shoot down his "aggressor."

While our companion pilot didn't nail his adversary in his dogfight near Brownwood, Texas, he did manage to stay clear of the electronic bullets and missiles of the other "bad guy." Soon, all four pilots were chatting over the same military radio frequency, checking positions and rendezvousing for our return hop to Dallas NAS.

Our adversaries were American fighter pilots trained in Soviet air-to-air combat tactics. They were flying A-4s, jets with flight characteristics and handling similar to some Soviet jet fighters. Our "mission" had all the elements of real air-to-air combat, except that the weapons weren't operational.

After the flight, the four of us linked up in two formations and headed for the barn. As we came into the downwind leg of the traffic pattern, Fossil requested permission for a military "break" over the runway. Permission granted, we guided the F-4 directly south over the north-south runway that extends into Mountain Creek Lake at the south end of the air station.

Screaming across the field at 240 miles per hour, we turned the Phantom onto its left wing, perpendicular to the ground, and pulled back on the stick rather quickly. This is about a 5-G maneuver and your eyes are pushed back into your head and your body is slammed down hard into the seat.

As we completed the 180-degree turn, the throttle came back, the nose pitched up ever so slightly, and we slowed down for the base leg and the turn onto the final approach. Our wingman was following the same routine about a mile behind us. In less than a minute we were tracking down the glide path and, as the terrain below us rushed by, we brought our F-4 right down to the deck, squeaking onto runway 17.

❖ ❖ ❖ ❖ ❖

There is something indescribable about walking around the flight line of a military air field—wearing your G-suit, swinging your helmet at your side. The feeling begins the moment you see those jet fighters sitting there just crying out for a crew. And while you wouldn't call it "jaunty," there is something special in the way fighter pilots carry themselves as they circle their planes. I guess it's a certain kind of walk—confident, and to a degree, cocky.

In the life-and-death arena of real warfare, that cocky attitude can mean the difference between celebrating at the officers' club that night or leaving bits of your body scattered around the patch of burned ground that marks the impact of your wounded bird—proving the brave chariot that carried you into battle was no better than the pilot who flew it.

A fighter pilot must have complete confidence in himself, his equipment, and his training. Without that, a moment's hesitation can cost him his entire existence. So, by necessity, a crackerjack fighter pilot must have the confidence that he is the better pilot, that although he respects his adversary, he will emerge the victor. To worry about failing is to hesitate, and in a business that must be played at maximum concentration and reaction, there is little room for error and a lot of room for disaster.

As the son of an Air Force colonel who trained pilots in combat tactics during World War II, my dreams were to be that cocky guy with the nifty helmet; the guy who made the right split-second decisions and who would finish each mission with his hair matted down on his scalp from the sweat and fatigue he had endured in high-intensity, air-to-air combat.

I would be that guy who would walk that certain walk away from my warbird, helmet at my side, and head for the officers' club to relive the flight. I'd be the one who would put down that cold bottle of beer, hold out both hands, and begin by saying that hallowed phrase used since biplane pilots did battle over the trenches of Europe in World War I—"There I was . . . "

On that day at the Dallas Naval Air Station, at the age of thirty-one, I lived the dream I had carried with me since I was a child, a dream that had never come to fruition. . . .

2

...To the Newsroom

"IT ALL STARTED AT A SMALL FIVE-WATT station." That phrase sounds like Ted Baxter, right out of "The Mary Tyler Moore Show" of the 1970s. I remember a show when the white-haired anchorman recounted how he got his start in broadcasting. Oddly enough, though, my story starts out very much the same way.

All my life, I had my heart set on being a professional pilot. The best route to reach my dream was, of course, through the military. I had enjoyed my upbringing in a military family, as an Air Force "brat." We moved every four years or so, and it was a good life.

In 1965, as I entered college at Baylor University in Waco, my focus was on following in my dad's footsteps and becoming a pilot in the US Air Force. I envisioned five years of active duty, then joining American Airlines or one of the other major air carriers and beginning a long and lucrative career as a commercial airline pilot. Heck, working a couple of weeks per month and making a handsome salary—that was appealing.

I joined the Air Force Reserve Officer Training Corps and took this part of my college curriculum very seriously. I decided to major in political science, since it seemed that would afford me a good diplomatic background if I later decided to stay with the Air Force as a career officer, hopefully stationed in foreign countries, sort of like what happened to my dad.

In college, I moved quickly up the ranks in the Air Force ROTC and soon had a leadership position within my unit. As a sophomore, I was named cadet of the year, a great honor. Everything seemed to be on track; older cadets praised my leadership skills, and the commanding officer gave me high marks in the various key areas that would ultimately determine my final acceptance or rejection as a pilot-candidate for the Air Force. My dream seemed to be getting closer and closer.

After my sophomore year, it was time for the Air Force flight physical, which was required for junior year flight training. That was when the roof fell in.

I went to the USAF's Wilford Hall Hospital in San Antonio. During the examination, doctors found on my x-rays that I had three seriously damaged vertebrae. The disc degeneration was so great that if I were ever forced to eject from a jet aircraft, the force could well cause paralysis or worse. Well, the doctor gave me the bad news—the Air Force couldn't use me. There were too many candidates qualified for the pilot's training course who didn't have the serious back problems I had. I was out.

I remember I actually started to cry at the hospital; the disappointment was so great. This had been my dream. The doctor did have some good news, however: I wouldn't have to face the draft. I was given a 4-F disqualification. This all happened in the midst of the Vietnam War. Although I was prepared to fly combat missions, I did not especially relish the thought of spending a tour overseas as a "ground-pounder" in the rice paddies and jungles of Vietnam—so many of my contemporaries did fight and die there. The doctor told me to go back to college and figure out a new career.

As fate would have it, three of my close classmates happily and proudly went on to pilot training and flew F-4s in Vietnam. They were all killed.

Later, when I visited Washington, DC to cover President Bush's inauguration, I went by the Vietnam memorial, found the names of my old friends and touched them on the wall. These three guys had been the success stories—the role models—in my world as a young cadet. They paid the ultimate price for our country. There was no American Airlines career for them after that war, no chance to raise a family, no life.

My eyes filled with tears when I saw the names of those men chiseled in the black granite. They had achieved the goal that I so wanted for myself, and in my eyes, that had already made them larger than life. But when I saw their names years later—just small inscriptions amidst thousands and thousands of others—I realized what truly made them heroes was not what they had achieved in their own lives, but that they had given it all up for the sake of their country—and for you and for me.

Back at Baylor in 1967, I didn't have a clue as to what to do with my life. I was twenty. It had never occurred to me that I would be anything but a pilot. I had no compass, no direction. Every profession I could think of then seemed too hard, too boring or just mundane. I knew I wouldn't be able to walk that certain jaunty walk as I got out of the elevator, making my way into an office juggling papers. It would never work. You just don't carry a briefcase the way you carry a fighter pilot's helmet. . . you just don't. . . .

During fall registration for my junior year, while standing in line with hundreds of other students, I heard over the loudspeakers that the campus radio station, KWBU-FM, needed five new announcers for the upcoming semester. Auditions would be held in "Old Main," one of the original buildings on campus and the home of the broadcast and journalism departments.

While standing in line there, wondering what classes I would take, I thought about the possibility of being on the air. Maybe being a disc jockey wouldn't be so bad. It might even be fun and give me something to do for awhile as I went about the business of deciding what it was I wanted to do with the rest of my life.

I headed over to Old Main along with fifty-five other hopefuls, read some copy given to me into a microphone, and introduced a few records on the audiotape. Lo and behold, a few days later I was informed that I had made the cut and could be one of the new campus disc jockeys. Did I want to do it? You bet! I immediately changed my major from political science to journalism.

Well, it didn't take long to figure out that I not only enjoyed being an announcer, but that it came relatively easily. KWBU-FM didn't have a very strong signal, but it did reach most of Waco. For ten hours a week, I read newscasts and hosted a radio program. My other duties included introducing and playing "soft pop" music (Peter, Paul and Mary—groups like that), giving students information on upcoming campus events, and reading news headlines from the Associated Press wire. The position was considered a campus job, so I was paid by Baylor University $1 an hour. Wow!

Six months after my foray into the world of radio broadcasting, one of my professors, Win Frankel, told me about a job opening at the local TV station, KWTX-TV, Channel 10. At the time, the station was a rare dual affiliate of CBS and ABC. The local program director could pick whatever shows he wanted from the program line-ups from each network. Win Frankel was a control-room director at KWTX, in addition to his duties as a professor of radio and television at Baylor.

The job opening at Channel 10 was for weekend anchor and week-day reporter and photographer. I jumped at the opportunity and made an appointment to meet News Director Ron Hall. Ron was the reigning anchorman in town, and Channel 10 news had the highest ratings. We cut an audition tape at the studio—I was so nervous I'm still surprised I didn't stutter. The audition must have gone well, however, because a few days later Ron called to inform me that I had the job. That was March 1968.

The job at Channel 10 was six days a week. I worked Monday through Thursday as a general assignment reporter, took Fridays off, and then went in to write and anchor the newscasts on Saturdays and Sundays. The starting salary was a big jump over the pay at Baylor. Now I was pulling down $1.65 an hour—plus overtime! That translated into roughly $100 a week. Boy, was I on my way. I guess you can see why I say "it all started at a small five-watt station . . . ."

The job at KWTX involved a lot more than reading the news. I was required to go out on stories with a 16-mm Bell and Howell news cam-era, get the facts, take pictures, write the story, and sometimes even develop the film myself and edit it for broadcast.

I worked my way up to do "packages," which included stand-ups with me in front of the camera and on-camera interviews with other peo-ple. This was all very similar to what is still the bread-and-butter of any television news operation. And because Channel 10 also had AM and FM radio affiliates, it was part of my job to give live reports on the radio while covering a story for the television station.

Being the rookie, I made more than my share of goofs on the air. One live report I still remember . . . and I still laugh about it. At the time, though, I thought I had torpedoed my broadcasting career.

I was sent out to a traffic accident with injuries on Interstate Highway 35. I arrived on the scene, shot some film of the car and the badly damaged motorcycle involved in the wreck, and called in on the two-way radio in the mobile unit to tell the folks back at the station I was ready to file a live report from the scene.

I would take my cue from the radio announcer, which went some-thing like this: "News is being made in central Texas, and now, live from the scene, a 'T-X Mobile News Report'." At that point, I turned down the radio in the mobile unit and began talking on the air. Well, the report started off okay, but went downhill quickly, eventually falling right over a cliff.

A pensive reporter for KWTX-TV in 1970.

I started out in my most authoritative voice: "This is Chip Moody and I'm on the scene of a major accident on Interstate 35, just north of the Waco city limits. A car and a motorcycle have collided, resulting in injuries to the driver of the car, his passenger, and the rider of the motorcycle." Sounds good so far. But then I went on, ad-libbing: "I can see some unidentified blood . . . " Huh? Unidentified blood? I couldn't believe those words were coming out of my mouth. But this was live radio and all I could do was to try desperately to redeem myself.

But trying to redeem myself only made matters worse. In the split second I knew I had made a stupid error, I intoned very officially: "That is, we don't know if the blood from the motorcycle driver is from his head or his shoulder." Boy, I didn't live that one down for years.

A few months later, at the scene of a house fire, I was giving another live radio report when I said, "Fire department officials here at the scene say an unidentified man— Tom Reynolds—was burned in the fire." In my head I'm thinking, "Oh no, I've done it again." But then I figured I could rise to the occasion, so I tried to cover up the gaff by saying, "'Unidentified' in the sense that we don't know his age and his exact address, although the address does appear to be on his house."

I knew my boss, Ron Hall, was either banging his head on his desk, or rolling around on the floor laughing. Later I found out he was laughing, a fact which did ease my embarrassment a little bit. After all, Ron once reported a devastating hurricane by saying on the air, "At last report, the big storm was moving through the Carolinas, into the vaginas." At least I didn't make that goof!

Those early days at KWTX-TV seem like another era now. Our newscasts were done in black and white, we used black and white film, and we had no real live video capability from the field. All that technology would come later with the introduction of the videotape cameras— "mini-cams" and "live vans" as we now call them. We didn't even have a TelePrompTer back in those days. Now, of course, we can bring you live reports from countries half a world away.

Being live on the air, whether it's radio or television, always carries a risk. There are more than a few examples of honest mistakes made by good reporters on the air. One of the cutest blunders on the air that I remember came out of California.

Many times you will see reporters and anchors out on the scene, working with a hearing-aid type device, in order to communicate with the producers and technicians back at the station. In television parlance, this device is commonly called an IFB, which in engineering terms means Internal Fold Back (which still makes very little sense to me even now).

So a reporter was on the air in California, and her IFB fell out of her ear. She calmly announced to the viewers, "Excuse me, I couldn't hear that, my IUD has fallen out."

At KWTX-TV it seemed to be smooth sailing for the young Chip Moody. But after about six or seven months on the air, my boss called me in to say he and the general manager had decided that my on-air anchoring really wasn't improving. In fact, my anchoring wasn't very good at all.

My ego was crushed. And to add to the humiliation, I was told that I was being taken off the weekend news until I could improve. I felt ashamed and embarrassed, but later my boss would tell me that he was proud I had hung in there in the following months and didn't quit.

I worked hard on improving my on-air delivery and finally, several months later, I was told that Ron Hall would be taking a vacation. Management decided I had improved enough to fill in for Ron during that time. So my career was back on track and I had survived my first major professional crisis.

I finished up my college studies at Baylor in 1970, while working for KWTX-TV. After working 48 hours a week, plus going to school . . . just going to work seemed like a vacation. But shortly after graduation, I received a call from the ABC affiliate in El Paso. They said I was one of the candidates for news director and anchorman at their station.

I had been at KWTX for more than two years by this time, and now that I had graduated, I was ready to take on the world. I accepted the job in El Paso, and became the youngest news director and anchorman in the state. I also got married to my college sweetheart, Vikki. I was at the tender age of twenty-three.

Although I was challenged professionally—working twelve- and fourteen-hour days to build and improve the station's news department—and although Vikki and I had a wonderful apartment with a beautiful view, we did not feel at home in El Paso. A feeling of being very removed from the rest of the state contributed to our general feeling of unhappiness. So less than a year after my arrival in El Paso, I sent out resumes to stations around the country, including channels 4, 5, and 8 in Dallas-Fort Worth.

Channel 5, which was then WBAP-TV, brought me in for an interview for weekend anchorman and weekday reporter—similar to what I had done in Waco. The difference, of course, was that Dallas-Fort Worth was one of the top 10 markets in the country. At the time, Channel 5 was the top-ranked news station in the area. It had been the first television station to sign on the air in Texas, and had the first regular newscast, "The Texas News."

When I was offered a job at Channel 5, I jumped at the chance to join the big leagues. That was 1971.

3

The Early Stories

No JOURNALIST EVER FORGETS THEIR FIRST big story. And I remember mine, as if it happened only yesterday. It was 1968, not long after I joined KWTX-TV in Waco. One night, we got a bulletin that an airliner had crashed between Waco and Dallas. It turned out that a Braniff passenger plane, enroute from Houston to Dallas, got caught in a thunderstorm and crashed near the community of Dawson, north of Waco.

I was one of the first reporters at the site. I had never experienced such a devastating scene. As a rookie reporter, I was in awe of the destruction around me—the wreckage, the bodies. Actually, there were only body parts, scattered around the area. All in all, 85 people died in that accident.

As I recall, only one person in that crash came out in one piece. That happened to be a woman who had died and been embalmed in Houston, and was being flown to Dallas in a casket for burial. Her body was the only one left intact. To add irony to all this, the crash happened near a place called Dead Man's Creek.

The scene was a madhouse: Reporters from Dallas, Fort Worth, Temple, and Waco swarmed around. I was in the middle of it all, filing radio reports and shooting film for the television news.

As a reporter getting paid $100 a week, I remember an investigator from the National Transportation Safety Board going through the wreckage and showing us a wallet he found with three $100 bills in it. To me, it looked like a fortune—almost a month's pay. I can still remember

21

thinking, boy, somebody had that much money on them at their death and never got to spend it. I also remember someone bringing back the captain's hat from the wreckage.

I was in a state of disbelief as I watched all this unfold before my eyes, but I felt a keen responsibility as a reporter to bring all the facts back to our Channel 10 viewers. It gave me a sense of maturity and professional duty, and I realized for perhaps the first time how unpredictable and interesting the news business could be, how a reporter's obligation was to be as accurate and factual as possible. You never know from one day to the next what's going to happen, who you're going to interview, where you're going to be, or what your day will be like. And no two days are ever the same.

Late that evening after the crash, as I got back to the newsroom and was preparing my report for the 10 p.m. newscast, I had a moment I'll never forget. As I looked at the Associated Press wire machine, it printed out "World Headlines"—and that crash was the first story. In those few seconds I realized what I was covering had been the top story in the world for that day. I knew I had received my initiation into real reporting.

The Lubbock Tornado

It was 1970. While still working at Channel 10 in Waco, we got word late one evening at about 9:30 that a tornado had hit Lubbock. Details were sketchy and communication lines from Lubbock were out. The extent of the damage wasn't yet known. Even the police, fire departments, and other emergency personnel were not completely sure of the damage's extent. As the hour wore on, and more details came in, it became clear that Lubbock had been hit very hard and there were a number of fatalities as well as widespread damage.

Earlier that day, we had also experienced some of the same storm system that hit Lubbock, which had moved east through our area. In the newsroom, we decided late that evening we should go cover the story and make a special report when we came back. Because flying was impossible in the still severe weather, we loaded our gear into the new mobile unit Channel 10 had just purchased. I remember General Manager Buddy Bostick telling us that because of the vehicle's new generation engine, we didn't have to use premium gasoline, we could instead use cheaper, "regular," lower-octane gas and still get the same performance.

We'd only had the mobile unit for about two weeks at the time. It was great to have a brand new car to use on routine news assignments, but we were routinely reminded by Bostick to pull up at the regular pump and get the cheaper gas. On the day of the tornado, we were at the end of a work day, and suddenly we were called out on a big story, hundreds of miles and eight hours away. Cameraman/reporter Dave Tolbert and I loaded up our gear in the new unit and headed out to Lubbock. We left about 2 a.m. and arrived shortly after daybreak.

We spent the day shooting film of the damage and interviewing victims, including Texas Tech students from Waco, trying to put a local spin into our coverage of the tornado. That afternoon, police started clearing the Great Plains Life Building in the downtown area, shouting through a bullhorn, "Evacuate the area, the building is about to fall!" Dave and I had seen terrible devastation throughout much of Lubbock, and this large building was twisted and tilted to a frightening degree.

Police evacuated several blocks around the building, in anticipation of the apparently impending collapse. We bravely found a nearby shoe shop with a blown-out window that afforded us a good view of the building. We set up our camera and prepared to watch the fall. Well, if you go to Lubbock today, the Great Plains Life Building (now called Metro Tower) is still standing. We waited two hours, ready to roll at any moment. Here it is twenty-five years later and we'd still be there today if we hadn't finally packed up the camera.

While the disaster teams were on the scene, we worked nonstop throughout the day, knowing we'd be putting together a half-hour special when we returned to Waco in order to bring central Texas viewers a more in-depth look at the damage and destruction.

Finally we were ready to head home. It was about 6 o'clock in the evening, and we had been awake about fifty hours straight. We were getting a little pooped, and as we headed out of Lubbock I realized we needed gas. As I pulled into the service station, I remembered the boss's reminder to go ahead and use regular gas. As I went by the pumps I noticed the prices, ranging from about 69¢ a gallon to about $1.10. I backed the mobile unit up to the 69-cent pump, naturally assuming that this was regular, being the cheapest. I put the pump on automatic and slowly walked toward the office. Then someone yelled, "Holy smoke, who's putting diesel in that new Ford?" I just panicked, ran back out, and pulled the nozzle out of the car, but the pump had already dispensed about two thirds of a tank of diesel fuel into this car that was designed to run on regular gasoline.

The attendant hurriedly advised us to start it up immediately, while we still had some of the normal fuel left in the fuel line, or he said we'd never get it started again. So we started the engine, and then started pumping in high-octane gasoline—while I jumped up and down on the trunk, trying to shake up the gas, mix it, and dilute the diesel. But the engine started knocking and sputtering, and a huge plume of white smoke started coming out the back, as this gasoline engine tried to process the oil-rich diesel. It only got worse, as more and more of the diesel fuel got into the fuel system. Here we were, dead tired, with this brand new car smoking and knocking, and I had put in some odd blend of fuel.

We started down the highway. I had the accelerator pedal to the floor, but the fastest we could possibly go was fifty-five miles per hour. The racket was incredible. Imagine a World War II bomber with two spark plugs missing on a cold morning. I thought pistons were going to come flying through the hood. Going down the highway, our mobile unit looked like a crop duster, with huge clouds of white smoke billowing behind us and the engine racket making it too loud for conversation.

Well, we pushed on at full speed because we were on a deadline. I knew in my heart I had ruined the new mobile unit, but I figured we'd just sort it all out when we got back to Waco. As we got closer to home, we stopped and filled up again with the highest premium gas we could find and tried to mix it up again by pushing up and down on the trunk, to hopefully stop the smoke and the noise.

It turned out okay in the end. I don't think we did any permanent damage to the vehicle or the engine. Well, maybe we did. . . . but probably the worst of it was the sight we made chugging down the highway at fifty-five, with cars whizzing by, their occupants looking at us oddly and noticing we sounded like an old thrashing machine.

In any event, we put our special report together when we returned, but to add misery to my already bad day, just as we opened our live report on the air, I realized I had forgotten to put on my microphone. I was sitting on it. During the first commercial break, after the introduction, I retrieved the microphone from underneath my rear end and got it in the normal position on my tie. I guess it's all a part of the price you pay when you stay up sixty hours to get the story. Your brain sometimes just doesn't function at its normal level.

Tragic Stories

Very early in my career in Waco, in 1969, I was called out to the scene of an apparent suicide in a middle class neighborhood. Because of my press credentials and my growing reputation as a newsman, I was allowed inside the house to look at the scene while the detectives, the medical examiners, and the Justice of the Peace, looked over the situation.

What I found in front of me was truly tragic. Here was a seventeen-year-old boy who I later understood had called his girlfriend and told her that if she didn't make up with him and start going steady again, he would kill himself. The girlfriend probably didn't take him seriously, but he meant what he said. And when she spurned him, he found a shotgun, went back to his bedroom, took off a shoe and a sock, loaded the shotgun, held the barrel to his chest, and then reached down with his right big toe and pushed the trigger.

There was a very small entry wound in the middle of his chest, but it blew out a large section of his back and he was killed instantly. Here was a kid who was only seventeen years old, but who was caught up in a teenager's passion and not thinking very clearly. The young man was a very good student, and also on the student council. This all happened twenty-six years ago, yet I still think about this boy, how he would be a man today—perhaps a successful, productive member of our society—had he not taken his own life.

While the unfulfilled promise of that young man still haunts me, I was moved even more by a story I covered in Fort Worth while working at Channel 5 (WBAP-TV at the time) around 1974. We got word of an "auto-pedestrian accident." As I recall it was on Northeast 28th Street. The tip was that someone had been hit by a car and killed. When we arrived at the scene, we discovered that a man of about fifty-five had in fact been hit by a car and was dead in the middle of the street. Police officers were taking photographs.

As our TV crew started shooting some film, a young woman came running up crying out loudly and hysterically, "That's my daddy, that's my daddy, that's my daddy!" I'll never forget that moment. The paramedics on the scene were about ready to remove the body, but to calm the daughter, they pulled out a hypodermic needle and gave her an injection. They decided to send her to the hospital, too—she was obviously in a great deal of emotional distress.

Then, to my horror, they loaded the man's body into this ambulance and put the young lady in the very same ambulance—with her dead father. I'm saying to myself, that has got to be a nightmare. Your father is suddenly run down and killed in the middle of the street. You arrive at the scene, you are understandably hysterical, then you end up in the same ambulance with your father's body, and you're both headed for the hospital. I just thought to myself, someone should have called another ambulance and sent them in separate vehicles—perhaps to two different hospitals.

The news business is terribly sobering because you get a close-up look at violent death and how quickly it can come. As a newsman, I have to try to shut it out so that I can communicate the facts to viewers. Other professionals confronted by tragedy have to cope as well. . . . At KWTX in Waco, we got a call from the authorities, who had found a body out in a field near the local Veterans Administration hospital. I went out there and realized firsthand how professionals who have to deal with death day in and day out really must develop a shield of humor to try to get them through.

When I arrived at the scene, there was just the skeletal remains of a person. As I started gathering the facts, I was told that apparently this man had wandered away from the VA hospital several months earlier, walked maybe a mile, and died in the field. Here his skeletal remains were found.

The local Justice of the Peace on call was Joe Johnson, a man who always took his job seriously, yet at the same time always tried to put people at ease. Joe looked over at me as he was examining the bones and said, "Chip, look at this." And I thought to myself, "Uh-oh, this must be some clue to a murder or some very important aspect of his investigation." He picked up the skull and turned it over and he pointed to a tooth on the right lower side of the jaw and he said, "Look here, this guy had a really bad cavity here."

Here I was, tensed for this Columbo-type clue, and JP Joe Johnson was instead putting us all at ease. When the ambulance showed up with the body bag, old Joe started singing from the old spiritual, "The ankle bone connected to the leg bone, the leg bone connected to the knee bone . . ."

I was getting an idea of how professionals deal with the unsavory parts of their jobs. Cops do it, undertakers do it, newsmen do it, too— you build up a little mental wall that shields you from the pain. It often works, but sometimes it doesn't. Sometimes the gravity and the gruesomeness, the horror of what you're actually seeing, can't be overcome by a little levity.

Comic Relief

At KWTX-TV in Waco, whenever a Signal 12, which meant a dead person, came across the police radio in the newsroom, the reporters and crews would spring into action. We would never know right away if the death occurred from an accident or some foul play like murder. Anytime we would hear the signal, we'd also hear the call for a Justice of the Peace to come to the scene to make an investigation and pronounce the person dead. That was the usual scenario.

Late one night, we heard a Signal 12 from a police officer reporting from one of the poorer sections of Waco. Quickly, I got out to the scene and was allowed to enter a small, wood frame house. Inside was a man, somewhere in his mid-fifties, who had died of what appeared to be natural causes. There was no violence involved, but what made this unusual was that this gentleman had apparently been sitting on the toilet with his pants around his ankles when he died.

He had fallen forward, arms outstretched, and there he lay for a day or so before neighbors noticed that he wasn't picking up his newspaper and called in the authorities. When the police showed up and looked inside, they found the man stretched out in front of his toilet. Rigor mortis had set in—his arms were stiff and outstretched in front of him.

I arrived on the scene with the Justice of the Peace and it was pretty obvious that the death was from natural causes, a heart attack. When the paramedics rolled this fellow over to put him on the gurney, they had to strain to get his arms to lay down on his chest. I think in some cases they have to break bones to do this because the tissue starts stiffening up so badly. Finally they got both of his arms down, strapped his body on the stretcher, and started wheeling him out of the house.

A large crowd had gathered outside—the flashing lights and the TV crews had attracted some attention. Well, they watched as we came out the door and started going down the steps with the gurney. Suddenly, one of the dead man's arms came loose and flew up into the air, throwing off the sheet that covered his body. Apparently, his arm had worked loose from the restraining belt, and because of the rigor mortis, the muscles had become frozen in such a way that the raised arm was by now its natural position.

I don't think I've ever seen sixty or so people whose eyes got so big or who jumped so high as that crowd did when that arm went flying up. It was scary for the crowd, but at the same time it was like something out of a sick comic movie. I had only been in the news business a couple of years and I thought, boy, there's never a dull moment in news.

Oh, I Have Slipped the Surly Bonds of Earth and Then Kicked the Trash Can

While anchoring at Channel 5 in Dallas during the late 1970s, I contacted the US Air Force Thunderbird Aerobatic Demonstration Team

Flying from Kansas to Texas with the USAF Thunderbirds.

about possibly flying in one of their jets the next time they came to Texas for an air show. I got the word that, yes, not only would I get a ride but because I was a pilot, I'd be able to fly with the team from Wichita, Kansas down to Carswell Air Force Base in Fort Worth for an air show. In other words, it wouldn't be one of the typical media rides, where the local news guy gets to go up in an Air Force jet for a 30-minute ride over the city. Instead, the US Air Force flying team said they'd enjoy having me join them for a cross-country flight.

This was a very rare opportunity for a reporter. The next civilian reporter to be offered a cross-country flight was Harry Reasoner, who got similar treatment when he did a story for "60 Minutes" on CBS. Let me tell you, I was really excited about riding with the Thunderbirds! Before accepting the offer, I talked to our new news director, Bill Vance, about it, but he was decidedly unexcited about it. He thought the air show and any "backseat" ride by a newsman were basically a waste of taxpayers' money.

I countered that the air show was not only a good recruiting tool for the Air Force, but it was also a chance for Texans to see some of the best pilots around. And besides, it was a routinely scheduled demonstration that the Pentagon and the White House had already approved. It's in the federal budget to do these air shows to demonstrate our military strength and skills of some of our top Air Force pilots. I explained to Bill that I'd been offered a long-distance trip, something most journalists would never get a chance to experience. But Vance said I could do it only if I'd pay my own way up to Wichita.

Although it seemed a bit odd for a reporter to pay his own way to cover a news story for the station, I bought a one-way airline ticket to Wichita, and when I got to the Air Force base, I spent the night in the bachelor officers quarters. The next morning, I went through a briefing with the Thunderbirds, then we loaded up, strapped ourselves into our T-38 Talon jets, took off, and headed to Fort Worth. I felt very much a part of this crack team. I was on cloud nine, eating, sleeping, and rubbing shoulders with these extremely talented Air Force pilots.

After we left Kansas, I remember we climbed up to 43,000 feet, which is the highest I had ever flown (most airliners travel at around 33,000 feet). At that altitude you can actually discern the curvature of the earth. Here we were, flying along in a tight formation of seven airplanes, and these guys were just a riot on the intercom, joking back and forth and singing songs. Imagine seven T-38 jets, beautifully painted red, white, and blue, skimming along the bottom of the stratosphere. We looked down on the earth through a cluster of clouds. On this incredible flight I was getting a rare glimpse into the elite fraternity of top-notch pilots and the US Air Force Thunderbirds.

The flight to Fort Worth took only about an hour—not surprising when you're doing 550 miles an hour or better. As we came across the Red River, the northern boundary of Texas, we started our descent into the Fort Worth area. I was snapping pictures with my still camera and also trying to capture some of it on film with a movie camera. We broke through the clouds and came in at easily 400 miles an hour on the south side of Fort Worth, traveling in a northerly direction from Camp Bowie Boulevard and the I-20 interchange.

We zeroed in and headed straight north to Carswell Air Force Base. As we got lower and lower, I could see familiar landmarks like car dealerships, restaurants, and intersections. Everything seemed to be in slow motion because we were going so doggone fast. It was a real rush as we made this high speed pass across around Carswell Air Force Base. We went right down the runway, one jet behind the other, and then we all split off to perform stunts, some of them doing the fancy timed aerobatics and team rolls and their famous "bomb burst": the jets go straight up and then "break"—with a fifth jet zooming up behind the others, doing rolls as it climbs into the sky. It's all very impressive and it's an awesome feeling to be in the cockpit taking part in it all.

When we landed, I was just bubbling with excitement. This was one of the neatest things I'd ever done. I was so proud that I had gotten this opportunity to fly. We taxied up to Carswell's tower where the VIP recep-

tion committee was waiting, along with TV cameras from the local stations. We popped open our canopies and I took a look around. What
did I see? A Channel 4 cameraman. A Channel 8 cameraman. A Channel
11 cameraman. What I *didn't* see was anyone from Channel 5, my own
station. Here I was, working on this story, shooting film up in Kansas,
taking footage as we flew. And my station wasn't even there when I landed to shoot the arrival and the aerobatics. I cannot remember ever being
more mad about something in my professional life than I was that day.
Every other TV station in town was there except mine.

I went back to the station and I asked the assignments editor why
we didn't have a crew at the scene. I told him I had a really great story
going, but now it was only half-baked because we couldn't finish it up
visually with film of the arrival and the show. That was when I was told
that our news director didn't think it was a story worth covering. When I
heard that I just hauled off and kicked a big trash can probably fifteen
feet across the room. I've never been so upset and I considered it a slap
in the face that—despite my participation, the importance of Carswell
AFB to the local economy and its strong, positive presence in the community—Bill Vance considered this a non-news story. Maybe it wasn't a
presidential election, maybe it didn't change the world, but it was a legitimate news story and our coverage of it would have certainly beat out
that of the other stations.

The incident was a double-edged sword: to be flying along at 43,000
feet with the US Air Force's Thunderbirds and feeling like you're part of
the team is an incredible feeling. At the same time to have your real-life
team, your own newsroom, snub you when every other news team in
town is there was a very hard blow.

I think that was the first time I said to myself, "Something isn't right
here at Channel 5, I'm not comfortable with this news director and this
television station." It was the first time I thought about leaving. Less than
a year later, I did.

4

Why I Left Channel 5

DURING THE MID-1970S, WBAP-TV Channel 5 was sold to the LIN Broadcasting Company as part of an FCC mandate for dividing major news outlets within a given community. The mandate states that an entity cannot own a newspaper, television station, and radio station in the same market, where that entity would then dominate. Channel 5 was owned by the *Fort Worth Star-Telegram* and the marching orders were that the paper would have to divest itself of the television station.

Channel 5 has been around since 1947. One of its hallmarks is being the home of the first regularly televised newscast in the Southwest. Entitled "The Texas News," it was in the early years a newsreel type of presentation, with the reporter or anchor doing voice-overs. One of the original voices was the late Tom McDonald, who died of Lou Gehrig's disease in 1991. He was a talented journalist, an awfully nice guy, and a good friend—in fact, he ended up being a next door neighbor after I purchased a home on the Meadowbrook Golf Course in Fort Worth.

For twenty years, Channel 5 had dominated the local news ratings, but in the late 1970s, WFAA-TV Channel 8 launched an expensive and aggressive effort to compete and win the top local news spot. WFAA brought in Marty Haag, who had been with the CBS Radio Network in New York, as news director. Marty began to change the way local news was presented. He wanted to have more in-depth reporting—not just the sensational, quick, sometimes overly graphic and bloody stories that many local television stations still indulge in, usually in an attempt to gain ratings at the expense of quality.

Marty Haag took Channel 8 and started rebuilding from the ground up. WFAA began producing a much superior product to what they had before. Over at Channel 5, all this was being taken into account as our ratings began to slip during the LIN Broadcasting transition.

With the change in ownership came a change in management and philosophy. Seeing the downward trend in ratings, LIN Broadcasting brought in Bill Vance, from Columbus, Ohio, as news director. Bill came in as a product of the 1970s' fast-paced news broadcasting style. When Bill came to town, he rented an apartment before moving his wife down from Ohio. One night, he called John Miller, our number-one producer, and me over to his apartment to explain where he thought our news operation ought to be heading.

John and I were shocked to hear that he had decided to get rid of Channel 5's signature newscast title, "The Texas News," and rename it "Action News." In our business, "The Texas News" name was a unique calling card, a tradition steeped in history and awards. You can see "Action News" in Albuquerque or Ames, Iowa. This name change was one of the suggestions recommended by TV consultants and it signifies the sort of newscast where you start throwing twenty-five-second stories at viewers. It's a very high-paced, "top 40" type of newscast. This was ostensibly done to build the audience, and sustain their interest.

John and I were more than a little concerned. We were both from the school of news reporting that gives the viewer a lot of solid information, rather than just showing quick out-takes of a fire or a wreck, with a lot of gore and little substance. We thought this sort of thing sacrificed content for quantity. Unable to countenance the new approach, John resigned in January of 1980 and went on to Channel 8 as a field producer. Today he is the executive news director for the station.

As Bill Vance continued to run the Channel 5 newsroom and we went to "Action News," a number of us became more and more frustrated and unhappy. The word had gone out that I was looking for a new job. I was under no contractual obligation to Channel 5 and I could leave with two weeks' notice.

A station in San Francisco called and they asked me to come out to audition for them. San Francisco is a huge television market and since I was born in nearby Oakland I thought it might be fun to live and work out there. When I got out to San Francisco, I visited with the news director for KRON-TV, one of the network affiliates.

During the interview, the news director said, "Chip, we give every new anchorman two things. One, a videotape machine and the other, a

new Porsche." Well, obviously that got my attention and I
went ahead and did a taping
there in the studios with
their folks. The news director
was favorably impressed and
said she liked what I did and
how I looked. She said she'd
be back with me within two
weeks.

Well, two days later, that
station was hit by a strike.
Three unions went on strike
at once: the writers, producers, and anchor people. So
the news director called and
said they really couldn't
afford to hire anyone until
the strike was over. She said

Channel 5, 1979.

if I was hired now, I may not be able to work for another six months
because of the union problems, and in the meantime they'd be paying
me this large salary and I could be sailing around the world with it.
The San Francisco station said when the strike was settled, we'd get
back to talking.

What I didn't realize was that someone in the San Francisco newsroom recognized me during my interview. Soon, word got back to the
Dallas-Fort Worth newspapers that I had been out there talking to those
folks. It was reported that a San Francisco station was courting Chip
Moody, hoping to hire him on as their anchorman.

I knew that the deal was up in the air because of the strike. But the
folks at KDFW-TV, Channel 4, figured maybe they could hire me away if
I was unhappy at Channel 5. That's when they called one of the national
head hunters for the television business, Sherlee Barish. She called me
out of the blue one day from New York, and asked me about my contractual obligations.

Sherlee and I had a nice talk and I got the impression that another
market was interested in me, be it Chicago, Boston, New York, Los
Angeles, whatever. I had no idea she was calling at the behest of Channel
4. But the key here was that she found out in our discussion that I was
under no contractual obligations to Channel 5. I had asked Channel 5 to

negotiate a contract with me six months earlier, but Vance had said we'd have to wait and see what the ratings looked like in May, which was a real slap in the face to me.

In any event, when Sherlee found out that I had no written contract with Channel 5, she told the executives at Channel 4 that I was available. All they had to do was make the right offer and I might go for it.

Well, that's where Channel 4 news director Wayne Thomas comes in. He camped out on my doorstep and tried to convince me to forget San Francisco and see that KDFW's offer was right for me. The salary was twice as much as I was earning at Channel 5. Plus, I had the impression that Vance didn't like me and really didn't think it mattered whether I came or went or disappeared into thin air. So, after really struggling with it for a night—I had been with the Channel 5 news organization for almost 10 years—I made my decision. Channel 4 was a station that was eager to have me; they seemed to appreciate my abilities as an anchorman. To be appreciated was a whole new feeling.

I went back to Channel 5 and talked to the general manager, Blake Byrne, and explained to him that I was quitting. I explained that Bill Vance and I just weren't seeing eye to eye on how the broadcast should be presented each night and what our priorities were. And I explained that Channel 4 was doubling my salary. Byrne countered, "We'll meet their offer." I said, "No." I figured Channel 5 could have done that a year ago, but right now, it was a textbook case of too little too late. So, in that sense, my decision to move wasn't a tough call.

So I went over to Channel 4 and, boy, did that get a lot of attention from the public! This was the first time a major Monday-through-Friday anchor guy moved from station A to station B. The headlines and feature stories that the move generated were really almost scary. Actually, it was all pretty humbling (anyone who knows me realizes that that is quite a statement!).

It was odd to find myself as the news story instead of the person delivering the news. I now held the top paid position in the market for anchor people. At the same time, the ratings shot up at Channel 4 and they spiraled down at Channel 5. I was gratified to see that quite a few viewers stayed with me. We tied or beat Channel 8 for several rating period time slots. And it was fun to be part of a success story. We took a third-place station and moved it up substantially in the ratings. That's what Channel 4's management was counting on and it happened. The sales people, the management people, the newsroom people—they all thought this was a special moment. The Channel 4 people made me feel very welcome.

My very first day on the air at Channel 4 was exciting in a couple of ways. Just before my debut 6 p.m. newscast, my sister Kate gave birth to her daughter Brooke. So, at the end of the newscast, I explained to viewers that I had just become an uncle for the first time. "My sister has given birth to her first child, Brooke. Seven-eleven. That's not *where* she was born—that's how much she *weighed*! Mother and daughter doing well—father [my brother-in-law Bard Holbert] doing 'so-so'. . ."

I was having a great time. We had a terrific team of personalities with great chemistry. Clarice Tinsley was there when I came over. Then we hired Wayne Shattuck as our weatherman and Dale Hansen joined us as sports anchor. Between the four of us, we had a good mix. We got along on and off the air, and I think that came across to our viewers. We had a terrific run at Channel 4.

Soon after I started at Channel 4, one of the longtime reporters over at Channel 5, Jack Brown, was getting very frustrated because many of his stories, which were usually newscast-ending vignettes about Texas, driven by unusual characters and needing at least two minutes of air time to tell a story adequately, were not getting aired or were being cut because more and more stories were being packed into the newscast, and the newscast would run out of time. This upset Jack, because he worked hard on those stories.

One day Jack called me at Channel 4 to express his understandable disappointment. So I told Jack to send an audition tape over to John McKay, the new general manager at Channel 4. Jack, who had been at Channel 5 for twenty-two years, quickly got the job at Channel 4, and gave his notice at Channel 5. Bill Vance posted a memo on the bulletin board at the station, saying, "Jack Brown has quit and left for Channel 4." Period. In a classic move and in his typical good, dry, understated humor, Jack tacked his own memo underneath Bill's, which read: "Dear Staff: I don't know what all this fuss is about. It's always been my policy to change jobs every twenty-two years. Regards, Jack." It's one of the best memos I've ever seen in broadcasting.

5

Hurricanes, Conventions, and Casino Bombs

IN THE EARLY MONTHS AFTER I HAD arrived at KDFW-TV Channel 4 in Dallas, a couple of important stories began to break.

I was scheduled to work with Clarice Tinsley in our upcoming coverage of the 1980 Democratic National Convention in New York. But, perhaps a week prior to that, a major hurricane was developing in the Gulf of Mexico, and by all indications, it was headed for the Texas Gulf Coast. As I was preparing for the early evening newscast, our news director, Wayne Thomas, came out to the TV newscast set and told me to prepare to fly down and do some field anchoring on the approaching storm.

This would be my first hurricane, and I had heard all sorts of stories about what happens when the skies open up and spill a huge amount of rainfall in the hurricane area. One of the stories I had heard is that snakes leave their underground quarters and move to higher land, to escape the flood waters.

I called home and asked Vikki to pack not only a suitcase to last me a couple days but my Old-West-style six-gun revolver as well. I anticipated that at some point in our news coverage, I would be face to face with one or more deadly cottonmouths—or perhaps some other not-so-friendly varmint—which would present a threat to my health and well-being. It would be prudent to arm myself to shoot any dangerous predator. I went ahead and did the 5 p.m. news, secure in the knowledge that Vikki was rushing to pack me a suitcase, my boots, a heavy-duty rain slicker . . . and my gun.

As we finished the
5 p.m. news, News
Director Wayne Thomas
called me back into his
office and told me that
he had checked with
the local airplane char-
ter companies, and
that given the circum-
stances and timing—
with this major storm
bearing down on the
Texas coast line—they
did not have a twin

KDFW-TV, Channel 4, in 1982.

engine prop plane that would be able to leave Dallas and still beat the
heaviest and most dangerous part of the storm as it zeroed in on Corpus
Christi. As he told me this, I looked at him and simply asked, "Why
don't we hire a Lear jet to get us there, if time is that critical?" Deep within me, I felt like saying, "Let's go for it, no matter the cost." Wayne
thought for perhaps thirty seconds, and said, "Okay, let's see what we
can do."

Meanwhile, I went back to the business of looking over the 6 p.m.
news script. As that newscast ended, Wayne came up to me and said,
"Okay, Chip. We've chartered a jet, so get out to Love Field as quickly as
possible." I felt very proud that the station had gone along with my suggestion despite the extra expense, which was considerable. Vikki showed
up at the station with my overnight bag and my gun, and I made a bee-
line to the corporate jet facility at Love Field.

From a broadcast standpoint, the plan called for me to land at
Corpus Christi, assemble whatever videotape our crew had already shot
along the coast, get the latest information on the hurricane, and craft a
report on the spur of the moment that could be shot by one of our cameramen. The cameramen would fly back to Dallas in the chartered jet
with the report and then, if all the communication lines held together, I
could also provide a live report on the 10 o'clock news that evening,
updating the information we had gathered along the coast that day.

As we made our airborne descent into Corpus Christi, I remember I
could vividly see from the airplane that the main interstate highway was
bumper to bumper in every lane. People were making a desperate effort
to get out of town. Here we were, the brave journalists, flying into

town—into the teeth of the storm. I thought to myself, maybe these Gulf Coast residents know more than I do!

We landed safely in Corpus, and I talked to our ground-based reporters and got enough information and video to put together a "stand-up report" on videotape. The Lear jet crew had to do a quick "turn-around" because the high winds and heavy rain from the hurricane were indeed bearing down on the area. With the videotape in hand, they hightailed it back to Dallas.

I discovered later that CBS News had waited too long to send its own crew into Corpus, therefore it fell to me and our crew to compile and broadcast reports on the hurricane to other CBS affiliate stations across the nation.

After the jet took off and headed back to Dallas with my stand-up report, we manned two mobile units and headed out to the coastline, prepared to record the arrival of the hurricane. Boy, Mother Nature can really kick up her heels when she wants to! As we moved closer to the shoreline, the winds became so strong that our mobile unit, which was a station wagon, almost flipped over. I know one side of the car, both the front and rear wheels, actually lifted off the ground a few inches. To be sitting in a four-thousand-pound automobile while it is tossed around like a plastic toy is something I will never forget.

As the storm approached, most of the city lost electrical power. I remember how odd it was to walk out into the street and see virtually no lights. Our motel room did not have lights or hot water. Everything was shut down. I recall that for a couple days my main food menu consisted of cold cans of beans and wienies, lukewarm cans of 7-Up, and grapefruit juice.

For most of the next day, we videotaped scenes of fishing boats out of the water, resting in the middle of thoroughfares along the coastline. Then, that night, as fate would have it, the actual eye of the hurricane passed over us, during our 10 p.m. newscast.

It was spooky. The high winds and fury of the storm in the hours preceding the eye were terrible, but then suddenly everything became so still. You could look up at a beautifully clear sky—it was the eye of the storm. However, in the next hour, we would once again be pelted with heavy rain and high winds.

Because we had access to a telephone communication blockhouse in a field a few miles out of town, we were able to send reports not only back to Dallas-Fort Worth, but around the country. The technology of television these days is still hard for me to comprehend. Here I was, in a small concrete building on the outskirts of Corpus Christi, sending my report to every part of the nation. If I had had time to think about it, I probably would have gotten nervous and goofed up the reports. Only later did I learn that the reports were carried in Seattle, San Francisco, Boston, Chicago, and most points in between. We were able to give viewers around the nation an accurate look at the intensity and destruction of the storm.

In the course of covering the story, I never did come across any snakes and, unfortunately, I wasn't able to pretend to be Indiana Jones or Clint Eastwood. I never fired a single round. But covering the storm was still one of the most interesting and rewarding aspects of my career. One thing is for sure: you never know what's going to happen next.

As we wrapped up our coverage of the hurricane, it was time for Clarice and I to go cover the 1980 Democratic National Convention about to begin in New York City. Clarice was already headed in that direction, and I flew back to DFW Airport. Vikki had a new suitcase packed with a couple of suits and ties, and I traded her for the wet, not-so-nice-smelling suitcase of clothes I had worn covering the hurricane and caught the next flight to New York.

Once there, I linked up with our crew, which was already there and in position. As the convention got underway, all of us were putting in fourteen-hour days, doing interviews, covering the various debates on the floor, and then writing and assembling reports that would be carried by satellite back to the viewing audience in Dallas-Fort Worth.

I think most viewers watch coverage of events like this without a full appreciation of the effort and coordination that make such reports possible. In fact, even to this day, I myself am amazed at how we can communicate by satellite to reporters in the field, and everything usually goes so smoothly. I tip my hat to the engineers and technicians who make this possible. I would be completely lost trying to do what they do. These folks are really the unsung heroes in getting you the latest news and live reports from here in the States as well as hot spots around the world.

For the most part—and to the average viewer—everything seems so organized and easy. But behind the scenes it is usually a scene of chaos and frantic last-minute changes, script writing, ad-libbing, and hoping that the whole presentation goes somewhat according to plan. What viewers don't see are the hours of work and frustration that reporters must spend in tracking down key political figures, shooting an interview, then assembling a report that puts things into perspective and tells the viewer what it all means. A report that airs on the evening newscast for two or three minutes has probably involved three or four people working several hours to gather, write, shoot, edit, and present the finished story.

During the convention, Clarice and I found ourselves swamped trying to follow political developments, tracking down key politicians for interviews, then rushing to compose the stories that would air that night. Sometimes we had to record our voice-over track, or narration, in a hotel room closet or bathroom (not too glamorous!) in order to have some peace and quiet. At the same time, the videotape editors were scrambling to get the story cut and ready to be "fed" to the station via satellite. Trust me, it's never as easy as it looks from your living room.

We wrapped up our coverage of the convention, and Clarice and I took a few hours to really do the only sightseeing we had time for. We went to the top of the Empire State Building, and then headed for the airport to catch the flight back to Dallas. The convention wrapped up on a Thursday night and the boss wanted us back to anchor the 10 o'clock news Friday night in the Dallas studios. I remember both Clarice and I felt we had earned a weekend to relax and explore New York City, but the boss back home wanted us back ASAP. We weren't thrilled, but as I said, these remote assignments are never as easy or as much fun as they may appear to the viewer at home.

When I got back to Dallas that Friday night, I talked to Wayne and reminded him that I had been working non-stop for ten or eleven days, covering the hurricane and then the convention. He agreed it would be fine for me to head to Lake Tahoe to enjoy the clean mountain air and play a few hands of blackjack. I invited my parents, who had never been out there before, and the three of us caught the next plane out to Nevada. We landed at Reno and rented a car for the one-hour drive up to Lake Tahoe.

As we approached the city limits of Lake Tahoe, I was surprised to see lots of flashing police lights and barricades across the highway. As I pulled up to the first police roadblock and checkpoint, I asked the officer what was going on. He said, "You mean, you haven't heard? There is a bomb at Harveys Casino, and the extortionists are demanding $3 million or they will detonate the bomb."

As I began to gather more facts from the people involved, it became a really interesting story. The extortionists had arrived at the casino with a large metal box, purported to be an IBM computer that the casino had purchased. For the security and office personnel on duty at that time, it sounded logical and legitimate. But the so-called "computer" was actually a large explosive device that, as we learned later, incorporated an extremely powerful military explosive called "C-4."

The law enforcement people at the roadblock were really more interested in checking out the people who were leaving the area than those
coming in. But they had a duty to advise us of the situation. When we
arrived in town, Mom and Dad played the slot machines and
saw some shows, but the reporter in me went to work. I started interviewing local city and police officials to get a better handle on what
was happening.

This was the scenario: the disguised computer bomb had been delivered as planned into the management area of the casino. Then, the
extortionists called to explain that unless the casino handed over three
million dollars, the bomb would be detonated. The police scrambled to
put sandbags around the "computer," and tried to decide what to do
next. The extortionists said if any attempt was made to disarm the
bomb, it would explode in sixty seconds.

In the early stages of this story, rumors began flying that the bomb
was perhaps a nuclear device; a miniature atom bomb. That, of course,
got everybody's attention. The Nuclear Regulatory Commission was
alerted in Washington, DC, and because of the possibility that this was
perhaps a small atomic bomb, they sent nuclear experts to Lake Tahoe
on government jets.

As all of this was unfolding, I began to wonder if this sort of thing
happened rather routinely in casino towns—like bank robberies in other
cities. Perhaps, I thought, this is not really a big deal. With all the cash
available at casinos, maybe this was a reasonably routine occurrence in a
city built around gambling.

Lake Tahoe does not have a local TV station, and, in fact, I'm not
even sure it has a local radio station. Therefore, as I assembled these
facts, I began to question the importance of this story. Harveys Casino
was off limits entirely to reporters, but right across the street was
Harrah's Casino and Hotel, which police had not ordered evacuated.

I tipped a bellman $20 and got access to a twentieth-floor room
overlooking Harveys Casino across the street. I then telephoned the
newsroom in Dallas and talked to our 10 o'clock producer, Bob Henry,
and asked him if he had seen anything on the news wires about this
bomb extortion plot in Lake Tahoe. He told me that nothing had come
across the Associated Press wires, or down the line on any CBS closed-
circuit feed. It was a whole new story to him. Again, I thought to myself,
well, maybe this was nothing really out of the ordinary.

But as I looked down at the roadblocks, the flashing lights, I changed my mind—this really was a major story. So, talking to Bob in Dallas, I arranged to do a live telephone report for the 10 o'clock news. It crossed my mind that I was possibly making this story out to be more important than it really was, but I went ahead and recommended to Bob that we go ahead and let me file the report back in Dallas.

The CBS News southwest bureau chief, Travis Lynn (a former news director at WFAA-TV), was watching the news that night when I came on with my report. Nothing had been on the wires. Nothing had come down the lines to CBS. Travis immediately alerted the West Coast bureau of CBS, relating to them what I had reported, and then the word went out across the nation on the Associated Press wire that a multi-million-dollar extortion plot was unfolding in Lake Tahoe.

I decided to stay up that night and keep in communication with local authorities for any new development. I spent a few hours playing blackjack at Harrah's. As the story broke along the West Coast, reporters and TV crews starting coming in from San Francisco and other California cities. Oddly enough, a reporter came up to me at the black-jack table late in the morning and asked me if I was aware that there was a huge bomb across the street in Harveys Casino and that it might go off at any time.

She had no idea I was the one who had broken the story or that I was a TV newsman. I calmly gave her a quick answer that would be a perfect sound-bite for the TV newscast in San Francisco. I told her, "I have just gotten through covering Hurricane Allen in the Gulf of Mexico and the Democratic National Convention in New York, and a little bomb across the street doesn't really worry me that much."

As the day wore on, I saw more and more out-of-town TV crews show up to cover the story. In the back of my mind, I started having just the hint of doubt that perhaps I had caused huge interest in a story that might not be fact; that perhaps this whole bomb story was an imaginative plot to try to bluff the casino into paying the ransom demands. I thought, "What if this is just a big hoax, and I have created all this commotion, and there is really nothing to the story?"

The nuclear bomb experts in Washington, DC, flew in a special remote-controlled robot to try to disarm the bomb. With a TV camera mounted on the robot's head, agents could command the little guy to do various things, while they were at a safe distance away. The bomb device apparently had a keyboard type of control panel, and if the right combination of letters or numbers were entered, it would not explode.

As the day dragged on, more and more reporters showed up. The nuclear bomb experts were busy with their robot, trying to have it punch in the right code to disarm the bomb. Well, something went wrong. The robot punched the wrong button and the "IBM computer" gave the message that it would soon explode, and that to avoid a loss of life, the area should be evacuated. That's precisely what the local authorities did, reinforcing their six-block blockade around the hotel and using police car speakers to warn nearby people that "the bomb was about to explode and to take cover."

The news media representatives were being kept behind a blockade four blocks from the hotel, and non-journalists, including my parents, were being kept behind another set of blockade barriers six blocks away. As the police announced that the bomb had been activated, I had a churning, mixed emotion run through my gut. I was, on one hand, concerned about the potential destruction and loss of life if this bomb actually went off. But at the same time, I worried that if this was all a bluff, I would look kind of stupid.

About that time, however, the whole building—as I recall it was about twelve stories tall—visibly shook. The windows blew out and we felt a shock wave, and then heard the explosion. I'll never forget the succession of those events: seeing the blast, feeling it, and then hearing it. The bomb, which indeed had been sandbagged heavily, directed most of its force upwards and blew through most of the floors above the management area where it had been delivered. Even though this was not a nuclear device, it was still one heck of a big explosion and certainly the biggest one I had ever seen. Fortunately, no one was injured. Inside, I felt an odd sense of relief, because I had been right in my reports, and had not sounded a false alarm.

In the meantime, there was a mad scramble by the reporters to get to telephones and file their reports. I had a sense of pride in "breaking" the story (I had won $800 at the blackjack table as well). Because of the bombing and the national coverage it got, my boss was proud and happy and even offered to pay for my airline ticket and hotel expense because it did turn out to be a legitimate story. I was more than glad to accept the airline ticket refund, the reimbursement for the hotel stay, and a couple extra days of vacation—after covering three major stories back to back.

(Eventually, three people [two men and a woman] were arrested, tried, and convicted in the Lake Tahoe casino bombing.)

6

Later Career Moments

Death on the Highway

As a reporter, it's inevitable that you will cover major traffic accidents . . . and death. There are two traffic accidents that stand out in my mind, both of which I came across by coincidence, meaning they were not assigned stories I had been sent out to cover.

The first one that stands out in my mind happened after the late news was over one night at Channel 4, as I was driving home on Interstate 30. It had been raining all day, but the skies had cleared toward evening and the Texas Rangers had just finished a game against the Boston Red Sox. As I left Dallas at about 11 p.m., I could see the steady stream of traffic coming from Arlington down Interstate 30. As I approached the Loop 12 cutoff, I noticed the traffic in the eastbound lane had come to a stop. There were a few flashing lights and I realized as I came over a small hill that there had been a bad accident in the eastbound lanes. I pulled over to see what had happened. It was a head-on collision.

It seems that a driver from Oklahoma was headed toward Dallas, eastbound, when he decided he was lost, did a U-turn, and then went back down the highway the wrong way. As he crested a hill, he hit a car full of people coming back from the ball game. The two vehicles met left headlight to left headlight. The car with the baseball fans spun around in the middle of the highway. The driver from Oklahoma skidded off into the median next to the guardrail. He survived. Later I was told by the police he had been under the influence of drugs.

The immediate concern for me was seeing if I could help anyone in the car that was coming back from the ball game. Several of the victims had been thrown out of the car, and as I walked around the scene I saw that the driver was dead, and there were two dead people in the back of the car.

I remember hearing the sirens as the ambulances tried to get to the scene, which was difficult because the traffic was so thick. A firetruck and ambulance both got stuck in the mud on the shoulder of the road. On the highway lay a young lady, barely alive, who I talked to. As I bent over her, she said her dad was a doctor at Baylor Hospital and asked if I could call and tell him she was on the way. While she explained this, I put my ear to her mouth, but then she died.

Some of the onlookers came up to me, recognizing me from television. Someone asked me to cover up the bodies, but I didn't have anything to cover them with. I tried to explain that there wasn't anything I could do to help these people. In the end, five people were killed in that traffic accident.

The driver of the car who was at fault did, however, survive. I'm sure he was charged with negligent or vehicular homicide, but I don't recall his name and I don't recall the disposition of the case. But I do know the emergency workers had to cut him out of his wreckage. They worked hard to save his life and did. I've always wondered what happened to that driver. I wonder what he's doing today back home in Oklahoma, if he thinks about the accident. He's probably holding down a job somewhere, and maybe this accident is always in the back of his mind. I would surely hope so.

While on the scene of that accident, I tried to gather information for a news story. When I talked to one of the witnesses, he said a taxicab was just barely involved. The cab was parked on the eastbound shoulder, a few hundred yards from the actual point of impact, so I went up to the driver and found out just how close the accident had come to being a story with national implications. The taxi driver, who saw the entire incident and was sideswiped by the driver of the vehicle that caused the accident, said he had been carrying from the ballpark two star players for the Boston Red Sox, Carl Yastrzemski and Dock Ellis. They came within inches of being involved and maybe even losing their lives. It was a close call.

Another accident I came across also happened one night after the late news. A woman had lost control of her car a ways ahead of me and went off the highway into a ditch, rolling over several times. There were only a few cars ahead of me which were pulling over to stop—they, too, had just seen the accident. I was about ten cars behind and didn't know what was going on. I think most people have a genuine concern, along with a morbid curiosity, about the people involved in traffic accidents. I stopped with everyone else and ran over to see what had happened.

The woman's car was upside down and very badly damaged. The driver was wearing her seatbelt, but she was hanging upside down and we could see that she was badly bleeding out of her mouth. At the same time, we could hear these gurgling sounds as if there was a build-up of blood in her lungs and throat and she might suffocate. We desperately tried to get in from the other side of the car, but it was impossible. I shouted that we could use a crowbar or a heavy metal bar.

One of the fellows at the scene brought a tool for changing tires and we tried to get through the rear window of the car. I had been warned over the years that sometimes it's not prudent to try to assist accident victims who have neck or back injuries because if there were complications, you, the would-be rescuer, could be held responsible for injuring the victim. But it seemed so irrelevant and so stupid to not try to do something. So we broke out the window behind the driver and I was able to get down, crawl partly inside, and reach around her seat and seatbelt, and hold her head at an angle to try to minimize the choking and gagging. At the time, I thought I was really helping this woman— she was probably about thirty-five years old. I thought that at least I could keep her alive until the paramedics arrived.

As I was laying on my chest, with my arm through the back window, holding her head back up, I could tell she was still breathing and this gave me hope. There was a crowd of about 15 people, all trying to help, and we were thinking we might be able to flip the car right side up. But then the paramedics arrived and they somehow ripped open the driver's door and pulled her out, got her over to the ambulance and placed her inside. But by then she had stopped breathing. The emergency workers jolted her with the electric pads several times, but I could see through the back of the ambulance that she wasn't responding. After three or four minutes, they closed the doors and drove off—without their flashing lights. That told me they had already determined she had died. You feel so helpless in a situation like that, and you realize how quickly your life can change and your life can be over. In a split second, she hit a curb, swerved out of control, flipped over and was fatally injured, living only a few more minutes. You wish you could help more, but sometimes there's nothing you can do.

Lee Harvey Oswald's Rifle

In 1983, while at KDFW-TV, Channel 4, we decided to do a twentieth anniversary special on the assassination of John F. Kennedy. As part of that assignment, I went to Washington, DC, to film part of the story at the National Archives.

One of the special things about being in the news business is that sometimes we have access to things to which the general public is not privy. We requested that the folks at the National Archives put up a display of items related to the Kennedy assassination down in the catacombs of the archives, and I felt privileged to be so near these items and to be able to explain what they all meant to our viewers back home.

We started filming the various articles on the display table, one of which was the Italian Mannlicher-Carcano bolt-action, clip-fed rifle that Oswald allegedly used to kill President Kennedy. There was also the blood-stained shirt of the late president.

And in small, plastic bags there were bullet fragments from President Kennedy's head and from the limousine. There was also a bag with the "magic bullet" that supposedly went through the president's neck and through Governor John Connally's back and wrist, coming out undamaged. It was an odd feeling to hold in my hand those pieces of metal that killed a president and forever changed US history.

I picked up the rifle—it was so small in size and weight, not unlike a .22 rifle, it surprised me. I held the rifle up and looked through the scope. At that moment, seeing the crosshairs, I was overwhelmed. I felt I could see history. I imagined that this was possibly the sight that Lee Harvey Oswald peered through at Kennedy's head when he pulled the trigger with the fatal shot. It took my breath away.

While in Washington, we also shot some footage at Kennedy's grave and the eternal flame. The cemetery's personnel told us that the Kennedy family had mandated that no one's face could be photographed with the flame at the same time. This seemed like an odd restriction, but we got around it. We'd pan from me doing a commentary about the assassination down to the flame, always keeping my face out of the same picture.

When we returned home, I received permission from the Dallas County Historical Society to do part of the story at the old Texas School Book Depository. We shot the scene from the window where Oswald allegedly perched when he fired the rifle. I sat in that window and looked down over the grassy knoll. At that moment, I felt very privileged to be so close to an event that had such an impact on virtually every American and millions of people around the world.

I guess questions will always surround the president's assassination. Was there a conspiracy? Was there more than one gunman? What was that puff of smoke from the grassy knoll? All the mysteries surrounding John F. Kennedy's assassination continue to this day, and perhaps will never be solved to everyone's satisfaction.

Virtually every night, I drive right down the middle lane of Elm Street as I head home from work, and I pass by the grassy knoll and the old School Book Depository. Hardly a night goes by that I don't think about all that took place there.

The Move to Houston

After I had made the move to Channel 4 in 1980, I was told that station consultants at WFAA-TV Channel 8 several years earlier had recommended to management that they try to hire me away from Channel 5. I also heard that the management's answer to the consultants was "No." There was an unwritten rule in Dallas-Fort Worth that the various stations didn't raid each other for anchors. But KDFW-TV apparently hadn't heard of that rule, and it was a big benefit to me both professionally and financially.

All of this did not go unnoticed at Channel 8, especially since the 6 and 10 p.m. news ratings at Channel 4 suddenly jumped, pushing us up from number three into a virtual seesaw battle with Channel 8 for the top spot. The sales department said the difference in ratings the first two years I was there resulted in an extra six million dollars in revenue for the station. They could charge more for commercials because so many more people were watching. Some of the guys in sales kidded me, calling me the "six-million-dollar man." Very good for the ego.

Then along came the next big change in Texas television. The AH Belo Corporation, which owns WFAA-TV and *The Dallas Morning News*, purchased five television stations around the country from Corinthian Broadcasting in one of the biggest broadcasting purchases in history, for $600 million—in Houston, Sacramento, Tulsa, Norfolk, and Indianapolis. The largest of the new stations was KHOU-TV, the CBS affiliate in Houston. The next move for AH Belo was renovation on a massive scale. The aim was to improve each of these stations and in the process improve company profits for stockholders. Now the WFAA consultants had their hands full with the responsibilities and demands of so many new markets.

KHOU was performing poorly in the news ratings at that time, trailing long-time leader KTRK-TV Channel 13 and KPRC-TVChannel 2. It

Chip Moody leaves Channel 4
Moody decision
Houston station wants Chip Moody as anchor
Houston station pursues Moody
p off Channel 4 block?
Why in the world did Ch. 4 let Chip go?
on TV station wants anchorman Moody
Moody to anchor newscasts at Houston station KHOU-TV
Moody decision on offer could come this weekend

didn't take long for the consultants and WFAA management to say to themselves, "Here's a chance to get Chip on our team, albeit in Houston, and get him off the air at Channel 4 and out of direct competition with us in Dallas."

So in 1984, I got a telephone call from the top management at AH Belo and Channel 8 asking me to a lunch meeting, and I agreed. They presented their idea, and it was an exciting and flattering proposition. They wanted me to join them and help them rebuild KHOU-TV. In terms of the TV industry, Houston does not have quite as large a market as Dallas-Fort Worth, but the two are close. The latest ranking puts Dallas-Fort Worth as seventh in the nation and Houston as ninth. Considering there are about 270 or so markets in the country, the difference in rankings between Dallas-Fort Worth and Houston is negligible. Plus, Belo was offering me a huge salary increase to relocate to Houston. It was really a case of apples and oranges; I had been in Dallas-Fort Worth for fourteen years and wasn't unhappy at Channel 4 or looking to move, so I really didn't feel motivated to make such a drastic change. Still, a virtual doubling of my salary was something I could hardly ignore. It was a tough, tough decision that I was wrestling with. I expected the decision to become even harder when I told the guys at Channel 4 about the offer. I figured they would probably offer me a pretty substantial pay raise to keep me; we were, after all, enjoying great ratings since I had come on board.

When I did actually meet with my bosses, they kept asking what Belo had offered me. I told them that it really didn't matter what the exact offer was because they were asking me to leave Dallas-Fort Worth—my home—and move my family to Houston. Naturally, there would be an incentive for me to stay at Channel 4, and I believed they should make me their own offer based on what I had contributed to our success. As the days dragged on, my bosses at Channel 4 kept insisting that I tell them what the offer from Belo was, and I kept saying that it didn't matter. After a week, I said they should make their own offer, and let me make a decision. I didn't ask them to meet or beat the salary increase to go to Houston, I just wanted to get an idea of what they felt in their heart I was worth to their operation. But no offer came. I was disappointed and surprised. Finally, after ten days, I asked again if they had come up with an offer, and the answer was, "No, we're still thinking." I explained that it was unfair to keep the other company hanging and I hoped to see something on my desk the next day. The next day came, and still nothing. So, I talked to the broadcasting division president and told him he had left me no option. I didn't even have an offer to renew my old contract. At this point, I felt my hand was being forced. The next day, I met with the Belo officials, signed the new contract, and resigned from Channel 4.

In the following weeks and months I was excited by the new challenge and promotion, sorry that I had to leave Dallas-Fort Worth, and busy as heck actually moving. Dan Rather had been an anchor at KHOU-TV, so the sense of tradition there was impressive.

The move to Houston was the first relocation for the kids—and they weren't very happy about it. While they understood that I had to go, they didn't want to leave all their friends, most of whom they had grown up with. When I was young, I was always sad when Dad was transferred to a new location, but after a year in the new place, I had found new friends and life continued. Trae and Tiffin adapted pretty well, but still maintained ties with their buddies back in Dallas, Fort Worth, and Arlington.

Vikki took the move as an exciting new challenge. She enjoyed the process of looking for a new house and exploring the various neighborhoods and shopping centers in Houston. She fully understood and accepted the reasons for the move, but deep down inside, I don't think she ever felt "at home." It would all change so suddenly. . .

Back Home

After we settled in Houston in 1984, I threw myself into this new position—and got involved in community events as well. Just as I was getting settled in the new job, and as all of us were getting acclimated to a new city and new surroundings, I faced something more challenging than a move to a new city and new responsibilities. It was in Houston that I was diagnosed with cancer, and suddenly all of that really didn't matter. But that's another story . . .

To be honest, those years in Houston are colored by my battle with cancer. By the time I had finished my chemotherapy and radiation treatments at MD Anderson and slowly began regaining some of the weight I had lost, the new anchor team of Steve Smith and Felicia Jeter had settled into a comfortable routine at KHOU-TV. In addition to my cancer battles, I lost more than a few dollars in the real estate crash, and never did get accustomed to that Houston humidity. I was homesick for Dallas-Fort Worth—so was my family—and I began to think of returning.

I knew, of course, that my health would be of concern to any TV station. But after a chat with then Channel 8 News Director Marty Haag, he agreed to gamble and bring me back to Dallas.

Vikki and the kids were overjoyed. Old friends would be right around the corner, and my parents, sister, and brother-in-law still lived in Arlington, so we'd be close to them, too.

While I recuperated in the hospital, Vikki found and leased a house on Lake Arlington, to give us time to search for a new house to buy. We always knew we'd be back in Arlington, because of its central location in the Metroplex and because we were attached to the area and the lifestyle. Vikki handled the movers and got the house ready to live in. For me to escape that hassle was the silver lining in the cloud.

That was 1987. Since then, there have been some health problems, but thankfully the cancer has stayed in remission. Sometimes I feel like an old gunfighter who gets shot up over and over again but keeps on coming back. The people in Dallas-Fort Worth who had been watching me for those many years before I went to Houston and the warmth and confidence of the team at WFAA gave me such a positive lift. I know it made a big difference in my recovery.

The Killeen Massacre

Whenever I talk to groups, I mention that one of the really interesting aspects of being in the news business is that no two days are ever the same. You have the same typewriter (or computer screen these days), the same news set, the same cameras. But the content of each day's news is different. Some days there is good news, some days bad news. Sometimes there is a natural disaster. Many times these stories break so quickly it's as if you are swept up in them.

On October 16, 1991, I joined some other local media and sports figures at the old Mrs. Baird's Bread bakery on the south side of downtown Fort Worth for a hospital fundraising effort. Executives with Mrs. Baird's had decided to relocate the venerable old bakery, and as part of the relocation, they decided to celebrate with a fresh bread sale to benefit Cook-Fort Worth Children's Medical Center. Local TV, radio, and sports figures were recruited to sell loaves of fresh bread on the street to passing motorists, will all the money going to the hospital. In all, we collected more than $30,000 at a dollar a loaf for that event. It was a good day that would quickly turn bad.

We arrived about 11 a.m., donned aprons, and began hawking bread. It was a lot of fun, but little did we know that 100 miles to the south one of the most terrifying incidents in domestic US history was unfolding. A mentally crazed former merchant marine, George Hennard, had crashed his pickup truck through the front of a Luby's restaurant in Killeen around noon. He pulled out a 9-millimeter Glock 17 semi-automatic pistol, and he walked through the restaurant, killing the men and women inside. It would ultimately turn out to be the worst mass shooting in US history.

In Fort Worth, we continued to sell bread, smiling and meeting citizens as they drove by, none of us aware of what was unfolding in Killeen. About 1 p.m., I wrapped up my two-hour shift, bought a couple of loaves of bread for myself, and headed off for downtown Dallas and the studios of WFAA-TV Channel 8. On the radio, I heard early reports that a gunman had killed several people at a restaurant in the central Texas town of Killeen, in Bell County. Obviously, it was a breaking news story I knew we would be covering later that day on our news at 5 and 6 p.m. But at the time, it wasn't clear just how major a story this would be.

By the time I arrived at the newsroom, executives at the station we work closely with in Waco (my alma mater, KWTX-TV) were telling us that they were at the scene—about thirty miles south of Waco—and that the death toll was accelerating as we spoke. Channel 8 News Director John Miller had already dispatched a couple of reporters and cameramen in mobile units, and they would be arriving by 3 p.m., which would be in plenty of time to send us reports from the scene.

As the death toll climbed into the teens, John looked around and said to me, "Let's send you to Killeen." He quickly ordered that a Lear jet be chartered at Love Field, and picked out a crew to go with me. We would be doing what we call in the news business "field anchoring," which involves one of the regular anchors going to the scene of a major story and helping coordinate and tie together reports at the location: the story could be a hurricane, a political convention, or, in this case, a major act of violence.

One of the really nice advantages of working at WFAA-TV has been its commitment to covering the big stories without any real concern about the cost. We do whatever it takes. I remember covering the tornado that hit Wichita Falls on April 10, 1979 while working for Channel 5. Although the station sent our helicopter, when I got to the scene I found Channel 8 had chartered not one, but two corporate jets, and was ferrying videotapes from the scene back to the station. Plus they had at least half a dozen camera crews at the scene.

At Channel 8, that was the philosophy in the Killeen case and it still is the philosophy today: pull out the stops, and do everything to give the public immediate and accurate information. Get to the scene as quickly as possible and get the best information available to the viewer.

As I headed out the door on that day in October, the death toll in Killeen, according to KWTX-TV and the Associated Press, was past fifteen and whoever had been doing the shooting inside the restaurant was involved in a shoot-out with law enforcement officers. We left Love Field for Killeen and touched down forty-two minutes later. We arrived at the restaurant only moments later, since it was only a couple of miles from the airport.

When we arrived, witnesses and survivors were milling around outside. The shoot-out was over. The gunman was dead inside the restaurant and so were a lot of innocent patrons. Nobody knew exactly how many had died, but a spokesman for the Department of Public Safety was trying to keep up with the latest information and briefed reporters as often as possible.

A terrible, horrifying picture began to emerge. After crashing into the dining area, the gunman announced something to the effect that "this is what Bell County has done to me, this is what Killeen has done to me, I hope you're happy." And then he started walking through the restaurant, shooting people as they cowered under their tables, or squeezed together on restaurant benches. He was well armed, and reloaded his Glock 17 pistol several times.

As I spoke with survivors, some still crying, some obviously shaken, others still disbelieving and trying to sort things out, the scope of the carnage became more and more clear. Some of the survivors had escaped by breaking out a window and crawling through. Others in the restaurant had no chance. The gunman walked up to numerous people, aimed his gun, and simply pulled the trigger. One older man was shot in front of his wife. He was just moments from dying and his wife cradled him in her arms. As she looked up at the gunman, he shot and killed her, too.

Employees tried to scramble to safety. One bus boy hid in a commercial dishwasher and didn't come out until many hours after the shooting had stopped. He was understandably frightened and still not sure if the shooting had indeed ended.

Next door to the restaurant, authorities set up an information center for civilians, writing down the names of survivors on one blackboard and the names of the wounded on another. They also commandeered a room to counsel relatives who showed up and did not see the names of their loved ones on the boards. They were quietly told of their deaths.

As fate would have it, it was Boss's Day in Killeen and it was also payday at nearby Fort Hood, so there was a larger than usual crowd at the restaurant. Authorities later said 162 people were in the building. As the horrific scene unfolded, a strange coincidence emerged—DPS undercover officers were attending a seminar at the Sheraton Hotel adjacent to the restaurant only 100 yards away.

When the Killeen police, local DPS officers and the undercover DPS officers got word of the massacre in progress, they responded quickly with guns drawn. They began a running gun battle, but used extreme caution so as not to shoot any innocent bystander or restaurant patron.

The situation, according to reports, was havoc. DPS Sergeant Jody Fore of Waco went to the rear of the restaurant, spotted Hennard, but could not get a clear shot at him. The officer did fire four rounds and apparently wounded Hennard, who crawled into the restaurant's bathroom. His gun was jammed, but once inside the bathroom he was able to clear the pistol. At that point, he put the gun to his head, pulled the trigger, and killed himself.

Incredibly, the shooting spree lasted only ten or eleven minutes. Twenty-two customers and workers were killed, twenty-three others were wounded, and Hennard was dead. Every available ambulance from miles around rushed to the scene. Army helicopters were dispatched from Fort Hood to transport some of the injured to Darnell Army Hospital. Metroplex Hospital in Killeen accepted seven wounded, Darnell admitted eleven, and five were transported to Scott and White Hospital in nearby Temple.

With our news teams now in position, the satellite truck up and operating, and field producers on the scene working with news managers back at Channel 8, assignments were quickly made. Crews were sent to the various hospitals and to the emergency Red Cross center set up at the Sheraton Hotel, where friends and relatives began streaming in for information about their loved ones. Reporters and camera crews were sent to Hennard's hometown in Belton, just a few miles away, to find out more about this former merchant marine, who had been disciplined for marijuana use and had been writing threatening letters and stalking area women.

We kept a couple of reporters and producers in the vicinity of the restaurant to gather additional information from various sources and witnesses, and to interview them or try to convince them to appear live with me on our breaking bulletins and regularly scheduled newscasts.

The Ford pickup truck Hennard drove still rested inside the restaurant. And even late into the evening, the DPS, Killeen police, and medical examiners elected not to move the bodies or otherwise disturb the crime scene until they had completed their investigations.

It was a bizarre feeling for this reporter to be standing just outside the restaurant, broadcasting live reports back to Dallas-Fort Worth, saying that twenty-two victims and Hennard himself were still lying where they had died; some were under the buffet line, others under tables, another under the truck. Others were killed as they tried to flee out the doors.

Late that night, authorities finally began moving the bodies from the restaurant and into special trucks for transportation to Dallas for autopsies. It was a sad and somber sight for the residents of Killeen and for viewers across the nation. But it was especially heartbreaking for those who had lost family and friends.

The massacre captured news coverage and interest around the world. Killeen will continue to bear the wounds and the scars of a man gone mad, a man who took twenty-two innocent lives during the lunch hour at a family restaurant. As a reporter and a person, it's a tragic story I'll never forget.

II

CANCER
MOMENTS

7

The Enemy Within

I_T WAS_ M_AY OF_ 1986. T_HE_ CANCER
that was growing within me grew without pain or discomfort.

I was at home in Houston one evening and looked in the mirror and noticed that the right side of my neck was swollen; it was noticeably larger than the left side. In a way, it looked as if I had the neck of a football line-backer on the right side, and a normal neck on the left side. I felt around, and deep inside the neck tissue, I could just barely discern a lump. It didn't hurt when I pushed it, and I thought to myself, this must be a swollen gland. But because I did not have a sore throat or a cough, the first seed of doubt was planted: perhaps it was something more serious.

During my years as a broadcaster in Dallas/Fort Worth, I enjoyed supporting a large number of charities and organizations in celebrity golf tournaments. I would play in perhaps ten or twelve tournaments a year. Although there were flashes of glory (perhaps I should say flashes of good luck with wonderful shots), I was an average golfer who enjoyed the game and the fellowship, along with helping out the various charity organizations, which included the Leukemia Society of America, the American Cancer Society, the Boy Scouts, the Boys Clubs, Big Brothers and Big Sisters, and others.

Because of my close ties to Dallas-Fort Worth, I stayed active in various charity events while in Houston. I flew up on occasion to help with a chili cook-off, or a golf tournament. That year, I had accepted an invitation to play in the Danny White Boy Scouts of America tournament, scheduled for the first week in June. There was a party and auction the night before the tournament at the Bear Creek Golf Course adjacent to

DFW Airport. I planned to attend, making a full weekend of it all.

As I prepared for my trip, the swelling in my neck gnawed at my subconscious. I decided I could make a quick visit to my personal physician in Dallas, Dr. Neal Sklaver, before tee-off time on Monday. Dr. Sklaver understood the tight schedule, and saw me without an appointment. He listened to my

Dr. Rick Hagemiester explains my cancer and the treatments to come in 1986.

lack of symptoms and felt the swelling. He said to give him a call back after I finished the golf game.

The tournament was providing rooms for the out-of-town celebrities at the DFW Hyatt Hotel, and after I had finished my round of golf, I went back to the hotel to shower and clean up, preparing for the post-tournament awards and dinner.

Anxious to hear what Dr. Sklaver had to say in the way of a diagnosis, I gave him a quick call. He said, "I'm not an expert in this field, and since you are living in Houston, I have set up an appointment for you with a doctor I know there. In fact, I'd like you to see him as soon as possible. I set up an appointment for tomorrow."

I could feel a sense of apprehension growing in the pit of my stomach. Obviously, Dr. Sklaver wasn't writing a prescription for a swollen gland. I asked him the name of the doctor in Houston and he told me a Dr. Helmut Gepford would see me the next afternoon. My heart skipped a beat and I asked Dr. Sklaver where this Dr. Gepford had his practice. The answer hit me like a sixteen-pound sledgehammer to the gut: MD Anderson Hospital. I knew exactly what MD Anderson doctors practiced. No broken legs, no pregnancies, no flu cases. MD Anderson treated cancer.

I sat in my room for what seemed like hours, letting Dr. Sklaver's words sink in. I missed most of the awards dinner—I had actually even won a small fishing boat for knocking my golf ball closest to the pin on hole #17. One of my golf partners, former Channel 8 and ABC anchorman Murphy Martin, noticed my absence and when I finally went down in time for dessert, he asked where I had been. I could only answer that I wasn't feeling well and had taken a short nap. Inside, the fear in my heart was growing, and it was hard to concentrate on anything. I was both anxious to see Dr. Helmut Gepford the next day and scared of what he might say.

After arriving back in Houston, I headed to the hospital. It sounds like a cliché, but I really did have butterflies in my stomach. Walking through the doors at MD Anderson, I felt fear. I found the doctor's office and we met briefly. He examined my neck and abdomen and told me to return over the next several days for a battery of tests.

I resumed my normal work schedule, but I secretly slipped away during the early afternoon hours for a series of tests, exams, CAT scans, x-rays. One test was a fine-needle aspiration, in which a long needle is inserted in a tumor, and fluid is drained off for examination under a microscope. Another was a bone marrow extraction, which is not much fun. They put a large, hollow needle into my hip bone and pulled out a vial of bone marrow fluid. Then there was the bronchoscopy, in which they put a long, fiber-optic tube into your lungs and look around.

The tests seemed to go on and on. The doctors said they were assembling as much information as they could in order to make the most accurate diagnosis possible. I did not tell anyone at home or at work what was going on. I didn't want to cause any undue alarm.

Finally, the tests were completed. I met with the doctor on Friday* of the same week of that first appointment. It was about 1 p.m. As we sat in the examining room, Dr. Gepford simply said, "You have cancer." I remember sitting there in silence for about fifteen seconds, letting the gravity of his sentence sink in. As I sat there, the first words out of my mouth were just, "Well, I guess we've got some work to do."

I asked the doctor what else he could tell me. He could only say we would know more as further results came back on the tests. At that time, doctors were not sure of the extent of the cancer. Within a few days it was narrowed down to Stage 3 Hodgkin's disease. In other terms, this was an advanced case of cancer of the lymphatic system, a cancer that attacks the white blood cells and the body's immune system. Without a proper immune system, a simple virus can kill you.

Dr. Gepford said the first move would be to have an operation on my neck to remove and examine the tumor. Assuming this surgery would take place in the next month or so, I told the doctor I'd get with my boss and figure out when I could take a week off for the surgery. I'll

* It was actually Friday the 13th.

never forget the doctor's reply when I told him this. He said, "You don't understand. We need to operate right away, and I have scheduled your surgery for Monday morning."

Until he said this, I hadn't accepted the urgency of my situation. I guess I had prepared myself for some cancer treatment, but it didn't occur to me that quick action was so critical. I was introduced to Dr. Rick Hagemiester, who specializes in lymphatic cancers. He would be in charge of my treatment throughout the next year and beyond.

When I met with Dr. Hagemiester, I asked him if he knew what caused this kind of cancer, and he said doctors were not really sure. It is an unusual cancer that, for the most part, afflicts people from the teenage years to about the age of thirty-five. I was thirty-nine.

In the process of my examinations at MD Anderson, it was determined that the cancer was in the lymph gland on the right side of my neck and that one tonsil was also affected. As surgery would later prove, my spleen was also totally involved. I got a pretty good cram course in pre-med, learning that the spleen is a kind of oil filter for the body, trapping impurities and cleansing the blood. My spleen had indeed been trapping impurities, in the way of cancer cells, but in doing so had become a large tumor in itself.

When I left the hospital the day I learned of my cancer, I was exhausted and scared. How would I deal with it, how would I tell everyone? I found my car in the parking garage at the hospital and made my way down to the ticket booth. Here I was, trying to absorb the fact I was now facing a major crisis in my life and trying to let this all settle into my brain and still do regular stuff like drive my car. Well, I drove to the toll booth and handed my ticket to the attendant and she said, "That'll be seven dollars." And I just said, "No. You don't understand. I have cancer. I am a patient here. I'm probably going to die soon. Parking should be free for the patients." And she said, "Well it's the same for everybody." I thought maybe I could use a patient ID bracelet or something. I found out that no matter who you are, going to the hospital is always expensive.

I drove away from the hospital thinking that now I must face the hard part: I was a son, husband, father, and employee. My family and friends would have to know soon. I returned to work that Friday afternoon and asked our news director, Alan Parcell (now with CBS News), if I could have a word with him. We closed the door to his office, and I explained that I had secretly been undergoing these tests at MD Anderson, and the diagnosis was cancer, with surgery scheduled in three days.

Alan and I then went to the station manager, Terry Ford, and explained to him that I had cancer, and I would be starting a long period of surgery and treatment in a matter of days. We scrapped my appearance on the newscasts that day, and he told me to just head home to tell my wife.

Vikki had noticed I wasn't on the early news and had wondered why. Perhaps I had been sent out on a breaking story or something. But when I arrived home very, very early, she knew something was wrong. I stood in the foyer of our home, I hugged her, paused for a moment, and said, "I've got some bad news . . . I've got cancer and they want to operate on Monday." I had been saying those words out loud in the car, rehearsing what I would say. My wife and family were, understandably, just beginning to feel the first shock wave.

Sadly, this was Father's Day weekend. I knew I would have to tell my parents in person, and soon. I caught a flight up to Dallas-Fort Worth on Saturday. Mom and Dad were delighted that I had decided to surprise them with a visit on Father's Day. That jubilant mood was quickly extinguished.

I explained to my parents as simply as I could that I had been diagnosed with cancer, and that I was scheduled for surgery in about forty-eight hours. Dad, the former Air Force pilot, was as stoic and as understanding as possible, but Mom broke down in tears. It was the worst Father's Day present I could have given them.

Things began moving fast. I flew back to Houston, and Vikki had already started a suitcase with pajamas, socks, books, shaving kit, and other stuff for my hospital stay. My parents made plans to come down to be there for my surgery Monday morning.

As it turned out, the doctors opened my neck and removed a tumor about the size of a small egg. It did not take the hospital experts long to analyze it, and discover it was malignant. Now we had our next decision; major surgery to remove the spleen and appendix was the normal procedure. Or there was another option, and that was to skip surgery, but undergo long-term, extensive chemotherapy, with the assumption that the cancer had spread beyond my neck.

My doctors felt we should remove the spleen, determine the extent of the cancer, and then formulate a plan of radiation and chemotherapy treatments. Dr. Hagemiester said if we didn't operate, he would be forced to proceed on the assumption of widespread cancer, and give me significantly higher amounts of chemotherapy and radiation. Depending on the condition of the tissue in the spleen after surgery, it might keep the radiation and chemo treatments to a minimum. It seemed to me surgery would be the best option at this stage, then the doctors would know for sure and they could formulate the best treatment plan possible with the medical evidence they had at hand.

As I was to learn, the doctors at MD Anderson are advocates of "aggressive treatment," that is, heavy doses of chemotherapy and radiation. They had seen all too often just how deadly cancers can be. It's a tough and formidable enemy, so doctors are not hesitant to fight back as hard as they can with whatever weapons they have at their disposal.

I would learn that chemotherapy was not just a single type of drug, but rather a combination of different drugs that kill cancer cells. Each cancer case is different, and a doctor will use his or her best judgment in formulating the best combination of drugs and radiation. In my case, Dr. Hagemiester said he would treat this as an even more serious case (Stage 4 Hodgkin's) just to be on the safe side. This meant a stout regimen of heavy-duty drugs. In cancer hospitals, a number of these drugs are called the "big guns" because they pack the most punch. At the same time, they are the most debilitating to the patient.

Dr. Hagemiester set me up on a prescription (or protocol, as he called it) that was nicknamed "MOPP" because of the four primary drugs used in the treatment. He did not elect to give me adriamycin (often called red devil, the drug that makes people lose all their hair). Instead, he picked nitrogen mustard for my "big gun." This is a second cousin to the infamous mustard gas of World War I, used to poison enemy troops. Make no mistake, nitrogen mustard is a deadly poison, but you must use powerful drugs to combat cancer.

I was afraid. Just the word "chemotherapy" is scary. For my very first treatment, doctors taped my arm to a structure reminiscent of a big, wooden school desk. My arm was taped down and made immobile because some of the drugs that would begin to flow through my body were very caustic and if the IV needle were to come out, the drug would seriously burn my skin. That wasn't too exciting to hear. Doctors started an IV, and about 200 milliliters of several different drugs began running into my veins. The last drug to be administered would be the nitrogen mustard, and the nurse brought it out in a special syringe.

The nurse inserted the syringe into the IV line and she told me it would take about ten minutes to deliver all the contents in—a process called a "slow push." Well, she got everything adjusted and inserted the needle into the line. As she did this, however, my blood pressure began pushing the plunger back up *out* of the syringe. The nurse, who was wearing protective plastic gloves, did not see what was happening. I could see that the syringe's plunger was backing up and that this drug was about to overflow onto the IV line and the floor.

I called her attention to it, and said I thought the top of the syringe was coming out. She looked at it for a split second—she was still holding the syringe in her left hand—and then, fearing the worst, she began backing up, now holding the syringe out at arm's length. The plunger came out and fell to the floor, and the nitrogen mustard started to flow out. The nurse let out a loud exclamation, dropped the syringe, and made a quick exit from the room.

It was obvious the nurse wanted nothing to do with this drug, and by the way she was acting, I expected the stuff to hit the floor and start eating through the linoleum like something out of the movie *Alien*. Well, it did overflow, but it did not eat the linoleum and it did not hit the nurse. The hospital staff came and wiped it up, and then they had to make a new dosage for me. I figured the stuff was probably like Drano, the way people were afraid of it. And, in many respects, that's about what it was like—very, very caustic. The drug actually destroyed some of my veins. People who have chemotherapy have veins so battered from the chemicals inserted into their bodies that they collapse.

I'll never forget that first chemotherapy treatment and the nurse who ran away from it. These drugs are indeed heavy-duty stuff, but I, and others who have been in my situation, cannot run from them.

As a result of my treatment, I did not lose my hair (although the doctors did provide me with a wig that made me look a bit like Phil Donahue). Thankfully, I didn't have to wear the wig (I did lose some hair during radiation, but I never did end up completely bald like those patients who have to take adriamycin).

The primary adverse affect for me was severe nausea and vomiting. In fact, I could almost time it to the minute after my chemo treatment at the hospital: in almost every case, it would be exactly ninety minutes later and I would be vomiting uncontrollably. For the week following each treatment, it was especially difficult to eat. Even the smell of food made me nauseous. On those occasions when I would try to eat something, I almost invariably threw everything up after fifteen or thirty minutes. Many times, food had a metallic taste to it, or tasted like cardboard. This led to a significant weight loss, of course, and doctors were very careful to make sure my blood counts did not get too low. Low blood counts could cause irreversible infection or death.

It was a balancing act for my doctors. They had to give me the most medicine my body could handle, without pushing too far. I remember commenting to a nurse that this constant vomiting and nausea was not too much fun. "It seems like they almost have to kill you to get you better." The nurse answered, "That's right, it's a tough enemy, and we have to push you right to the limits if we're going to save your life."

❖   ❖   ❖   ❖   ❖

When cancer hits an individual, it has a reverberating impact that dramatically affects his or her family. Vikki, Trae, and Tiffin had to wrestle with my mortality every day for perhaps a year. But Vikki was a solid rock through all this, buoying up the kids, my parents, and me.

After the initial shock of the diagnosis, we tried to keep things at home as normal as possible. Trae and Tiffin were in the fourth and fifth grades then. Vikki worked hard at insulating the kids from the true seriousness of my illness that first year. Although Mom, Dad, and Vikki paid me regular visits in the hospital, the kids didn't come along too often, because the situation and the scene were pretty scary for children that age. Vikki would create games or projects to keep their minds off the fact that Dad was in the hospital minus a couple cancerous organs, tubed up with IV lines, with large metal staples running down his abdomen from the first of several surgeries, and drifting in and out of reality depending on doses of painkillers.

I think that Trae and Tiffin knew deep down that something serious was going on—and that I was facing a tough fight—but I don't think they consciously thought about me dying. It's normal for youngsters to suppress thoughts like that, rarely bringing such fears to the surface. It's easier to deal with a nasty situation if you don't look at it straight in the eye, or dwell on it.

But the strain of trying to maintain some sense of "normalcy," combined with an undercurrent of despair, was heavy, and prompted Vikki to set up some family counseling sessions for her and the kids. Talking about possible changes and life and death helped everyone cope a little better with the possibilities of the treatment not working or the cancer spreading. Yet when they visited me in the hospital, they always had smiles and nifty presents. That renewed my determination to get through the operations and the chemo and the radiation—to come through okay for a new chance at life.

I couldn't have made it without those three keeping the faith and giving me quiet encouragement and confidence.

8

Megan Mills

THIS IS A VERY TOUGH STORY FOR ME TO tell. When I first got to Houston, in Dan Rather's old anchor job at the CBS affiliate, KHOU-TV, it was incumbent upon me to go out and visit with sick children. My first year there, MD Anderson asked local celebrities to come out and participate in a parade around the hospital complex to kick off Christmas card sales raising money for the children who were patients. I've always enjoyed being with people, and this volunteer time was meaningful and enjoyable.

At the parade, I rode around in an antique fire truck with a young lady by the name of Megan Mills, who had lost a leg to bone cancer. She was nine years old. Megan and I visited as we rode around in the truck and became fast friends. I had no idea at the time, of course, that I would also be a patient at the hospital's cancer center only a year later.

When I first met Megan at the parade, I was basically being "a good guy" for my job and doing my bit for the community. I felt compassion for Megan and the other people at the hospital, but it never occurred to me that I would soon be in their shoes. Later, when I entered the hospital for surgery, Megan was still there and it was good to have a friend. "Now we're both in the same bucket," I told her.

When I was first hospitalized, I was going through what you could call minor testing, in the sense that I didn't have to be anesthetized. I think I went through just about every test that MD Anderson had—or at least nine out of ten. But I'm sure there were some other tests that were more painful or extensive than mine. The tests that I was going through included bone marrow extractions, sonograms, x-rays, and fine needle aspirations.

There was another procedure I went through, in which they cut open the top of one foot, find a lymphatic vessel, and put in a special liquid that doctors use to evaluate the lymphatic system. This test is called a lymphangiography, as I recall, and it is not a lot of fun. You're on the table for at least four hours while this special dye courses through your lym-

I met little Megan Mills in an MD Anderson parade in Houston in 1985.

phatic system. With follow-up x-rays, doctors can see if there is a problem or if cancer is re-occurring. It's an arduous ordeal, but the doctors say the test gives them clues about where the cancer is.

I later underwent my first major abdominal surgery and it was probably two days before I was cognizant of what was going on around me. I had talked to Megan before the surgery and wanted to talk to her while I was recovering. She was, after all, my comrade in arms. When I was coherent, I told the doctors I wanted to go see Megan in the pediatric ward.

A few minutes later, one of the hospital's patient care coordinators came in and told me I couldn't see Megan: She had died. Her death hit me like a ton of bricks. I remember visiting her before my own surgery when she was due for a major bone marrow extraction. Megan knew what was ahead and she knew it would hurt big time. She was in tears when the gurney had arrived, and I had to leave the floor because I couldn't stand to see her in such pain. I honestly don't understand how the nurses and doctors in the pediatric cancer area can do what they do. It's a tremendous reward when a child survives, but boy, it is really tough when the kids die. I know how painful it was for me when Megan died.

Later, I was back in the same MD Anderson parade with the fire engines and the kids with no hair. I was wearing a hat myself on that day. I didn't need it that badly, my hair wasn't falling out, but suddenly I had a much better understanding of the physical and psychological battles that cancer patients face every day, every week, and every month of their treatment.

Why I made it through the cancer, I have no earthly idea. Twenty-five years ago, Hodgkin's disease was usually fatal within one year. Doctors didn't know how to treat it. That is one reason I do so many fund-raising activities, golf tournaments, and cook-offs to raise money for cancer research and to assist patients and their families. At some point in the past, somebody had done that for me. Without research dollars and the generosity of others, I wouldn't be alive today. While doctors still don't have an answer as to what causes Hodgkin's disease/lymphatic cancer, they do have a pretty good solution for how to cure it or keep it in check. Before, it was terminal. Today, if you are diagnosed with Hodgkin's early, you're probably going to survive.

I had the surgery, I had the chemotherapy, I had the radiation. My chemotherapy at MD Anderson lasted for two months. That was followed by daily radiation treatments for another eight weeks—twenty-eight days to the head and twenty-eight days to the abdomen. When it was all over, the doctors said they saw "no sign of active disease." That's more clinical terminology for remission. (Unfortunately, doctors never use the word "cured" when referring to the cancer.) Anyway, the probability of survival increases as the months and years go by with no recurrence.

The aggressive treatments I underwent have caused some problems down the road. But that's the price you pay and you've got to accept that, otherwise you just die. Although I'm not thrilled with my current health situation, I can say I'm awfully glad to be here—period.

Cancer is a tough, tough battle. One of the hardest things I had to do was watch other people share my pain. My wife, my children, friends, relatives, mother, father, brothers, sister, co-workers—they all came in to the hospital to see me. My biggest challenge was to present a positive outlook. That's all I concentrated on. I never cried, I never let on that I was scared. I said to them and to myself, "This is something I can handle."

Some of our TV station reporters would get off at midnight after working the late shift and show up at the hospital at one o'clock in the morning to see me. The nurses on the overnight shift were wondering what the hell was going on. These were people—among them Cinny Kennard, who is with CBS now—who tried to give me encouragement. I don't think I ever lost faith that I could beat this thing called cancer. Cinny's smile and kind thoughts made a big difference. I met people who weren't going to make it, who didn't make it, and I just thought, all I've got to do is just press forward and be positive. I don't know what else you can do.

In a hospital room two doors down from mine, Roger Maris, the New York Yankee home run hitter, had died of cancer a few years earlier. His death especially illustrated to me how we're all vulnerable, we're all human. Anyone can get cancer. And when you do, you have to accept that and then move on. The best thing you can do is have a positive attitude. I've been accused of thinking of myself as being indestructible. And I do think that, to an extent. But that's starting to wear a bit thin these days because I know none of us are going to live forever. You just hope to have a good, fulfilling life and do the best you can while you're here.

So we see a progression, we see advancement—I'm not sure what more somebody could want in life than saving another life. If I could do that, and that's what I'm working at, that is very, very substantial. It gives me a satisfaction that cannot be rivaled. You can hit a home run, you can throw a touchdown, but if you can save somebody's life, *that* is a grand slam home run, *that* is a touchdown in the Super Bowl of life.

That somebody could be a child like Megan Mills, and I wish it had been.

III

CHILDHOOD AND FAMILY MOMENTS

9

Growing Up

I THINK EVERYBODY KNOWS THAT VERY few red-blooded American youngsters want to be born around Christmas, because more than likely they wouldn't be getting as many presents as they would if they were born any other month but December. And no kid wants to be born on April Fool's Day—and be called an April fool the rest of their days. But boy, I came close: I was born on March 31, 1947, the first-born child of Robert (Bob) Phelps and Darlene Moody.

Dad came from La Grange, Illinois. He joined the United States Air Force at the outbreak of World War II and was chosen to train instructor pilots during the war. He was to be a career Air Force pilot. Mom, née Darlene Stark, grew up in the small farming community of Unityville, South Dakota. To help the war effort, she took a civil service job as an Air Force secretary. Mom and Dad wound up at Randolph Field just outside San Antonio, and they met each other singing in the Randolph Field Chapel Choir. They wed on May 5, 1944 (and have recently celebrated their golden wedding anniversary).

Dad's career in the Air Force meant that we traveled a lot. In fact, all four Moody children were born in different states. I made my appearance about three years into Mom and Dad's marriage, while Dad was assigned to Travis Air Force Base in Northern California. Just six weeks after I was born, he was transferred to Florida. My brother Kelly was born way up in South Dakota, although at the time, Dad was stationed at Hickam Air Force Base in Honolulu, Hawaii, and was flying missions out of Kwajalein Atoll. As soon as Mom was able to travel, the three of us

My first tractor! Unityville, South Dakota, 1948.

moved to Hawaii. I still remember a bright red tricycle and a fireman's hat that I wore just about everyday. It wasn't long before my sister, Kate, was born in Hawaii—we've always kidded her by calling her the "beach doll." Four years later, it was another transfer back to Texas—this time to Kelly Air Force Base in San Antonio. And, in 1954, the final member of the family arrived: Bruce Randolph Moody, the "Randolph" in honor of where my parents had met.

Dad was later stationed at the Pentagon on the Potomac River in Washington, DC—the moving/traveling was still not over! In 1960, he was assigned to the Military Assitance Advisory Group (MAAG) with the United States embassy in Brussels, Belgium. In 1964, we came back to Texas: Dad's mission was to oversee the closing of James Connally Air Force Base in Waco. There at Waco I spent my senior year of high school, and then entered Baylor University.

Lots of people have asked me where I got the name "Chip." Well, it's really kind of simple. My full given name is Robert Phelps Moody II, but on the way home from the hospital, Mom looked down at her newborn and pronounced me "a real chip off the old block." And so it was, the name "Chip" stuck. I once asked my par-ents what they would have named me if I

Age two in Honolulu, Hawaii.

had been born a girl. Mom said it was up in the air, but Dad said his choice would have been "Melody." I'm just happy I turned out to be a guy named "Chip."

Growing up in the Moody family was quite an adventure. With so many moves and upheavals, we do have a lot of stories. But through it all we had fun.

Kid Stuff

If you happen to look real close, you can still see an egg-shaped scar in the middle of my forehead. The story of the scar sounds like something out of a cartoon. I was in fifth grade and we were living in Arlington, Virginia—when Dad was working at the Pentagon. One night, my brother Kelly and I decided to make popcorn balls—the kind where you heat up a corn syrup concoction, pour it over popcorn, and mold the goop into balls.

We let the mixture reach a pretty good temperature—almost boiling—leaving the metal spoon in the pan. My brother reached over to stir the stuff with me standing behind him.

He grabbed the spoon, screeched when he burned his hand and threw the spoon up. The thing twirled maybe twice in the air and landed on my forehead. The scalding syrup caused the rounded end of the spoon to actually stick to my forehead. Well, I went running around the kitchen in pain. Desperately, I grabbed the spoon and ripped it away—pulling off about four layers of skin. For the next several months I had a real prominent egg-shaped red scar on my forehead while the skin healed. The incident was just one of those kid things that happens to most of us, but I did learn one thing: you need to use your brain, not your head, making popcorn balls.

At about the time of the popcorn incident, I also came close to burning down our house in Arlington—twice.

The first circumstance was rather unique. I had seen a war movie on television where an oil tanker had been hit by a torpedo and much of the ocean was aflame. For me to see flames on water, well, that made quite an impression. So I went down to the basement, found a large plastic washtub, filled it with water and in it floated a model ship I had built. I got the family's eight-millimeter movie camera out, set it up on a tripod—thinking I'd make my own movie—and then poured oil over the water and tried to light it with a match. Nothing happened. I tried again and again, but the oil slick on the water wouldn't ignite.

So I decided to try some gasoline. Big mistake. I poured the gas into the tub, put a match to it and WOOMF—just like the movies! The whole tub of water was aflame. I forgot all about the camera.

Moments later I realized, much to my horror, that the edges of the plastic tub were slowly melting. It dawned on me that, as the edges curled down, the flaming water would at some point spill out onto the basement floor and start burning everything it came in contact with. I went into a panic. I obviously couldn't pour water on this fire. What to do? I happened to look up on the wall and saw a snow coaster—one of the big aluminum discs that we'd use to sled down hills in the wintertime. I grabbed the disc off the wall and put it over the tub and smothered the fire. It couldn't have been more than a minute later that water started trickling out around the edges of the tub. Boy, I came so close to setting fire to the place. I'm certain I was within thirty seconds of destroying our house.

The other time was on a New Year's Eve, I don't remember the exact year. My parents were out at a party and Kelly and I decided we would help with the Christmas cleanup, so we went around the house collecting all the excess Christmas tree limbs that my mom had put on windowsills and other places for decoration. We put them all in the fireplace and decided to burn them and surprise Mom with a clean house. Well, if you've ever burned dried pine wood and needles, you know they go like blazes—no pun intended. This fireplace full of Christmas tree limbs erupted in flames—flames so big, they were coming out of the fireplace and scorching the mantle. Our only solution was to run to the kitchen, grab the biggest pans we could find and fill them with water—I got a Turkey basting pan—run back and forth, throwing water on the flames, trying to quench the fire. We got the fire out, but in its place was a huge, wet mess of ashes and debris: the mantle was badly scorched, the carpet was soaked and everything was covered with black soot. So much for the Christmas cleanup. Mom, of course, wasn't impressed.

OUCH!

At the age of seven, I was with my parents in San Antonio on an afternoon cruise, rowing a boat on a nearby lake. We all had cane poles with some fishing line, a hook, and a little bait. We went out there not expecting to catch a big one—just to have some fun in the sun.

It was a quiet, warm day and we drifted along close to shore, throwing our lines out. At one point, I pulled my pole back and the top of it hit a large wasps' nest nestled in the branches of a tree above us. And that nest—it was one of those gray cocoon things—fell down and hit me squarely on the head. It broke open and the wasps, well, they just went crazy. Because I couldn't really swim well at that age, Mom was afraid to throw me overboard. But she did her best to try to cover me up as the wasps were attacking.

The rest of the family escaped with just a few stings, but I got nailed big time. I had more than twenty-five stings on my head and another ten around my body. My head swelled up and I remember thinking to myself, I look like Mr. Pumpkin Head. It was a terribly painful couple of days afterward; I cried most of the time.

Because of all those stings I endured as a kid, I thought I was immune to further stings. Once, while in the ninth grade in Brussels, I sat around talking to some friends and a yellow jacket landed on my right forearm. Everybody said, "Chip, get rid of it." Well, I launched into this story about how I had been stung as a child and therefore bees and wasps knew that I had already taken my punishment and that they wouldn't sting me anymore.

Here I am, telling this silly story, thinking to myself it's true, and meanwhile we're all just looking at this yellow jacket on my right forearm. Of course, the bee curled up its tail and stung me. I couldn't believe I was so stupid. That was one lesson it took me awhile to learn!

Would You Buy a Doughnut from this Kid?

"Hello, my name is Chip, and I'm wondering if you would like to buy some fresh doughnuts?" That was my opening line as I went house to house while in the sixth and seventh grades in Arlington, Virginia. A lot of kids then (and today) made a few dollars by setting up a newspaper route or by mowing lawns. I had decided that one way I could make a few extra bucks every week would be to start a door-to-door doughnut route in my neighborhood.

Since I have never been one of those people who enjoys getting out of bed at the crack of dawn—which is what some of my friends who had paper routes had to do—I started my doughnut route *after* school. I would finish classes and then spend a couple of hours every Monday, Wednesday, and Friday, going from house to house along different streets in the neighborhood, selling fresh doughnuts I purchased from a local bakery.

Would you buy a doughnut from this kid?

It didn't take long to establish a regular customer base. The doughnut company charged me twenty-three cents for a half-dozen, which I turned around and sold for thirty cents a half-dozen, including glazed, powdered, and jelly-filled doughnuts. The bakery would come by my house Mondays, Wednesdays, and Fridays to drop off doughnuts and collect the money I had earned from previous sales. I would place my

doughnut order with the bakery based on what I knew my regular customers would want as well as my own gut feeling on how many extra
boxes I might be able to sell.

Many of my regular customers had standing orders, and if these
folks weren't home when I came by, I would leave their order on the
porch and collect the money the next week, or whenever I saw them
again. I don't know how much my buddies were making delivering
newspapers everyday at some ungodly hour, no matter the weather, but I
do think I did a whole lot better by working a few hours, just three days
a week, after school. In fact, I know I got the better deal.

"Doughnut delivery kid" was my first real job, and I took on all the
responsibilities of finances, bookkeeping, and deliveries. At seven cents
profit per half dozen doughnuts, I worked hard to sell as many as I
could. I learned very early in life that reasonably hard work, combined
with discipline, could pay off with tangible rewards. In fact, I earned
enough money to buy myself a go-cart.

I remember one day a lady who was buying doughnuts looked
into her purse and found an old nickel to give to me along with a quarter for my payment. It was so old it looked like a foreign coin, but it
said "The United States of America" and had a "V" on one side. I later
found out it was called a "victory nickel." I put that nickel in a separate
pocket and checked with a local store that sold stamps and coins and
found out that the old coin was worth more than two dollars in the
world of coin collecting.

That incident started me on the hobby of coin collecting and it was-
n't long before I was not only keeping a close eye out for coins that
doughnut customers gave me, but I had enough capital that I could go
to a bank and pay for $5 or $10 worth of rolled pennies. I would take
the pennies home or to the local drug store (and buy a cherry Coke) and
carefully check each coin and set the more valuable ones aside.

During those early years, I discovered quite a few coins which were
reasonably valuable from a numismatic point of view. It was a fun hobby,
just like collecting football or baseball cards. Somehow those trading
cards got away from me, lost in a move. But I still have a pretty nifty
coin collection, with old Indian head pennies, victory nickels, buffalo
nickels, Mercury dimes, and standing-Liberty quarters.

I learned some things delivering doughnuts back in the fifties that
many youngsters today should learn themselves: how to be reliable,
honest, and dependable, as well as how to give your customers a good,
fresh product at a fair price. Now, I may have looked a little like Ricky

Nelson going up and down the streets with my wire frame shopping cart of doughnuts every Monday, Wednesday, and Friday, but I was also the first kid on my block to be able to go out and buy my own go-cart. Hard work and steadiness do indeed pay off and I am sure that hasn't changed from 1957 to today.

It's very rare that hard, honest work doesn't pay off. Heck, wasn't it Ross Perot who delivered newspapers from horseback as a young, enterprising businessman?

The Cool Club

The songs we were listening to and dancing to in my youth were "Great Balls of Fire" by Jerry Lee Lewis, "At the Hop" by Danny and the Juniors, "Don't" by Elvis, "Diana" by Paul Anka, and a host of others songs that really formed the core of rock and roll's golden era. Dad was a colonel in the US Air Force, stationed with the embassy in Brussels, and I was a teenager trying to find my way into adulthood. Those years abroad will forever stand out as the formative years of my life. I later realized that mixing with other cultures was an amazing opportunity and skill. Being in a foreign country, sometimes traveling on my own by train to Paris or London, forced me to be self-reliant, adaptable to changing circumstances, and able to think on my feet.

I guess it's been said that a newscaster has to have a certain amount of self-confidence, since we're in contact with the public a lot and have to be in front of a camera. There just has to be a certain self-assurance that must go along with the job if we're going to communicate the facts clearly and responsibly to hundreds of thousands, if not millions, of people.

Perhaps when I look back on my life, maybe that self-confidence started growing in those early years in Brussels. I would probably pinpoint it around the eighth grade. It was 1961. The cliques, the hops, Elvis's songs, the duck-tail haircuts, the phenomenon of juvenile delinquency, they were all happening during that time. I decided we needed to have a club of the "neat" guys in school. Our international school was filled with a wide assortment of children from the diplomatic community, many of them there to learn English. So I started "The Cool Club." Of course, you had to be "cool" to be in the club and, since I had formed the club, I was King Cool.

All the club members were hand-picked by King Cool, and I was very discriminating in my choices. Well, as the weeks went on, it became fairly prestigious among the eighth and ninth graders to be a member of the club. You didn't necessarily need to have great grades to become a member, but you were expected to be a good athlete and have a little panache and personality about you. As the competition grew for membership in the Cool Club, a lot of guys starting bringing me gifts. Usually this amounted to bags of fine Belgium chocolate, but two Pakistani students—the Kahn brothers, whose father was a very powerful man in Pakistan—brought me huge shoeboxes full of pistachio nuts. Not a bad incentive, I thought, so I invited them to join our little club.

My girlfriend, whose name was Bunny Mallow and whose father was a major in the army, became the unofficial Queen Cool.

After the membership drive, our little club numbered about 20 or 25. Part of the rules were that you had to wear black and white in some form or fashion every day, be it saddle shoes, or a black shirt and a white tie, or a black and white belt. Occasionally, as King Cool, I would wear entire outfits that were black and white, from my saddle shoes and white socks, to my black pants and white belt with little mirrors on it, along with my cool black corduroy shirt with pearl buttons. Sometimes I'd add my black corduroy jacket from my school days at Williamsburg Junior High in Arlington. My name was on the front, the school's on the back—quite impressive, I thought.

The thing is, our club became controversial because the kids who weren't asked to join became unofficially known as the Un-Cools. Well, it divided the student body somewhat and got back to the parents and the community. One Sunday, our club became the subject of a sermon at the community church. The message was, to my chagrin, that we should not be so separatist, should not set our own standards. It was aimed at you-know-who.

Toward the end of the school year, one young man by the name of Andy Box, as one of the more nerdy guys in school, had unofficially become King of the Un-Cools. My dad met me one day after school, the day report cards came out, and he looked over mine, which was full of C's, a few scattered B's, maybe an A in gym, and a D somewhere. Not exactly the kind of report card you'd want to hang on the refrigerator. Well, Dad casually informed me that the King of the Un-Cools, Andy, had come home with straight A's. Dad wanted to know how it was possible that someone who was "uncool" could have such good grades, while the King of the Cools was merely an average student.

I kind of let the Cool Club slowly disband after that, having learned a lesson that maybe being cool wasn't always what it was cracked up to be. Still, organizing the club was my first venture into leadership or self-assertion you might say. I guess there are a lot of words that fit there, but maybe some of my self-confidence came from that first experience as a leader in my school in Brussels, Belgium.

Oh, those were the days. An aside—one of the girls at school brought me the song "To Know Him Is To Love Him," with all the words written out as "To Know Chip Is To Love Chip." She thought it would get her into the club. It did.

Sportsmanship

While in school in Europe, I learned to play soccer because it is the most popular sport there and there were many teams around. It gave us a great physical outlet and a lot of local competition. Because ours was an international school, we attracted a lot of other international schools to compete with us. We'd also play foreign national teams—high school squads made up strictly of French, Dutch, or German kids. We'd play in Brussels, Amsterdam, France, or other places. My teammates and I got a terrific exposure to European soccer this way.

Our team did okay. We certainly didn't win all our games; in fact, we lost more than we won. But I sure had a good time and got around the language barrier, because there really isn't one in soccer. It was a good learning experience for all of us, and looking back over my whole experience in Europe, my living there had a tremendous influence on my life because of the responsibility I achieved. Living in a foreign country, you learn to blend with different cultures and assert yourself in difficult situations. You're expected to think on your feet a lot more and you find yourself in strange situations more often, be it shopping, dating, or traveling. Without a good command of a foreign language, you must still learn to rise to every occasion.

We also played baseball. We had a league in Brussels, and then we would take an all-star team of Americans on the road to Air Force bases and Army posts in places like Frankfurt, Wiesbaden, or Kaiserslaughten in Germany; as well as in Laon, France; Amsterdam; and Antwerp, Belgium. We'd play against other young Americans who were the children of military and diplomatic personnel. It was always a great occasion for us, because it gave us a chance to play other Americans in America's sport.

One year, I was having a terrific season behind the plate. I was a catcher and hitting the ball awfully well. I went on to win the Triple Crown for that year, which was the most home runs, most runs batted in, and the highest batting average. I was using the Bobby Brown model bat, a thin bat named after a player with the Yankees in those years.

(Twenty years later, I was sitting in the private box of Eddie Chiles, the late owner of the Texas Rangers, at Arlington Stadium when the new president of the American League was there, none other than Dr. Bobby Brown. I was very honored to meet him and told him how I wished I had saved some of my Bobby Brown bats, since they had meant so much to me in my baseball career growing up.)

Back to the early sixties. I was having a banner year. When the season was over, one of my friends on the team was transferred to an air base in France. Rocky Hill was his name, a second baseman, who I would have to play against the following year. He told his teammates at his new school about the catcher who could really hit the ball, and warned them to be on the lookout for me. By the time we arrived in France for a game, word had spread. Rocky met me and told me everyone would be looking out for me, expecting some amazing plays, and that the team was on their guard, putting their best players up against me.

Come about the eighth inning, we're losing about six to one or two. It was not a close game at all. I had done doggone nothing the entire game; it had been a miserable batting performance. I kept feeling the pressure that the other team was waiting for some Willie Mays-Mickey Mantle heroics out of me. We came up to the top of the ninth and our last chance to bat. I came up to bat for the fourth time, the pitch came in, and I swung, popping the ball straight up into the air, not far between the pitcher and the catcher. Now at this point, I could have hit a home run and we still wouldn't have won the game—we only had one guy on base. But when I popped it up like that, my anger got the better of me and I slammed the bat down on the plate, broke it, and stomped off. The catcher made the play and I was out, 0 for 4 that day. Boy, was I mad at myself.

The coach saw this display of temper and I was benched for the next two games for unsportsmanlike conduct. This came as an even bigger shock, because obviously the coach knew what a valuable member of the team I was. So I was not only embarrassed at my performance, but then I was even more humiliated by being benched by the coach. To add insult to injury, the coach was my dad.

That episode taught me to use some control in sports situations. Try to win with humility; try to lose with dignity. And be humble in whatever you do. This was a turning point in my being a better sportsman.

The Wall

While I was in high school in Europe, the Berlin Wall went up virtually overnight. We were just a few hundred miles away in Brussels, Belgium, when the Communists decided to erect a wall to halt the exodus of East Berliners to the West in mid-1961. The blockading of Berlin came swiftly and it was of great concern, not only to the Free World, but to those of us stationed in Europe as part of the American diplomatic corps.

I was sixteen the first time I saw the Berlin Wall in 1962.

As a family, we went to Berlin to see the Wall in early 1962. We took a bus trip that took us to various parts of the structure. One of the most graphic things I remember about that trip was seeing a sidewalk leading up to a church and the cinder block wall cutting a swath across the walk, blocking those on the west access to the church. On the other side, I could see an East German soldier in the tower of the church with a machine gun. Thirty years later, that graphic image is still embedded in my memory. It still signifies to me the tremendous and terrible separation between the Communist world and the Free World.

On our trip, we were allowed to board a special bus to travel inside East Berlin, and we had to go through Checkpoint Charlie, a primary crossing point between East and West Berlin. While we were on the bus, a guard came on board and collected all the cameras (to prevent us from photographing the dreariness of East Berlin) and American currency. All was placed in a separate envelope for each passenger. The ultimate objective of the tour was to take us to the Soviet War Memorial in East Berlin that commemorated the hundreds of thousands of Soviet soldiers who died in World War II— especially those killed in the final stages of the war as the Soviets and the Americans closed in on Berlin and the Nazi headquarters.

The East Germans wanted to show off the memorial, but at the same time they wanted to hide from us the tremendous poverty and lack of economic strength in East Berlin. West Berlin, on the other hand, was a very upbeat, thriving Westernized city. The contrast between the two

Berlins was a touchy point for the Communists. As we moved from the neon lights, the movie marquees, and the department stores through Checkpoint Charlie and into East Berlin, I recall vividly that it seemed we went from color television to black and white. It was like stepping back in time. Everything was dreary and dull. The people walking the streets didn't smile and they wore gray and black clothing. There was no happiness.

We drove by bombed-out buildings that had not been repaired in fifteen or twenty years—since World War II. The Communist system had not generated enough money to rebuild East Berlin. As we drove by dozens of shells of buildings, it was terribly depressing, and you could see that on the faces of the people as we looked out the windows of the bus.

Finally, we arrived at the Soviet War Memorial, an awesome and powerful construction. Huge bronze statues of soldiers greet you as you walk toward the memorial. Beyond it, a field stretches for perhaps three or four football fields in length. This is a mass grave for the Soviet soldiers and hallowed ground. The East Berlin soldiers gave us our cameras back so we could take pictures of the memorial because it was something the Communists were proud of.

After we took pictures and walked around, the soldiers explained what the memorial was all about. Beyond the statues and the mass grave is a shrine extolling the sacrifice of the Soviet soldiers. We stayed there maybe an hour, then we boarded the bus and the guards once again took our cameras and put them back in their own special bags. We weren't allowed to take pictures of anything else.

On our tour, we drove down Stalin Allee (later Karl Marx Allee), a wide boulevard that our West Berlin tourist guide told us had been constructed primarily to highlight East Berlin's claimed economic strength for Nikita Khrushchev's visit and for the Free World broadcast media. As we drove past grand buildings meant for Khrushchev and photographers it all looked very impressive. But when we did a U-turn and came back around in the alley, we saw that fifty percent of these buildings were, in fact, just facades, just like a Hollywood movie set. Our West German guide explained how the Western journalists at that time would only be permitted to photograph the motorcade down this grand avenue—they would not be allowed to see behind the facade the Communists had built.

I remember seeing potholes and craters in the streets from the bombs of World War II that had not been repaired. It felt like I was traveling to a different time, as if I had stepped into a surreal, black-and-white world. There was a part of that teenage me that hoped an East German would try to make an escape and I would help. I envisioned a photographer from the *Stars and Stripes* newspaper getting a picture of me—a sixteen-year-old kid—helping an East German flee safely to the West. It was a fantasy of mine, imagining helping somebody get across the Wall, over the barbed wire. It was a half-dream, half-hope to help someone escape the gray, numbing land of East Berlin.

Then it was back through Checkpoint Charlie and back into the bright lights of West Berlin. In a space of half a mile, it seemed like twenty years. I realized how lucky we are as Americans to have the freedoms, privileges, wealth, standard of living that we do. I felt that at sixteen, and I feel that just as strongly today. It was one of those times when you want to run the American flag up and let it wave with pride. It became so clear to me how different our governments were and I felt like a real patriot. I was, and still am, very proud to be an American.

The Crumbling Wall

There is, of course, a happy coda to my early experience in East Berlin. It was within my lifetime that I saw the Berlin Wall go up—and come crumbling back down. Almost thirty years after visiting East Berlin and the Soviet War Memorial, the facade that was Communism in East Berlin finally collapsed in 1990. Having seen the Berlin Wall as a teenager, I wanted desperately to be there and see the structure come down. I went on my own—not as a reporter, but as an American citizen—to see the conclusion of all that had taken place since the Wall was erected.

I brought my own tools to carve out a piece of history for myself when the Wall came down.

I knew that pieces of the wall would be keepsakes and I took along my own hammer and a huge screwdriver so that I could make sure I got some pieces of the Wall to bring back to America. During the celebrations, I stood up on the top of the Wall near the Brandenburg gate with some other Americans who were there and proceeded to chop out as many chunks of concrete from the Wall as I could.

After the Wall fell, capitalism became apparent almost overnight, especially near Checkpoint Charlie. Suddenly there were tables and vendors selling Soviet paraphernalia—hats, belt buckles, and big chunks of the Wall. Because many parts of the Wall had been painted by the West Germans with messages and graffiti, those were sold for more than just plain pieces of concrete.

As I walked along this area near Checkpoint Charlie, I stepped through one of the three or four large openings cut into the concrete. I couldn't get over what I saw on the other side: people spray painting the concrete and immediately hacking it out and taking the chunks to a table near Checkpoint Charlie to sell. It was a sham, but it was capitalism. Here they were, they knew there was a demand for pieces of the Berlin Wall and that painted ones would bring a higher price. These were the new entrepreneurs, I guess you could say.

There was one guy from whom you could rent a hammer and a chisel and he would let you use it for a few minutes to carve out your own piece of history. I forget what the cost was, but again here was a guy who was taking advantage of the moment, a moment in history, and also a moment in capitalism. I got a chuckle out of this, and was glad I had my own hammer, chisel, and big screwdriver. I had somebody take some pictures of me with those tools so I could say, "Yes, this didn't come from a construction site in Plano, this was actually part of the Berlin Wall!"

Learning the Lesson the Dirty Way

When I was a teenager, my family would visit my mother's home state of South Dakota. We had a small family farm there, not a working farm, just a vacation place for the family, and we enjoyed Fourth of July celebrations there and picnics—family events like that.

I guess I was fifteen or sixteen, and I was visiting a friend's working farm up there. Now, I've always enjoyed machinery, tractors, motorcycles, planes, trains, and automobiles . . . and I figured I would volunteer to help my friend with some of his farm chores, maybe get to use the tractor. I felt that I was old enough and knew enough—I enjoyed farm labor and I wanted to be a contributing worker.

The farm's owner was Alden Skoglund, a long-time farmer in South Dakota who certainly knew his business. I asked if there was anything I could do to help him out on his land, it being a "real" farm and everything. He said I could help spread some manure that day. Well, it wasn't my first choice in jobs, but I figured I could handle that.

Alden showed me a large pile of manure that had been collected during the past year and then pointed out the manure spreader. The spreader works as its wheels turn by engaging a gear and pulling the manure down a bed into a spindle-like contraption at the end, which then flings the manure out into the field.

Alden showed me the front-end loader, which is a separate machine that you use to load up the manure spreader. Once you've loaded it up, you hook up the spreader and head out on the tractor to start spreading the manure. Alden told me to fill up the spreader, hitch it up, and pointed to a long field in the distance. Now, as you drive down the long country roads of South Dakota at sixty miles an hour, those green fields just seem to fly by. You can see the tractors out working in the fields as you whiz by in your car, but when you're actually on the tractor going down the field, that stretch of land seems a lot longer. Alden told me to keep the tractor in third gear when I got out to the field. With that, I was left to start my day as a farmhand.

First, the manure. That pile had been building up for several months and had a very thick crust on it. It's hard to say this delicately, but when I broke through, steam came out and there was a very pungent odor (pungent times 100 might be a better way of putting it!). But this was a farm smell, and I figured I'd better get used to it, so I loaded up the spreader, hooked it up to the tractor, and headed out.

In third gear, it took me about half an hour to do one load. After about three or four loads, I thought this was going too slow. I'm moving along about four miles an hour and thinking it's crazy to spend all day doing this. So I figured, why don't I go a little faster and get this done quicker? So I loaded up the spreader again and decided fifth gear would be better. Instead of four miles an hour I figured I could do about eight miles an hour, and cut my time in half. I guessed I would save myself half a day's work.

It only took a few moments to realize I probably should have listened more closely to Mr. Skoglund. I started up the row, engaged the manure spreader and took off with the John Deere in fifth gear. Manure immediately started falling out of the sky: The spindle was moving at a higher rate when I was in fifth gear and spreading that manure out, back, and even forward in front of the tractor—and right into my face and onto my head. I'm sure there's a moral to this story . . . at the very least, it's "never spread manure in anything but third gear." I know I went back to third gear to finish the job after that fiasco.

I guess the *real* moral from this story is to learn from your elders and pay attention to those who know their work better than you do—they usually know what they are talking about. The other thing I learned is that I'm far better suited to the newsroom than to working the farm.

Car Talk

My family moved back to the States after spending four years in Brussels, Belgium, and I enrolled at Richfield High School in Waco. After being in Europe for most of my high school years, it was quite a culture shock. In Europe, I could go to London in two hours. I could zip over to Paris in three hours.

Nevertheless, I made it through my senior year and, after graduating from Richfield High School, I enrolled at Baylor University in 1965. For my freshman year, my parents had given me the old family car, a 1957 Mercury station wagon. It was a big, two-toned blue job, but this was my transportation and I made the best of it—even taking my dates out in it.

One night I went to pick up a date and left the car running outside the girl's dormitory. I walked in to the dorm's reception area and the lady who ran the reception desk called up for my date. As I waited patiently, a guy came running through the door yelling that somebody's car was on fire. Well, I ran outside and sure enough there was my 1957 Mercury station wagon with smoke pouring out of the exhaust pipe. The guy who sounded the alarm had assumed the car was on fire from all the smoke billowing around, but fortunately the smoke was only an exhaust problem. I made it through my date that night, but I decided right then I needed a better mode of transportation.

One night a few weeks later, my roommate's friend came by and told us he had just blown the engine in his old Austin Healy sports car. I said I thought I might be able to rebuild it, but he insisted the car wasn't worth a hoot because the engine was gone. Even so, I said I'd buy it from him and he said okay, a six-pack of beer would do it. So for six

My 1956 Austin Healy convertible, purchased for a six-pack of beer.

beers, I had me a 1956 Austin Healy convertible—although one that didn't run.

That beauty had blown not only a gasket, but had sent a piston rod through the side of the engine block. In other words, the engine was virtually useless. But during the next year, I worked hard on this carcass of a car. I took off all of the side panels and doors. I found a new engine block at a junkyard south of Fort Worth. A friend of mine who knew something about rebuilding cars hooked up with me and we made a real strong effort to rebuild this car. Hell, I bought it for a six-pack of beer, so I figured I could put a few dollars into it.

I took the engine block and had the piston cylinders drilled out a little bit bigger than normal—racing pistons, they call them. We started rebuilding the car and it took a good year to do it. We had the little Austin Healy stripped down to just its frame and tires. But I didn't give up because I wanted a nifty little comfortable car to drive. We pushed ahead with this rebuilding effort.

When I finally got to the point where I thought the vehicle would start up, I hooked up the gas tank, the fuel line, and the fuel pump. This was going to be the big test. Amazingly, the engine turned over. I couldn't believe it. I mean, I was just in heaven. After spending months putting this engine together, it actually worked. Of course, the car had no muffler, no inspection sticker, not even a body—the seats and side panels were still on the floor of the garage.

But the engine was in the frame and we hooked it up to the manual transmission and I put a tin bucket on the floorboard, sat down, and backed out of the driveway and started around the block. Since the car had no muffler, it was making a terrible racket. Still, I sputtered off in my Austin Healy feeling like I was on top of the world. And then, wouldn't you know it, before getting a few blocks, a cop pulls me over for not having an inspection sticker. Well, of course I didn't have a sticker—I didn't even have a windshield! Here I was, sitting on a tin bucket, and this cop also cites me for not having a muffler!

Well, I stated my case something like this: "Officer, there are teenagers out there who are up to no good. Here I am spending my time, the few dollars that I have, to build a car to give me transportation and you're going to penalize me for that. I've been working many, many months to make this car run and now that it does, and I'm just taking it for a test drive, and you want to give me a ticket!" My plea didn't work. I was given two $10 tickets, one for lacking an inspection sticker and one for not having a muffler.

I went downtown a week later and talked with a Judge Valentine. I again challenged the traffic ticket, saying, "Here's a guy doing something useful, he's not out partying and doing drugs or getting drunk. Here's a guy who is working hard to give himself an adequate mode of transportation and gets pulled over because I had done my best and was a productive citizen." Judge Valentine was about as impressed as the officer had been. His verdict? "Let's split the difference—ten bucks." It was a small victory at least. I loved that car and drove it throughout college.

Publicity shot of "The Texas News" anchor team at Channel 5.

Anchorman to anchorman: I interviewed NBC newsman Chet Huntley in 1973.

Max Palmer was a big man in more ways than one. At a towering 7'8", the reformed alcoholic became a traveling evangelist, the "Goliath for Christ." I interviewed him early in my career.

Anchoring election night at Channel 5 with Russ Bloxom in 1978.

Channel 4, KDFW-TV publicity shot, 1981.

KDFW-TV promoted my partnership with Clarice Tinsley on a Dallas billboard in a 1980 campaign.

When I took over Dan Rather's old job in Houston, he said, "I hope it's as good to you as it was to me."

With Lisa McRee, Dale Hansen, Troy Dungan, Tracy Rowlett, and Gloria Campos in a 1990 WFAA-TV publicity shot. (Photo by Bob Mader.)

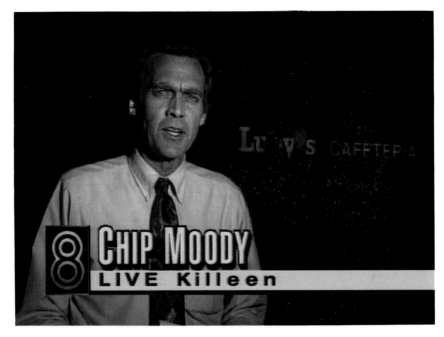

Reporting live from the Killeen tragedy.

Hosting the Adolphus Hotel Children's Medical Center Parade with Lisa McRee in downtown Dallas.

*Thanking President Jimmy
Carter after an interview.*

*President George Bush and I
share a laugh.*

*With former Texas governor
Ann Richards after an
interview.*

Gloria Campos's winning smile is contagious.

With Channel 8 sportscaster Dale Hansen outside the newsroom.

Winning the Buck J.T. Marryat Award for outstanding contribution to communications, a lifetime achievement award from the Dallas Press Club and American Airlines.

Celebrating with fellow Channel 8 reporter Bill Brown after winning the Dallas Press Club "Katie" Award for Excellence in Reporting, 1992.

My parents, Bob and Darlene Moody, at Kelly Air Force Base, San Antonio, 1944.

Baby Robert Phelps Moody II— with dirty feet.

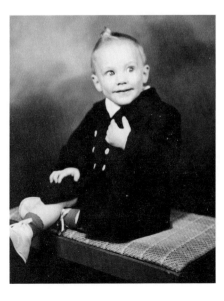

One year old and dressed to kill.

My first swimming pool.

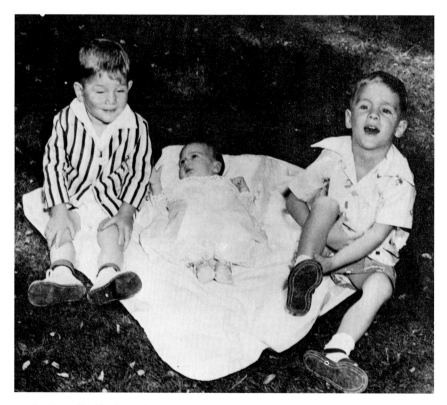

My brother Kelly (three), newborn sister Kate, and me (four) at Hickam Air Force Base, Pearl Harbor, Hawaii.

Tenth grade and having a bad hair day.

The newlyweds—enjoying our wedding cake on October 11, 1970, in Waco, Texas.

Trae and Tiffin.

Demonstrating gun safety to Tiffin and Trae, 1979.

Trae at age eight.

A family ski trip to Beaver Creek, Colorado, in 1984: me, Vikki, Mom, Tiffin, Trae.

Our first Christmas in Houston, 1985.

Christmas morning, 1985.

At a Houston Halloween party, 1985. We were Clint Eastwood and the Woman from Mars—in costumes created by Vikki.

Trae orders pizza from our garage in Houston.

*Me and the kids skiing at Zermatt,
next to the Matterhorn,
Switzerland, 1992.*

Tiffin and Trae today, with Munchkin.

10

Family Ties

I AM IN THE INTENSIVE CARE UNIT AT Baylor Hospital today. It is early January 1995, and I am waiting for word from my doctors about what can be done for my bleeding ulcers. If doctors cannot cauterize the ulcers, they'll have to operate. I have my fingers crossed I won't have to undergo major abdominal surgery again.

During my stays in the hospital I always have a lot of time on my hands. I often spend it thinking of my family—my wife, my two children. I think back on the vacations we've taken together and the little incidents that occur in every family that brings everyone together. Thinking of them helps days like this pass more quickly.

Ace, Deuce, Trae

Vikki and I got married right after I graduated from Baylor and was just beginning my broadcasting career. Like a lot of young couples, we decided to wait until I was more established before starting a family. We had been in Dallas-Fort Worth for about five years when we discovered that Vikki was pregnant. It was 1974. We were excited about the upcoming arrival of our first child and decided to pursue the Lamaze natural childbirth courses in anticipation of my being a partner in the delivery process. Because of the timing of my wife's pregnancy, the classes were in the fall—she was due in late January—and I had to miss all the football games on Sundays!

But I went willingly to the hospital for these two-hour classes in which a group of about fifteen couples laid around in a carpeted room and the husbands learned to tell their wives how to pant and puff. We were taught special blowing and breathing exercises— "pant-pant, puff-puff"—that would, according to the experts, "lower the mother's lactic acid output." Lactic acid causes the labor pain and if you have more oxygen, it reduces the amount of lactase and, thus, the amount of pain. We also learned massage techniques for the belly and the back in an effort to make our wives as comfortable as possible, and we learned how to help in the delivery room. This was all a new challenge for me and, although I missed the football games, I enjoyed the classes.

All my training came into play on January 17, 1975. I was at work at Channel 5 doing some writing for the evening newscast when Vikki called, around four in the afternoon, and told me her water broke. Now, the women reading this know what that means—so for the men out there, I'll just say it means the baby is imminent. I informed everybody at work that I had to bail out to go help deliver a baby. When I got home I confronted one of the first lessons I had learned in Lamaze class: the mother is always more calm than the dad.

I ran into the house expecting a mad dash to the hospital, but Vikki was calmly painting her fingernails and working on her hair. Well, the class instructor had warned us that women will do this primping stuff at the onset of labor and delivery, but I was getting rather frantic. I told Vikki to forget all that nail polish and hop

A step back in time—me and the kids at my childhood home in Brussels, Belgium in 1982.

into the car, because she was going to have a baby!

I called Vikki's doctor's office and told the folks there the contractions were coming about four minutes apart. The nurse said to first come by the office, which was just down the street from Arlington Memorial Hospital. We walked into the doctor's office fifteen minutes later. I noticed there were a couple of people in the waiting room ahead of us, so we sat down for a few minutes. I could hardly sit still, although Vikki was pretty calm. Finally, I got up and told the nurse the contractions were now two minutes apart, and to please do something!

The nurse, being used to pregnant women and their nervous husbands, did not flip her wig. She did, however, acknowledge that contractions two minutes apart meant that a baby was about to enter this fine world, and she told us to get over to the hospital immediately. I bundled Vikki back into the car and zipped on over to Arlington Memorial Hospital's emergency room. I realized things were happening pretty quickly, so as we hurried into the emergency room I announced loudly that my wife was in labor and her contractions were two minutes apart.

The nurses knew exactly what to do: They put Vikki on a gurney and started wheeling her down toward the labor and delivery area, while I explained that I was a Lamaze-trained partner so I could assist in all this. A nurse grabbed a hospital gown, a mask, and a couple of these silly-looking paper boots you put over your shoes from a supply closet and urged me to hurry up, get dressed, and wash up, because things were about to happen.

I opened up the hospital gown and it looked like it might fit a twelve-year-old kid. My arms hardly fit through the sleeves, and when I finally got the dinky thing on, it left a huge opening in the back. But I didn't complain—there was no time to get a larger size! The nurse hollered over her shoulder, to get those boots on and wash up. I looked around, saw the sink, and walked over to it. There was a long, tall stainless steel goose neck spigot and a stainless sink. But, much to my surprise, there was no way to turn the water on.

I looked at the sink and thought, hmm, maybe this is like the urinals at the airport where you walk up to them, and when you walk away they will flush. So I got to moving around in front of the sink, approaching it, thinking that as I came closer the water would start flowing. In the meantime, of course, the clock was ticking. As I'm doing this slow jig in front of the sink, an orderly walked by and I begged him for a little help. He told me the sink had a knee lever, and sure enough underneath the stainless steel bowl was a curved lever that you hit with your leg to turn on the water.

What you do is slide your knee into the curve of the lever and give it a little Elvis wiggle and the water starts coming out. If you wiggle one way it's hot, the other way is cold. On the floor is a soap button that you hit with your foot. So you've got one leg kind of moving around getting the water going while the foot of the other leg stamps on the floor and gets the soap coming. It looks like a miniature Elvis routine, but it's got to be done if you're to go into the delivery room.

Once I was washed up, I looked around and saw there were no towels. Great, I thought, this is getting crazy, even a little surreal. The nurses continued to shout at me from the end of the hall to hurry up, my baby was coming! So, my hands dripping, I ran down the hall in my silly-looking outfit. By the time I got into the delivery room, the baby was right on top of us. About the only thing I had time for was a "hip, hip hooray!" before our son, Robert Phelps Moody III, appeared. (Again, a nickname was in order. This time it was "Trae"—as in ace, deuce, trae.)

Being a rookie, I wasn't prepared for the shriveled-up, plum-colored baby that I saw. I actually had a moment where I thought he might be dead. But before I could let that thought sink in or get too worried about it, the doctor yanked him up by his ankles and gave him a whack on the rear and he started crying. The odd purple color started dissipating and Trae started exhibiting some forms of life and getting reasonably pink in color.

After the delivery, I suddenly felt very tired. And then I suddenly felt really dumb because I hadn't done anything—Vikki had done it all. Then the adrenaline kicked in and I was very excited, and I spent the rest of the evening with my sister, Kate, who also lived in Arlington, recounting the heroics we went through to get Trae delivered. It was an especially happy occasion, because January 17 was Kate's birthday as well.

There were a couple of things I didn't learn in the Lamaze class—the wash-up routine and the purple baby. Two weeks later, we were able to go back to our class to tell them how the experience went—Vikki and I were the first couple in our class to deliver. I explained the ups and downs, the pros and cons and what to expect, and I think it was illuminating for the rest of the class.

The next fall, Vicki was pregnant again, and once again I was back in Lamaze classes, missing Sunday football. We were told that the second baby always comes much quicker than the first. I thought to myself, if this second kid comes any quicker, it's going to be me and a guy at the toll booth at the end of the turnpike delivering it. With Trae, we arrived at Arlington Memorial at approximately 6:00 p.m. and he was on the ground by 6:08 p.m..

As it turned out, Tiffin Anne, our daughter, was a breach baby. I went through all these classes and then they had to do a Caesarean section. Once again, I was unable to help—it was congratulations to Vikki for doing all the work. When Tiffin was born, I wasn't even allowed in the operating room. My daughter came out with bright red hair, so at first it was very easy to spot her in the nursery. After a few days, there were about five redheads in the nursery and I couldn't quite pick her out as quickly.

I'm delighted that Tiffin's beautiful red hair has stayed just as bright red-orange as it was the day she was born on January 30, 1976. Now it's down to her waist and she is a very, very attractive young lady.

After Trae and Tiffin, we decided no more kids. I think those two wore me out. Plus it seems we are just the right size for a typical suburban American family. And we're doing fine—despite my crazy schedule. We're a pretty diverse family when all is said and done—four distinct individuals pursuing their own interests and talents.

Vikki plays classical piano, loves to read, enjoys creating art projects, and designs and makes costumes and clothes. Once for our annual Halloween party, she spent hours making me my own Elvis jumpsuit, complete with standup collar, brightly colored studs, and eagle belt buckle. We have a mutual hobby of collecting eagles, and she has worked more than twenty-five years hunting and building our collection. She's also a natural at caring for injured birds and animals. Trae and Tiffin's friends all call her "Mom."

Trae, Vikki, and Tiffin at home in Arlington.

In these past few years, Vikki gave up working for her favorite charities, The Children's Advocacy Center of Dallas and The Yellow Rose Gala benefiting breast cancer research, to center her attention on my health, or lack of it. Yet during this time we purchased an older home and spent three years transforming it into a beautiful home together. She has a natural talent for remodeling and did much of the design, preparation, and actual work on the renovation. In fact, this work has prompted her to begin architectural design courses. When she hasn't been driving back and forth from Arlington to Baylor Hospital to care for me, she enjoys theater, museums, travel, art, skiing, music, and more. Next on the agenda is learning gourmet cooking to help put some meat on my bones!

Vikki has never complained about my odd working hours, caring for me, then Mom and Dad, through grueling cancer treatments, or struggling to keep me alive and healthy in these recent years. Being married to me hasn't been an easy road, but she always looks for the positive, believing that everything happens for a reason, and that we learn from events—good and bad—to help ourselves and others. Although she is quickly gaining on the big "50," she hardly looks forty. Vikki is truly young at heart, generous, and honest. She has always supported and encouraged me to follow my dreams no matter what they have been— from flying my own plane to founding my endowment fund.

These days, Trae is interested in cars, music, and one special girl (what would you expect from a twenty-year-old young man?). He is an honest, thoughtful, unassuming guy who cares a great deal about his family and friends. Like a lot of guys his age, he's trying to figure out what he would like to do in life. Instead of working as a broadcaster, like the old man, he is leaning toward the music industry. Tiffin is showing great talent in art, and has designed some program covers for charity events as well as logos for a couple of local bands. It's fun to see her work shown in galleries and published in the newspaper.

Troy in Paris

I guess moving so much in my childhood made me a keen traveler in adulthood, and my family sure enjoys it. In 1982, on the spur of the moment, I asked Vikki if she'd like to go to England for a few days. She had never been overseas, and it didn't take her long to respond with an enthusiastic, "You bet!"

After two days in the London area, seeing the Tower of London and Buckingham Palace, I mentioned that we were just a short flight from Paris. I have always ad-libbed my way through most vacations, and this was just another example. We quickly booked a flight from London to Paris, anticipating a two-day visit, and then we'd head back to the United States.

Over the years, during my time in Europe, I had discovered a really neat way to show first-time visitors to Paris the Eiffel Tower: you take the subway from the outskirts of town and you get off at a stop called Trocadero. This way,

What a coincidence! Vikki and I ran into Troy and Janet Dungan at the Eiffel Tower.

you stay underground until you draw near the grandest feature of Paris, and then up close in all its glory stands the Eiffel Tower.

Vikki and I walked up the subway steps and through a busy intersection and climbed the back steps of the Palais d' Justice. Suddenly there it was—a magnificent view of the Eiffel Tower with the city laid out behind it. Vikki was suitably impressed. We paid our money—it costs a few dollars—to take the elevator up to the top, where there is a viewer's gallery. From there, you see a tremendous view of Paris, including the Seine, Notre Dame, the Palais d' Justice, the Louvre. It is a breathtaking sight and another one of "those moments" you don't ever forget.

As Vikki and I stood gazing out into Paris, I suddenly heard, from behind me, the voice of a man: "Son of a gun! To think I came all the way to Paris, France and who do I run into but Chip Moody!" I turned around and to my great surprise, there was Channel 8 weatherman Troy Dungan and his wife, Janet! I had been working at Channels 4 and 5 over the years, and because of our similar work schedules, Troy and I had never actually met in person. Of course, we knew each other by watching the competition on TV.

Although we worked only a few miles apart in Texas, we had never shaken hands. So our meeting on top of the Eiffel Tower had to be a chance in a million, like winning the Texas lottery. I mean, it's not like running into someone at Galveston Island, or while skiing at Breckenridge. You only spend about half an hour or so on the Eiffel Tower, so it was really quite astounding for Troy and I to meet there.

If we had had a good bottle of French wine between us, I am sure we would have toasted the occasion right then. Little did we realize that just a few years down the road, we would be working together. I don't think we need the theme from the Twilight Zone to accompany this story—but it would not be out of place.

Throw Chip from the Train

I remember one family trip around 1983 and a little incident on a train. Vikki, Trae, Tiffin, and I were taking our first trip to Europe as a family. Being the continental traveler I was, having spent much of my growing up years in Europe, I was excited to show my family the hot spots and show off my knowledge. I mapped out a very ambitious plan to see as much of Europe as we could in two weeks. I've since learned to slow down and smell the roses.

We flew from Dallas-Fort Worth to London and spent a couple of days there. We had difficulty finding something really good to eat—

something that would satisfy the kids. Somehow the Brits' form of cooking is just not the same as American cooking. I believe we ended up getting a McDonald's or two, just to satisfy our hunger, rather than eating kidney pie or some other British bill-of-fare (although I'm guilty of being fond of fish and chips).

My complicated itinerary called for us to leave Victoria Station one morning, take the train to Dover, then catch the hydrofoil ferry across the English Channel, and, finally, board the train from Ostend, Belgium, to Brussels. The start of the trip was great—we took some lovely pictures on the train trip down to Dover on the coast. We transferred to the hydrofoil ferry for the relatively quick trip across the channel—just an hour, compared to the typical four-hour ride on a conventional ferry. We watched the white cliffs of Dover grow smaller as we crossed the channel.

This was before the big mess I got us into on the train—see, we're still smiling.

We were due in Ostend around 1 p.m. After a smooth crossing, I saw we had arrived about ten minutes early, and glancing at my watch I saw we had over an hour to kill before our 2 p.m. train left for Brussels. Vikki, the kids, and I dawdled around, sightseeing along the nearby docks after we got through customs. We gradually made our way over to the train station. I figured we could find a nice compartment on the train, drop off our luggage, and still have time to spare for a little more sightseeing. I saw a long train that said "Ostend-Brussels." Obviously, this was the two o'clock train.

We made our way to the platform. I was dragging two huge suitcases behind me. Trae and Tiffin each had one, and Vikki had one. Whew. We stepped up to the back car, climbed on board, and began making our way down the narrow aisle with our luggage in tow. I was surprised to see that, even at this early hour, the train was quite full.

As the four of us, plus bulky luggage, wove our way down those narrow aisles in search of a compartment, I thought this was a lot of trouble. I would get off with the kids and the luggage, while Vikki would continue through the train to find a compartment. Then I'd move the luggage onto that car. So I threw the luggage off the train, and Trae, Tiffin, and I hopped off and began walking along the platform.

Suddenly, the train started moving! I couldn't figure out what was going on—we had at least forty-five minutes before the train was due to leave. But the train began picking up speed—obviously this one was leaving *now*. I began jogging alongside of the train waving my arms. I was wearing cowboy boots, and if you've ever tried to run in cowboy boots you know how awkward that is. I probably looked like the British comedian John Cleese doing one of his comedy routines.

I yelled at Trae to jump on. He ran along and grabbed a railing, pulling himself up and onto the train. I began grabbing luggage, heaving one bag after another onto the train—one suitcase landed right on top of Trae. Tiffin went next. I grabbed her under the arms and hoisted her up on top of the bags. Now the train was really starting to move and I'm sprinting alongside! With a burst of speed—as the doors closed—I grabbed hold of the door handles, banged hard to open them, and pulled myself on board. My heart was pumping, I was sweating. It was a real rush. But I was reunited with my family and all was well—although I still couldn't figure out why the train pulled out of the station so early.

While I'm catching my breath, I suddenly hear the brakes squeal and the train grinds to a halt. We were not quite out of the rail yard. This confused me even more. Suddenly a conductor came running up to me and started jabbering away in French. He was very upset: "Why were you running alongside the train, playing these games, jumping on when the train was moving?" he yelled.

Fortunately, I can speak a bit of French—just enough to get by. I started to explain to him what had happened, that I had to catch up with my wife and family and that the train had left early! He yelled that the train certainly did not leave early. I looked at my watch and said, "It's only 1:10—the train doesn't leave until 2:00!"

The conductor rolled his eyes and here's why: When we crossed the English Channel there was a time change. It was 2:10 Central Europe Time, and the train, in fact, was a few minutes late. So here I was, the great European know-it-all traveler, and I had forgotten all about the time difference between England and the Continent. Apparently the yard master had watched the whole scene unfold and had radioed the locomotive captain to stop.

I could image everyone watching this bowlegged American cowboy running after the train and throwing luggage on left and right and then jumping onto a moving car. What a sight. So I learned a lesson: Pay attention to time zones or else look silly in front of the world! Believe me, Vikki and the kids had a good laugh at my expense.

Gypsies, Tramps, and Thieves

Here's another good lesson in being very careful when traveling abroad. My brother, Kelly, who is a French teacher at a boys school in Columbus, Ohio, routinely takes some of his students to France to study, practice the language, and learn about the culture first-hand. On one of his trips, my family and I were in Europe and we coordinated it so that we could all meet up in Paris. Vikki, Trae, Tiffin, and I were looking forward to a rare, international rendezvous. Kelly had about a dozen students with him, and when he could get free, we would travel around Paris a bit.

When we managed to link up, we began making our way across the city using the subway system. A strange scene began to unfold as we traveled on one subway car. It confused me at first, but then it became frighteningly clear what was going on.

The subway car was reasonably crowded. At the far end, we could see a group of about ten

Trae, my brother Kelly, and I after we met up in Paris.

gypsies, ranging in age from five to about twenty-five—boys and girls. The group was making its way down the aisle, going up to people, begging for money, and trying to talk to them. One girl, who appeared to be the leader of the gang, had a newspaper she kept pushing in peoples' faces. Everyone kept telling these kids to leave them alone and go away. It was really angering the passengers.

The girl got to me and shoved the paper in my face. I politely pushed it away and she turned to Kelly and shoved it in his face. About the same time, the car began slowing down. At the next stop, the doors opened and, quickly, the whole clan of gypsies ran out! Kelly, looking concerned, patted his pockets and the small, over-the-shoulder carry bag he had with him. Suddenly he yelled, "They've stolen all the passports!" He had been carrying his students' passports, plus all the spending money for the trip, in that bag. He had been pickpocketed in a matter of seconds.

The game went like this: the older kids distracted the passengers with newspapers, while the little kids picked their pockets. Kelly lunged for the automatic doors and, just before they shut, managed to get out. I wasn't as quick—the doors closed on me and the subway train began moving out of the station. I felt so helpless and sick to my stomach for my brother. At the next stop, I had Vikki, Trae, and Tiffin get off and wait, while I took the next train back.

The gypsies had all run in different directions when they hit the pavement. Fortunately, Kelly speaks excellent French and started yelling to anyone within earshot to stop these kids, that they had stolen his wallet and passports. Some of the people in the station grabbed these kids as they were running away and managed to catch the culprit and get the money and passports back. A boy of about six had it all stuffed in his pockets. We found out later that a girl had done the pickpocketing and passed it on to the little boy, who had instructions to run off and hide.

By the time I got back to the station, the excitement was over. I found Kelly sitting calmly having a beer at a sidewalk cafe just outside the subway station. He said he was catching his breath and saying a prayer. I was really proud of how Kelly handled the situation and glad he knew so quickly that he had been a victim of the pickpockets and sprang into action. But it taught all of us a lesson: be ever careful when traveling on the Paris Metro—thieves are on the prowl.

Nine Lives

I was on vacation with Vikki and Tiffin in Europe in the winter of 1993, traveling around the Bavarian Alps from Garmisch to Munich. I had wanted to continue on to a mountainous, picturesque destination, but Vikki insisted that we stay in a big city with big hospitals readily available. She had a feeling something was not right with me. After we left Garmisch at about 9:00 p.m., I felt a fullness in my stomach even though I hadn't eaten a lot that day. I felt a little bit nauseous, but I really didn't pay a lot of attention to it at the time.

When we got to Munich and got off the train, about an hour or so later, I knew our hotel was only a few blocks from the station and suggested we walk there. On the way, I noticed that I was terribly weak. I had to stop every hundred yards or so to sit down and catch my breath.

I couldn't figure out exactly what the problem was. I thought, is it jet lag? Am I just that tired? Have I not eaten enough? I made it to the hotel and my room on the fifth floor. I tried to go to sleep, but had a gnawing feeling in my stomach. Half an hour later I was still feeling uncomfortable and suddenly I had to vomit. What happened next is not pretty, but it is part of my life and I'd like to talk about it. But I think I should warn you that the next couple of paragraphs are going to be tough reading.

Well, I started throwing up and what shocked me was that I didn't have the strength to get to the bathroom. I was there in my bed in the hotel room throwing up and it just kept coming and coming. The scariest thing about it was that what I was throwing up looked like calf's livers—the sort you see in the grocery store. No kidding. It was like large coagulated chunks of liver, the color of which looked like a cross between fire-engine red and black, you might describe it as black cherry.

For a panicky moment, I thought I was actually throwing up organs. That was the very first thing that crossed my mind—my whole body has suddenly started to reject itself. Both Vikki and Tiffin were terrified and so was I. Vikki notified the hotel desk and they called the paramedics. When they walked into the room, I stood up to greet them but then immediately had to sit right back down. They tried to find a pulse but couldn't. They wanted to put an IV in because they could see that I was losing a lot of blood. What I was throwing up turned out to be large coagulated clots of blood.

Later, I learned that I had an ulcer in my stomach that had eaten away part of the stomach wall. As luck would have it, the ulcer was right over a major blood vessel. The ulcer ate through the stomach wall and then hit the vessel—there wasn't any pain when this happened so I never realized it—and blood started flowing into my stomach and coagulating there. So when I felt uncomfortable on that train ride from Garmisch back to Munich and weak on the walk from the Munich train station to the hotel, it was actually my stomach filling with blood. And it wasn't surprising that when I threw it up, the first things that came up resembled chunks of liver.

At the hotel, the paramedics tried to get an IV started but couldn't. They rushed me down the elevator into their ambulance and, accompanied by the "bee-bop, bee-bop" sounds of European ambulances, Vikki and I were whisked away into the night. (Tif stayed at the hotel in case any calls came in or, considering the worst, to make transatlantic calls out.) They took me to the main hospital in Munich, which turned out to be a blessing because that particular hospital is extremely advanced in the treatment of stomach problems. My doctors in Dallas have told me I was very, very lucky to be at that hospital with this problem because I could have bled to death in another hospital.

When I arrived at the hospital, I was put in the intensive care unit and nurses got an IV started. One of the things that they do very well in Germany are what we call here in the States "endoscopies." This entails putting a tube about the diameter of your thumb down your throat and into your stomach and intestines. At the end of this tube is a light and a fiber-optic camera lens that shows doctors what is going on. It has little gizmos that can reach out, take biopsies, and do other useful things.

In any event, they sent one of these tubes down my throat. This wasn't the first time I had had this procedure done. I had it done at Baylor a couple of times before. When doctors got down there, they could see that I was bleeding badly from this ulcer in the side of my stomach. In a process almost like bicycle tire repair, they put some glue over the hemorrhaging area of the ulcer and then put a patch over it. I'm not sure what the patch was made of, if it was artificial skin or rubber or some other medical stuff. But whatever it was, it worked like a Band-Aid. Along with all of this, I was also given eight pints of blood.

I stayed five days in ICU in Munich waiting to improve. The doctors couldn't have been nicer. And the nurses were wonderful—thankfully, a number of them spoke English and we were able to communicate. They said I was pretty lucky to have been that close to a major hospital to get this treatment. Otherwise, I could have just lost all my blood into my stomach, thrown it up, kept bleeding, and died.

So after five days in ICU at Munich and another day in a regular room, I told the doctors it was time for me to go home. They looked at me and laughed. I told them, "No, you don't understand, I'm a big TV star in Dallas-Fort Worth and I have to get back to do the news." They replied that they'd rather me stay for another week to make sure the bicycle patch on my stomach held up. The doctors said that if the patch in my stomach came undone while I was flying home, I could be dead by the time I landed. But, ever the optimist, I said I'd take my chances. I told them they'd done a great job, but I had to get home. And I told them I honestly felt good enough and confident enough to fly—besides, I'd just rest on the flight.

The hospital's administrators weren't familiar with American insurance companies, so my insurance didn't work and they needed cash before I could leave. Fortunately, I had a couple thousand dollars in traveling cash on me and was able to pay the bill and leave. As I think about it now, it was very inexpensive; I actually had enough money in my pocket to pay for my ICU procedures and stay. Now, I don't know when, or if, all the healthcare problems in this country will ever be resolved, but I'll say this: it was rather impressive to be charged a flat rate of approximately $500 a day for the services I got.

It turns out this fee setup is pretty standard in Europe and takes care of just about any ailment—whether you come in for a broken leg or for chemotherapy or with a bleeding ulcer. Whichever physician sees you, whatever treatment is authorized, whatever technical support is needed, all the patient does is pay the flat fee. It was a real eye opener compared to our American system.

From a newsman's standpoint, I was intrigued by this European system. I hear that the fault of that system is that for normal ailments you don't get quick treatment. The system's detractors point out that you have no choice over your doctors and you wait in line for certain procedures. If it's not a life-threatening problem that you have, or if you are having elective surgery, or surgery that can wait six months, you're put on a waiting list. So the difference over there is, you do not get the prompt, grade-A treatment you would usually receive in America.

But the real story here is that I had a very, very close call in Munich. I must really be fortunate, really blessed. I dodged a couple of real bullets. Had this incident occurred in nine out of ten other places, it's very likely that I couldn't have gotten the treatment, couldn't have gotten the bleeding stopped in time, and perhaps would have bled to death. Back in the United States, my primary gastrointestinal doctor, Bill Santangelo at Baylor University Medical Center, said I was extremely lucky because the Munich hospital is a leader in the West in handling gastrointestinal disorders. Some of their professors give lectures worldwide as well as write many papers, really setting the pace for other Western doctors in this area.

All in all, it was a very unexpected week in Munich—all of it spent in the hospital (except for a quick trip with Vikki and Tif to a cafe and park that Hitler used to frequent—a real treat for a history buff—before catching our plane). But I got very good care and I'm still here to talk about it. I think my doctors here would also say I don't realize just how close I came to not making it. I'm ever the optimist and perhaps I need to be a little bit more the realist. But when you're as confident and as cocky as I am, you think you're invulnerable, you're Superman. None of us are. And that's something that I've got to realize as time goes on.

"Unity Farm," Unityville, July 1994.

I've been fortunate in surviving some critical situations over the years and I've got to wonder about the old cat with nine lives. How many have I used up? I think that with just a little change here and there, a little change of location, timing, diagnosis or treatment or just a little change of fortune, there are probably three or four times in the last nine years that I could have died. I should be very, very thankful that that didn't happen—and I am.

IV

ADVENTUROUS MOMENTS

11

Daredevil Deeds

Ever since I was a little kid I've loved excitement and adventure. A big part of me, of my personality, is a crazy streak that's filled my life with thrilling moments and memories that still make my heart race. You wouldn't know the real Chip Moody if you couldn't get at least a glimpse of some of these adventurous moments.

Cowboys

I think most young boys dream of being cowboys. Back in the fifties, when I was a kid living in San Antonio, I remember getting a set of cap guns and twin holsters for Christmas. And to me, at that time, that was probably the neatest present in the whole world. Cowboys were heroes to me. I remember seeing the movie *Shane* as a youngster and I was so impressed with it. I thought that Alan Ladd, as a cowboy, was perhaps the neatest guy who'd ever walked the earth.

I have always associated with cowboys, horses, and guns. Even as I grew into adulthood, I maintained an attachment with the Wild West. I enjoy the cowboy values and the cowboy dress and the cowboy skills. One of the skills, in Hollywood terms, is the "fast draw." Whether it's Clint Eastwood, Alan Ladd, or Gary Cooper playing cowboys—they were quick with a gun. I always had an image of myself being a cowboy and being a "fast-draw" type of guy.

In 1986 I had a chance to live out my fantasy. I was doing remote broadcasts for KHOU-TV from the Houston Rodeo and Stock Show for a week, anchoring the news from the Astrodome. One of the features of the week was a fast-draw artist, an expert named Bob Graham, who had been in many professional fast-draw competitions. This was his hobby and he was putting on a demonstration at the Astrodome. Well, I wanted to get in on this and perform myself during one of the newscasts.

Bob instructed me a little bit on some of the finer points of fast draw. In a competition, you are positioned in front of a machine that consists of a light bulb on top and then below that, two flat pieces of metal that are connected by a couple of springs. Those metal pieces are held apart by a balloon and in the front metal piece there is a large circle cut out that exposes the balloon. This contraption is wired electronically and when someone punches the button behind you, the light comes on and then a large clock starts running.

The only way to stop the clock is to break the balloon and let those two metal pieces come together, which stops the clock. The cowboy is positioned about fifteen or twenty feet away from the target and

Fast draw—.52 of a second! With pro Bob Graham.

the judges are behind him. The cowboy tells the judge when he's ready but he can't touch the gun until the clock starts. The gun is in a side holster, and when you're ready, you wait for the light, then, in a single action, you draw, cock, and fire the thing, hoping to hit the target and explode a target balloon. If you do, the clock stops and gives you your time. He who has the fastest time, wins.

The first time I tried it, I missed the target, which wasn't surprising. The second time, I tried to shoot too fast and shot right into the ground in front of me. But the third time, I nailed it. And I nailed it good: .85 seconds, which is less than a second to react, draw the gun, cock it, fire, and hit the target. Wow! I felt like I could've been right there with Gary Cooper in *High Noon*.

A couple of years later I tried it again at my house at a party for my golf tournament sponsors. Bob Graham came up and brought his equipment and I got my time down to .52—about half a second. I felt like I was really into the big leagues. Bob, however, and those who do this in competition around the country, have to be down in the range of about .30 of a second or less to have a chance at winning a contest. The guys who take this seriously are very, very fast. But, I thought my own efforts were pretty good—as a matter of fact, they were damn good. Maybe I have a new career?

Incident on the Guadalupe River

One of the most picturesque and enjoyable weekends you can spend in Texas is taking a canoe, raft, or inner tube down the Guadalupe River near San Marcos, just north of San Antonio. The US Army Corps of Engineers is responsible for the amount of water released from the dam on Canyon Lake, which determines the rate of flow along the Guadalupe.

During dry years, the release of water through the dam is minimal. But there are times when heavy rains necessitate that the Corps release an above-average amount of water into the Guadalupe, which then dramatically increases the river's flow. This is exactly what the white-water enthusiasts in Texas wait for: a good, solid, steady release of water that makes navigating the river exciting and fun.

The Corps tries to strike a happy balance, especially on weekends, so canoe riders and rafters can enjoy a fun ride without any special dangers. The Corps uses a scale ranging from 1 to 5 to let people know what the flow will be like. A "1" means the river will not only be running slowly, but in some cases, it may be necessary for people to "portage" their craft—walk around—some very low or dry areas. A "2" rating is better, and so on. For most people, a "3" is really the best overall rate, combining excitement, speed, and some possible spills, without dangerous undercurrents or waterfalls.

At a "5" rating, however, the river is quite dangerous. Because of large quantities of water being released from the dam, recreational activity is strongly discouraged at those times. In fact, when the river has a "5" rating, many raft companies along the river refuse to rent equipment to would-be customers because of the dangers.

There is one other warning the Corps uses: simply the letter "F." This is a fairly rare designation and means the river is in flood stage, and that there are especially strong currents, undertows, and dangers to anyone attempting to boat, raft, or swim on the river. The river is out of its banks, and normally placid or calm areas along it can become treacherous, and the exciting areas can be literally life-threatening.

Looking back on the summer of 1978, perhaps it was the adventure of the movie *Deliverance*, or simply wanting to experience something special and achieve the difficult that prompted me to organize a rafting trip down the swollen and dangerous Guadalupe. Because of sustained and heavy rains to the north, I knew that the Guadalupe would probably be in flood stage for at least two weeks. This gave me time to call my two brothers in Ohio and arrange for them to fly down to Dallas. The plan was to pack up a heavy-duty raft and a few camp-out accessories, and then head south for an adventure on the Guadalupe.

We drove to the small, quaint community of Gruene to get a look at the fury of the river. The bridge that crosses the Guadalupe River here was underwater and we could see and hear the power of the water being released from Canyon Dam upriver. The sight of the river flowing over the bridge gave us pause. But with so much time and expense already invested in getting Kelly and Bruce down to Texas, buying a new raft, and driving at least four hours from home, we were not easily discouraged.

It just took a little extra stupidity and bravado to look upon all this not as a danger but as an exciting and rare adventure that would test our courage, strength, and skills. The decision was made. We would launch our raft up from Gruene just below the dam. Once we reached the bridge at Gruene, we would leave the river. On reflection it wasn't a very smart decision, and it could have been deadly.

We found an abandoned park area from which to launch our raft and first discovered just how powerful this current was when we pushed our large raft out across the normally dry picnic area and toward the middle of the river: The raft was pulled away from us and wrapped itself around a tree. The current was so swift, we could not even pull the raft away from the tree. We finally deflated the raft, pulled it back on shore, re-inflated it, and started over. We should have quit while we were ahead.

On our second attempt to launch, we managed to get past the trees and out into the middle channel of the river. We climbed into the big raft and began moving down the river. The twists and turns were exciting and challenging—this is what we had come for! It dawned on us that we had the entire river to ourselves. But of course that was because everyone else was a lot smarter than we were . . . we had ignored two very strong warning signs—the flooded bridge and the incident with the raft wrapping itself around the tree. Still, we continued to press on, not unlike gung-ho pilots trying their best to accomplish their mission.

I had rafted the river before, so I knew some of the more exciting and tricky spots, which I expected to be especially challenging on this day. Oddly enough, the opposite was true. The big rocks that would normally cause white water and rapids were so far under the water, that these spots were abnormally tranquil. Instead, new and unforeseen areas of danger appeared before us.

At one point, I shouted that we needed to move to one side of the river to get a better look at what we would be facing in the next quarter mile or so. As we made our way out of the center of the channel, I saw to my horror a number of nasty-looking sections of barbed wire coming closer on the left. Normally these fences would end where the normal level of the river began, but with the river now five or six feet higher than normal, these barbed wire fences simply disappeared into the water at a 45-degree angle.

We were moving along at a pretty good clip, and the big raft was very difficult to maneuver. Despite our efforts, we could not alter our course enough to miss the barbed wire. I was positioned on my knees at the front of the raft and in a matter of seconds I felt us slide across the barbed wire. As the jagged metal barbs tore into the bottom of the raft, they also sliced deeply into my right knee. Suddenly, we were treading water, thrashing about in what remained of our raft. We swam, paddled, or tried to walk to shore.

As I got out of the water, I realized I had a serious medical problem. Looking down at my knee, it looked as if someone had used a sharp knife to cut through a pound cake. My leg was bleeding badly and the largest gash was do deep I could look down inside and see white stringy things (ligaments, I guess), plus the muscle tissue and red flesh you would expect to see with a deep cut.

We used strips of our T-shirts to wrap around the wound to staunch the flow of blood. We weren't anywhere near civilization, and the only road was about half a mile away. We had no choice but to set out on foot across some rough terrain, hoping to reach the road and find help as soon as possible.

After about twenty long minutes of walking—actually, I was hobbling—we found the road. As we walked south down it, a passing motorist stopped to ask if we needed help. A look at the bloody rags covering my leg only emphasized our answer that yes, we really needed a ride to the nearest doctor. (In 1994, that same motorist who helped us in 1978 happened to be attending a Dallas charity function that I was also attending. He introduced himself and wondered if I remembered him giving us the ride into town. Of course I did. Now, although I do not remember his name, I would like to thank that man once again for helping me out of a bad spot. If you read this, give me a call. I'd like to thank you in person.)

We reached a clinic and the nurses and doctors quickly took charge. In minutes I was on one of those cold steel tables with the doctor threading up what looked like a huge curved needle you might use to repair a chair or couch—Yipes! But, with some xylocane to numb the area, the doctor very routinely sewed me up. I got the distinct impression that I was perhaps the 250th person he'd done this to—I wasn't the first river rafter whose excitement had exceeded his better judgment,

All sewn up, we now deliberated what to do next. Our raft was useless, and our adventure on the river had only lasted thirty minutes at the most. Well, put it down to Texas stubbornness or not being too bright, but we were not going to be cheated out of our trip. We drove into the nearest town, found a truck stop, and asked if they had any used inner tubes to sell. They did, and we bought half a dozen, lashing them together with rope.

With our handmade raft, we went back to river. This time, we managed to stay out of trouble and had an exhilarating day. We did see some splintered canoes wrapped around trees in midstream and more than a few wrecked canoes on the banks. It was a mean little stretch of river that week. As I recall, several people drowned, but I don't remember the number or the circumstances. I've still got two large scars next to my right knee as a reminder to pay attention to warnings. Sometimes I am surprised I am here at all!

All Aboard

If you have ever been out to Fair Park in Dallas, you have probably seen the railroad museum on the north side of the grounds. I've always enjoyed looking at the huge old steam locomotives, passenger cars, cabooses, and freight cars that comprise this exciting collection of machines from a bygone era.

One day, one of the top executives at the Age of Steam Railroad Museum, Kelvin Kerr, called me at work and told me that the Union Pacific Railroad would be bringing the largest operating steam locomotive in the world, The Challenger #3985, through the Dallas-Fort Worth area. Kelvin wondered if I might be interested in riding on the train on its run from Fort Worth to Dallas. Every year, Union Pacific puts the Challenger, which is based out of Cheyenne, Wyoming, back in service to make excursion tours through different parts of the country, giving train buffs young and old a chance to recapture with their eyes and ears that golden age of train travel.

It was quite a thrill to ride in the engine of the Union Pacific Challenger.

It took perhaps a second to say, "Yes, count me in!" I have always been excited and fascinated by the size and power of these monstrous machines that belch smoke and fire and haul tremendous amounts of freight and were such an important part of the historic development of America and the Old West. Plus, I've always been fascinated by mechanical things—from cars and airplanes, to motorcycles and go-carts, to tractors and railroad locomotives.

In the split second I agreed to be on board, I also asked if it would be possible to ride in the cab of the locomotive. Kelvin said he'd look into that request. Thirty minutes later he called me back and said Union Pacific officials thought that because it was so hot and dirty up in the cab, I would probably come out looking the worse for wear at the end of the run from Fort Worth to Dallas. They said I would probably be smarter to enjoy the ride in the observation car, and then disembark at Union Station in downtown Dallas in time to walk over to the Channel 8 studios and appear on the 5 p.m. newscast without looking greasy, grimy and dirty. Besides, once I was in the cab, I would have to stay there for the entire trip.

I got their drift and decided I should just be happy and excited to ride along in the passenger section and enjoy the comfort and hospitality of the railroad. As we talked, Kelvin said that if I could manage to get up early the day after the trip from Fort Worth to Dallas, and head over to Union Station about the break of dawn, he would do everything he could to convince Union Pacific to allow me to ride up in the cab for part, if not all, of the ride on the next leg of the tour, from Dallas to Longview. I quickly agreed, and planned to do without my usual eight hours of sleep, just to get the chance to ride up in the cab of this great train.

On the day of the first leg of the trip, I arrived at the old Texas and Pacific train terminal in Fort Worth at the appointed hour, knowing I could look forward to some nice hors d'oeuvres and hospitality courtesy of the museum, the Union Pacific Railroad, and the crew of the powerful and majestic Challenger locomotive. I brought my own home video camera along for the ride. After shooting exterior shots of the engine before we left, I boarded and resigned myself to riding in one of the beautifully restored passenger cars. Don't get me wrong, I thought that in itself was pretty special. But I really did want to be up in the cab, the cockpit, the place where the action was.

We pulled out of Fort Worth in a plume of smoke, steam, bells, and whistles, just about on schedule, and I started shooting videotape from one of the domed observation cars. It was exciting to be enjoying a slice of old-time Americana. We were only about ten minutes into the trip when suddenly the train slowed to a stop—yet we had all been told that this would be a nonstop trip. As a newsman I was perhaps more curious about the unscheduled stop than the average passenger.

I walked to the front of the train, wondering to myself what might have prompted the engineer to stop. I soon learned that, tragically, the train had hit and killed a man who had been walking on the tracks. He had tried to jump out of the way of the huge locomotive at the last second. The trip was delayed as the railroad radioed for an ambulance and police.

Talking with the Union Pacific engineer, I learned that this had been the first fatal accident involving the Challenger in its long history of regular service and in the history of its nostalgic tours around the country. Despite the quick emergency aid by a railroad physician who happened to be on board, and the aid of local paramedics who quickly arrived on the scene, the victim was beyond medical help. The tragic accident took the shine off of what most people had expected to be a truly fun and exciting train trip.

Channel 8 had cameras ready at Union Station for our arrival in Dallas and it was a picturesque moment, with the big locomotive belching out a huge column of steam and smoke as it rolled into the station, and the modern skyline of Dallas its backdrop. But there was a shadow cast across the scene. That evening on the news, we covered both the train trip and the fatal accident.

After finishing the late news that night, I headed home and got to sleep as quickly as I could, looking forward to the chance of riding in the locomotive cab the next morning. When I arrived at Union Station, I met with the Union Pacific public relations director, who said he had gotten clearance for me to ride up in the cab for about one hour during the trip to Longview.

We departed Dallas under the cliché of "a full head of steam," and the fourteen-car train began its journey northeast. About thirty minutes out of Dallas, we stopped and I was summoned up to the spacious but all-business cab of the locomotive. I got a quick orientation on the various controls and soon we were pushing in the throttle, pulling the long cord with the red wooden handle that blew the whistle, and chugging our way along the tracks.

It was an exhilarating time for me, walking around the big cab, leaning out the windows, waving to bystanders who had lined the track anticipating the passage of this antique of rail history. Although I could tell a number of people along the way recognized me from television, I kind of wanted to be accepted as part of the locomotive crew.

I was invited to take the right seat in the cab and blow the whistle and otherwise act like I really knew how to control this five-hundred-ton locomotive and the long trail of passenger cars we were pulling. If you have ever fantasized about what it might be like to be up front in a real locomotive, I can tell you it is everything you ever dreamed it would be. It's all there: the heat, the many dials, the various pressure control valves, knobs and gauges that tell you about things like tinder box temperature, steam pressure in the lines, and approximate speed.

I want you to try to imagine what one million pounds really means. The average car we all drive is something in the neighborhood of four thousand pounds. If you start multiplying, it becomes apparent that this locomotive is a very, very heavy piece of machinery. Here's another comparison that might give you an idea of the tremendous size and weight of this monstrous locomotive: one of the largest airplanes you'll see at Dallas-Fort Worth International Airport is the DC-10 jumbo jet. American Airlines uses these for transatlantic and cross-country flights. It's the big jet with an engine on each wing, and a third engine mounted in the tail section. Well, one of these birds at takeoff weighs about 440,000 pounds. So, the Challenger locomotive, with all of its heavy cast iron parts and huge drive wheels, weighs as much as two DC-10s.

For me to seem to be in control of such an awesome piece of machinery was exhilarating. The noise, the heat, the whistles, and waving at the hundreds of people who had lined up along the railroad line to see this thundering relic of a bygone era made it a day to remember. I got to blow the whistle quite a bit, make a few throttle adjustments and play engineer.

My thanks to Union Pacific, the Age of Steam Railroad Museum in Dallas, and Kelvin Kerr for this once-in-a-lifetime chance to step back in time and get a hands-on experience of an incredible example of one of this nation's most glorious of eras . . . the age of the steam locomotive.

Bombs Bursting in Air

Reading this book, people will realize that I'm basically an overgrown kid. I delight in riding trains, flying airplanes, shooting six-guns, and driving tractors. I also, like most kids, love to set off fireworks. But even more than that, I love the thrill of putting on a show for my friends up in South Dakota.

I was lucky enough some years ago to make the acquaintance of Roy and Mary Trout, owners of Atlas Enterprises in rural Fort Worth. Their company is one of the premier fireworks companies in the country. Every year, I buy fireworks from them for a Fourth of July fireworks display at my farm in Unityville, South Dakota. (You know where Unityville is—it's 5 miles south of Canova, 16 miles south of Howard, 28 miles southwest of Madison, 9 miles south of Salem, and just down the road from Winfred. If that doesn't pinpoint it, just drive north on I-35/US 81 for 825 miles, then turn left and in 3 miles you're at my farm.) All the nearby farmers and their families come for the event—we usually have a crowd of about two hundred. The ladies bring marshmallow treats, red Jell-O with slices of banana in it, and other favorite Heartland desserts, while the men grab a cold beer or lemonade and talk about the rain—or lack of it—during games of horseshoes. The kids are in the playhouse or arguing over go-cart rides. The grand finale is the fireworks show.

The Trouts have always made sure that I have a good selection of fireworks to entertain my South Dakota friends. It's amazing to see a big yard full of fifty or sixty children each waving a sparkler! And the Trouts usually slip in a couple of extra goodies for extra dazzles—stuff you won't see at the corner fireworks stand.

I have also called on Roy and later his son, Royce (now president of Atlas) to help me out at my golf tournaments. No other golf tournament that I know of has a fireworks show—not to mention the huge one Atlas provides. Over the years, they have contributed tens of thousands of dollars' worth of fireworks and pyrotechnic expertise to my tournaments to make them extra special. I can't thank the Trout family enough, not only for being generous supporters, but good friends and wonderful people.

One year, the Trouts put on a tremendous Fourth of July fireworks show in New York, shooting them off from huge barges in the harbor. They lit up the entire New York metropolitan area. NBC televised it. It was an incredible event to watch on television, and I wish I could have been there in person, but I was preparing my own show at the farm. Actually, I'm glad I was in South Dakota and not New York. My friends there think the show I put on is the best around, and I keep trying to do it up just a little bit bigger and better every year. I've actually started throwing in patriotic music, trying to imitate the pros. Last year, everybody sang "America the Beautiful" in the middle of the show, and it was very moving.

Let me just say here that it's not a cliché: the farmers of the Midwest really form the heart of America. These people have a different set of values than many of us have in the big city, where things run at a faster pace, where perhaps there is too much of a focus on the dollar and big cars. The people on America's farms work fourteen-hour days with no guarantee that the crops are going to come in. They love going to community little league baseball games, playing in pickup softball games, and all those things that make middle America so great. Their minds are not on material things, but on family and friends—and fireworks, of course! True American values live on in my neck of the woods around Unityville, South Dakota. So grab a sparkler and give a "Hip, Hip, Hooray!"

12

Flying High

FLYING HAS ALWAYS BEEN MY PASSION. Although my career as an Air Force pilot was cut short before it really ever began, I never lost my love for soaring through the skies. It has remained an important and exciting activity for me—and given me plenty of good stories for parties.

Danger on the Wing

In the early eighties I was co-owner of a four-seater Cessna 182 and many times I would take the airplane down to Mexico or to the Grand Canyon or up to my farm in South Dakota—places like that. On more than one occasion I would finish up the news, say on a Friday night, and then go to the airport and jump in the airplane, take off, and head up to South Dakota. My normal stop for refueling was always Salina, Kansas, which used to be an Air Force base in World War II. It was used mostly for bombers and had a big, long runway.

One time after refueling in Salina, I flew on into Howard, South Dakota and landed on a small grass strip near the farm—just for fun. If you're a pilot and have a feeling for the old days of aviation in its infancy, you love grass fields. It's hard to describe—nothing like landing or taking off on a concrete runway. Landing on that grass element made me feel like a Roaring Twenties barnstormer pilot.

There were no fuel pumps in the Howard area, but I thought I had an adequate amount of fuel to make another trip a few days later. Kelly was coming in by bus from Columbus, Ohio to Sioux Falls, South Dakota, which was forty miles away, and I was to pick him up at the bus station there.

A few days later, I headed out to the small grass strip where the plane had been tied down. I did a routine pilot walk-around. There are certain tests, like checking for water in the gas tank, you must do as a pilot before taking off. Everything checked out as I did the walk-around, so I got into the airplane and cranked it up.

Immediately I noticed that the fuel gauges were strangely low. I couldn't quite figure that out. I got out of the airplane and crawled up on the wing and looked down into the gas tanks and I saw fuel in both wing tanks. I figured, well, I've only got about forty or so miles to go to Sioux Falls and the main airport to pick up my brother, and I'd probably be okay. I could see fuel, I could see a reflection from the top of the fuel tanks from where I was looking.

As I turned on all the switches in the cockpit, both tanks registered less than a quarter of a tank in gas. I thought that must be an error; from the looks of it I had enough gas. I really didn't have to go that far. My mistake was to assume that I did have enough aviation fuel to get to Sioux Falls.

A good friend of mine and a farmer in South Dakota, Dick Pearson, asked if he could fly to the Sioux Falls airport with me, which I said would be fine. He never had been up in a light airplane before and wanted to go along. Then the three of us would fly back to the farm in Unityville.

As I said, I made a mistake believing I had enough fuel to make it to Sioux Falls. And here I was taking up a friend who had never really flown. But we took off with good intentions. When we were maybe two-thirds of the way to Sioux Falls, the engine stopped. My words—which I think are probably universally used by pilots when something goes wrong—were simply, "Oh shit."

I was roughly 6,000 feet above the ground and suddenly I had no power. I radioed the Sioux Falls airport and said I was declaring an emergency, that my engine had quit, that I would attempt an emergency landing quickly. They had me on radar and they could see where I was. The flight controller told me to try to make it to Interstate 90, which is a big highway that runs through South Dakota. But, as I looked out in the distance, I could see that I might not make it. I had to figure out an alternative plan fairly quickly.

As all pilots will tell you, and anybody who reads this book who has been through pilot training knows, you immediately go through the Engine Out Emergency Landing Procedure when you're in trouble. It was during this emergency that all my training paid off. I suddenly real-

After take-off in my Cessna 182.

ized that I had very few options and I had to find a good place to land in what is called a "dead stick landing," which means that you have no power, but you have to move the plane, position it correctly and land somewhere without crashing.

When I talked again to the Sioux Falls control tower, they recommended trying to land in the median strip of Interstate 90 which was now maybe six miles ahead. I told them I didn't think I had the altitude and the speed to make it. At the same time all this was happening, I "trimmed" the airplane, a term for getting the best glide slope speed. The first thing I did was adjust the controls and position the flaps. There are a number of things that you go through to obtain what you would call your óptimum glide ratio.

As I was going through this, I told the Sioux Falls control tower that I could see the interstate at a distance. As I got closer to it, I realized in fact that I would never make it. You have to take into consideration that there are a lot of factors that go into flying. One of the most important is the wind, especially in a light plane. I saw a field that I thought I could land in when I realized I wasn't going to make the median of the interstate. But that was two, maybe three miles away and I just didn't think I could glide that far.

I was in the area of Hartford and, thankfully, South Dakota in that area is fairly flat, fairly regimented in the sense that land is platted out in quarter miles or in half miles or miles. So I had some straight rows of land to look at. I looked first for a field, but then I spotted something that looked from the air like a sidewalk.

In fact, it was a single-lane, dirt farm road, maybe twenty feet wide. But it didn't have telephone poles along it and it didn't have many trees. So I banked the airplane to the left and began to make my approach. Now all my many hours of training really began to take over and it's a good thing too, because the next several moments would be the most critical. A dead stick landing is extremely dangerous. You only get one shot at it, there are no second chances. There is no room for mistakes because, with no engine power, you can't pull up, go around and try it again. A dead stick landing is actually the way the space shuttle lands. After re-entry, the space shuttle is nothing more than an oversized glider. However, there are lots of people from NASA, along with some very sophisticated, high-tech equipment, available to guide that giant glider safely to the ground.

In my case, it was just me, my training, and a small dirt farm road. I would either get it right the first time, or my passenger and I would be seriously injured, or maybe worse—dead. The funny thing was, I wasn't the least bit nervous. No sweat on the brow, no clammy palms, never even a thought of not making it. I was completely focused on landing the airplane. Surprisingly, Dick was not nervous either. In fact, he appeared remarkably calm for someone who had never even been in a small airplane before.

Quite frankly, even if I had been worried, there was just no time to think about it. It had only taken six or seven minutes from the time I first ran out of gas at 6,000 feet above ground to when I successfully made the dead stick landing on the dirt farm road. It was a smooth landing at that! Not bumpy at all. But most importantly, it was a safe landing.

After I landed, I was able to communicate with another pilot who was flying above me and explain the situation to him. He translated the message to the Sioux Falls airport that I had landed safely. I thought, if I get some fuel, I could probably get to the airport. I think Dick was rather impressed with how the whole situation was handled. In fact, he has gone on to build his own airplane and is a fine pilot to this day and has two airplanes up in South Dakota.

In any event, I landed on this dirt road and there's a farmer out in the field on his tractor. I know we surprised him. The farmer got off his tractor, came over and asked if we needed some help. I told him we were fine, but needed some high-octane fuel. He took his tractor into town and found some people to bring out a portable gas truck to fuel the airplane. I asked them to give me the highest octane stuff they had, and paid them about $80.

Then it was a matter of just cranking up the airplane and taking off down this skinny dirt road and head into Sioux Falls. We took off with lots of dust and rocks and gravel flying behind us down this little country road. It was a sight that I don't think this farmer had ever seen before and probably will never see again while he is out doing his work in the field.

After taking off, we continued on to Joe Foss Field in Sioux Falls. As we headed toward Joe Foss Field, I flew over the bus station and I could see Kelly standing out in front of the station waiting. But there was no way I could holler down to him, "Sorry I'm late," or honk my horn. Kelly had no idea how I was going to pick him up or where to go. I went ahead and landed and of course I called the bus station. I asked them to page my brother and tell him to catch a taxicab or something out to the airport because that's where we were.

I was, of course, slapped on the wrist upon our arrival at the airport. An FAA representative wanted to talk to me about why we didn't have enough fuel. I explained that during a three- or four-day period at the Howard air strip, I had to assume someone had siphoned off most of the gas, and with no fuel pumps, I was not able to re-fuel there.

I told the guy from the FAA that, geez, I just did what I could and I thought I had enough gas to get to Sioux Falls without making an emergency landing. That didn't happen, obviously. I was gently criticized by the FAA, but there were no fines or penalties involved. I should have topped off those tanks, even if it meant spending extra time finding some fuel in the Howard area. It might have taken me only an hour or so to find some premium gas and bring it to the airport. Still, I was proud of my performance as a pilot in an emergency situation. Sure it was scary, but at the same time, I had this inner confidence that somehow it was going to work out. I credit my flight training, my flight instructor, Tom Toler, and the discipline that goes into flight training.

I explained to Kelly why we were an hour late and we made sure the tanks were full and then headed back to the farm. We made a fine landing on the grass strip at Howard and I think we had a margarita to celebrate.

There's a regular section in the popular magazine *Flying* entitled "I Learned about Flying from That." Well, that sure sums up my experience, because I did indeed "learn about flying from that!"

A Tale of Ice and Hearses

It was 1982. I owned a Piper Cherokee 180 private airplane, a single-engine four-seater. Kelly was down here in Texas visiting from Ohio. Vikki, my brother-in-law Bard Holbert, Kelly, and I decided to fly to the

Colorado Rockies for a ski trip. We were all very excited as we left my parents' house in Arlington and headed off to the airport. There at the Grand Prairie Muncipal Airport we packed our skis in the plane, loaded the luggage, and cranked up the engine. I guess it was about 9:00 a.m. when we took off. We figured we may not beat a Lear jet, but this sure beat driving.

We had clear conditions when we started out, but what happened about forty minutes into the flight was a real eye-opener. As we were heading west and north, I was climbing through 6,000 feet and the weather was reasonable. We had a very high overcast and plenty of visibility, but there was a pocket of freezing precipitation between 4,000 feet and about 8,000 feet above ground level. As we were flying out northwest, I noticed a slight build-up of ice starting on the windshield.

Any pilot worth his salt knows that icing is very dangerous. When I radioed the flight service station back in Fort Worth, the weather advisor on duty confirmed that there was a layer of freezing precipitation. Well, I'm cruising along at 6,000 feet and suddenly it's getting very, very icy—in an airplane without de-icing equipment. I had the defroster on, but the windshield started turning opaque, and as I looked out the side window, I could see that ice was starting to form on the leading edges of the wings. These are real danger signs for pilots.

So, rather than continue on toward Denver, I elected to start flying lower, anticipating that as I got below 4,000 or 3,000 feet, I could kind of hug the earth, find warmer temperatures, and fly below the freezing precipitation. When you fly at a low altitude, you don't get as good mileage or speed, but I thought for safety's sake I better drop down and the ice would disappear and I could continue on. But even as I descended to about 3,000 feet, the ice continued to build up. The windshield became more and more opaque, as more and more ice collected on it. The defroster was of no help.

As I looked out the side window, I could see the freezing precipitation flying right past us and that ice was continuing to accumulate on the wings. So I descended even lower with the intention yet again of finding a warmer level of air to melt everything off. I got down to about 1,000 feet above the ground. At that altitude, you're cutting it close—risking running into TV and radio towers and stuff like that. Also at 1,000 feet, you've got to really know exactly where you are at on your aviation maps.

I anticipated that as I got lower, the ice would melt off and everything would be fine. But it only got worse. And worse. By this time, we were flying over the border of Texas and Oklahoma. Suddenly I realized I could not even see out the front of my airplane. I'm down to 1,000 feet with three other souls on board and I could be in deep trouble unless I made a good—and quick—decision. I got on the radio, and there was an airport nearby, an "uncontrolled airport"—no control tower.

Using the standard radio frequency for pilots departing from or arriving at an uncontrolled airport, I announced my position to any other pilots in the vicinity and said I was coming in to land. The runway was clear, but looking at it straight ahead was like looking into an ice cube. I couldn't see a thing. So I looked out the left side of the airplane as I was landing and did my speeds and descent rates by the book, with Kelly looking out the side window.

The runway was straight ahead, and here I was looking out the side of the airplane at a ninety-degree angle to our approach path. Still, I made a great landing. Bard was impressed (he was riding co-pilot), although he couldn't quite figure out how I landed this airplane looking out the side window. I guess you could compare this to driving on the highway, and staying in your lane by looking to the side. I lined up the runway by compass heading and parallel taxi ways, reduced my power settings just like I would normally do, brought the nose up as we came close to touchdown, landed with no problem, and then braked to a stop.

We taxied the airplane over to one of the larger hangars, and the airport technical crew turned on some big heaters, which melted the ice off the airplane in about an hour. In the meantime, I called the flight service station and talked to the weather people, telling them what I had experienced and asking what I would experience further west. After their briefing, I figured that if I could climb through this one layer of freezing precipitation quickly, we'd be in the clear.

After we got the airplane de-iced, we refilled with aviation fuel, and everybody got back on board. I told my family that I would climb as fast as I could to get through this stuff and avoid the problem again. When I took off, I did a maximum speed climb for that particular airplane, and it didn't give the precipitation or ice time to build up. In twenty minutes we were above the precipitation layer and in bright blue skies. It was clear sailing all the way into Denver. For the rest of the flight, we flew strong and steady.

But our problems were not over entirely. As we approached the Denver area, the airport I had planned to land at, Arapaho County, was in the process of shutting down because of heavy snowfall. I radioed the control tower from about sixty miles out and was advised of the airport's situation. I was told that in fifteen minutes it would be at "the pilot's discretion" whether to land there or not. There was a heavy build-up of snow and ice on the runway, a build-up that was also gradually covering the landing lights.

Dusk was approaching, so the light was not great, and the increasingly snow-covered runway and lights presented a problem. But we were committed. As we came within five miles of the runway, we were informed that the airport was, in fact, being closed and any landing was "at the pilot's discretion." I could still see the runway and I could still see the runway lights—barely—and I knew I could handle the landing.

I got tower clearance and we landed without incident. We taxied over to the Fixed Base Operator (FBO), which is the gas station, repair hangar, and occasional motel that is at the center of any small airport. As we turned off the engine and started to unload, we realized that there were quite a few people stuck in the same predicament who had either just arrived or were trying to leave and could not. The entire building at Arapaho County Airport was filled with stranded people—all the rental cars were spoken for.

I had originally hoped to rent a car at Stapleton Airport, the major airport, but that was out because it was fifteen miles away. Oddly enough as I was standing around in the FBO office, I saw a guy kind of looking around and I asked him if he was waiting for somebody. And he said, there was a flight due in, a large Cessna, with an embalmed body in a casket. He said he was with the funeral home and was supposed to pick up the body that night. He said he had just learned from the tower that the Cessna pilot turned back because the airport was closed. I told him we were in need of a ride to Stapleton to pick up a rental car and could he help? He said, "Sure, if you don't mind riding in the hearse!" We didn't. We loaded up and this gentleman gave us a free ride to the big airport in this hearse with all our ski equipment and suitcases on board. He dropped us off, we picked up the rental car, and we headed out to the slopes.

The Fighting Falcon

Over the years, I've helped out General Dynamics (now Lockheed) in their United Way campaign on different occasions. The Fort Worth division has raised millions and millions of dollars for charity over the years and occasionally I would emcee their rallies. In 1992, I was the master of ceremonies for a company-wide celebration honoring everyone for how much money they had raised for United Way that year. It was well in excess of a $1 million and I was there to give out some individual achievement prizes and recognition plaques for people who had really helped make the drive such a huge success.

After the event, some of the corporate executives asked me to stay on for lunch and we went over to the VIP cafeteria. During our talk, one of the vice presidents said, "Chip, we really appreciate your help and we'd like to give you a gift. We know you're a pilot—would you like to fly our F-16 Simulator?" Well, the wheels in my head started turning and I looked at him for a few seconds before saying, "You know I actually flew the F-18 made by McDonnell Douglas that the US Navy's Blue Angels are flying. I flew that plane last year, and, boy, that is one nifty airplane. It really is a great fighter, very responsive . . . "

As I kept going on about the Blue Angels flight, the company executive, getting my drift, started smiling. He finally said, "Wait a minute, you're telling us you don't want to fly this *simulator*, you want to fly the real thing." Bingo! They said it would take a couple months to get the paperwork set up, but if I was patient, I could do it. Few civilian pilots get to fly the F-16. I was, of course, on cloud nine.

It was arranged within a few months, and I was told to show up one morning at the General Dynamics plant on the west side of Carswell Air Force Base for the flight. My father came along on the appointed day: As an ex-Air Force pilot he wanted to enjoy the thrill of seeing his son go up in what is perhaps the best dog-fighting jet fighter in the world today. I met with the General Dynamics executives and chief test pilot Bland Smith, and we spent half an hour in a pre-flight briefing on the layout of the cockpit, what my responsibilities would be, how the ejection seat worked, and other basics. I got a good look at all the instruments that I would be using, and that was critical, since I would be in the back seat flying the airplane for some of the mission.

We strapped on our G-suits and buckled up. There are about nineteen seat straps that lock you into an F-16 fighter or any other modern fighter. You're actually sitting on your parachute and you're hooked up with audio into your helmet and oxygen into your mask. On the F-16, it's kind of neat because the seat is set back at a thirty-degree angle—sort of like an easy chair. This helps pilots better handle the high-G maneuvers that the F-16 does so well.

We strapped in and started to head out to the runway. Bland let me taxi out and I was soon to find out he would let me fly almost the entire hour and a half we were out. I taxied out and lined the fighter up at the end of the runway, headed north. We waited for some spacing between

American Airlines and Delta Airlines flights headed into or out of DFW Airport. As I sat in the cockpit of this powerful jet, I knew we were going to shoot straight up to an altitude above where the commercial airliners were flying, so we had to make sure they were out of the way when we shot up.

We did a full military power take-off. Bland fired us up, hit the throttle, then kicked in the afterburner. As soon as we were airborne, he tucked up the landing gear and we stayed at about 100 feet over the runway. The runway at Carswell is around 12,000 feet long, and by the end of it, we were doing more than 400 miles an hour. Then we yanked back on the stick and headed straight up to 16,000 feet—it only took about 20 seconds. It was like being launched on a rocket.

We rolled over onto our back and then straightened up and I looked down at General Dynamics and Carswell. Bland said, "Okay, we're heading west—the airplane is yours." I was in heaven. I quickly did a couple of rolls, and demonstrated to Bland that I wasn't entirely a rookie at this, and in fact knew most of the basics of flying an airplane. Bland explained some of the sophisticated capabilities of the F-16, like the electronic bombing and how well the plane can fly on the computer. You give the computer a target and it can, in fact, find the target for you. We electronically "blew up" the dam at Possum Kingdom Lake.

It was a blissful hour and a half for me. Bland was happy that I enjoyed the maneuvers and aerobatics. He said that sometimes some of the VIPs or Air Force generals who he has taken for rides in the F-16 would throw up when they started doing anything very fancy. But for some reason, I've never had an air sickness problem and always just enjoyed the heck out of aerobatics.

One maneuver that I had never done before is called a "pop-up, tuck-under break." The Blue Angels do it and it works something like this: You pull the nose of the airplane up just a little bit, and then you quickly roll the plane 270 degrees to the right—not a full roll. Then you pull back on the stick and because you're in that position, your wings are perpendicular to the ground, the plane turns immediately to the left. It's a pretty fast maneuver—you roll right but you turn left.

I asked Bland if I could try it. I took a deep breath, thought it through, and pulled back on the stick. We did the three-quarter roll to the right, a sharp left-handed turn, and I could see the horizon straight up and down. It was one of the neatest feelings that I've ever had, because not only was it at 400 miles an hour or more, but I actually did the maneuver pretty well. I let out a whoop and said "piece of cake." We got it all on videotape so I could watch it later and enjoy that moment when I performed what was one of the sexier aerobatic maneuvers you can do in a jet.

Then it was back to Carswell Air Force Base and an instrument landing that Bland said I did as well or better than some commercial pilots who had flown the simulator the week before. We taxied in and got back to the hangar, and when I came off the plane, my dad was waiting in ambush with a huge bucket of water, which he poured all over me—just like you see on the sidelines of a football game when the coach gets a bucket of Gatorade poured on him after winning a big game. Usually pilots are thrown into a swimming pool after their first flight on a new plane—it's part of an initiation ritual among Air Force pilots. So this was my unofficial initiation into the F-16 club. But I also got a plaque and a 9G pin to wear and the congratulations of both the pilot and the executives at General Dynamics for not only flying the plane but flying it well. It was a day that I'll never, ever forget.

Never Say "Huh?"

I received an invitation a few years ago to fly with a group of Air Force Reserve pilots out of Carswell Air Force Base. It would be a simulated low-level bombing run down at Fort Hood—a war games exercise with tanks and all the ground infantry. When I arrived at Carswell, I learned we would be flying in vintage F-105 Thunderchief jets. These are the huge, heavy, fast jets used a lot in the Vietnam War. These F-105s, nicknamed "Thuds," were not designed to be great dog-fighting planes; their job was to go in fast, deliver a heavy bomb load, maybe strafe enemy ground positions, and get out.

As we were going through the pre-flight briefing at Fort Hood, I saw that our mission called for us to bomb some "enemy" positions outlined on a map. The group of fighter-bombers I'd be flying with would go down to the mock battle, peel off

After flying in war games exercises in an F-105.

in formation, and drop the bombs on targets at a specific time as part of the exercise.

The pilot I'd be flying with explained to me that these F-105s were older jets, and things can start going wrong inside. And he said bad things can happen very quickly. He told me that if we ran into a problem and had to bail out, he would say, "Eject! Eject! Eject!" I was to eject immediately. The pilot added one more warning: "Don't ask me anything—just do it! If you even say, 'Huh?' you're gonna be talking to yourself."

After he yelled to eject, that pilot was going to be long gone! It was one of the funniest lines that I had heard in my years of flying, but it was good, serious advice. I've taken it to heart—even when I'm not in a vintage jet. When an expert tells you to do something in a serious situation, you'd better act quickly. Never say "Huh?"!

The War Lover

One of my favorite motion pictures is *The War Lover*, starring Steve McQueen and Robert Wagner. It's the story of an American B-17 bombing crew in England during World War II and the talented but cocky pilot of the plane named Buzz Rickson, played by McQueen. I always identified with that role and felt a kinship to Rickson. McQueen played the part so convincingly, as a pilot who is very, very good, but that's all he really has in life—his talent as a pilot. His life is built around being a good bomber pilot.

Moments before taking off in a vintage World War II B-17 Bomber.

The movie itself was beautifully filmed, with some great shots of B-17s in combat. In the end, Rickson, with a very shot-up B-17 after a raid, orders his crew to bail out of the badly damaged plane that in all likelihood won't make it back to base. After the crew abandons the airplane, Buzz goes back to the controls and tries to get the B-17 safely back to the airfield. He felt that he was invincible, and he took the controls of this badly shot up plane and tried to get it back. Instead, he ends up crashing into the cliffs of Dover. It's a tragic story, and one I think of when remembering my own trip on a B-17 bomber.

There was an air show a few years ago that my friend, Jan Collmer, helped organize to benefit the Frontiers of Flight Aviation Museum at Dallas's Love Field. Jan and I have been friends for a long time—he is a corporate president by day, but his first love, like mine, is flying. He's also an ex-Navy pilot who flies in airshows on the weekends and has a great deal of flight experience.

At the benefit there were a lot of planes on display, including the Stealth Bomber and a vintage B-17 bomber owned by the Lone Star Flight Museum in Galveston. I got to tour the B-17, which was really exciting. Jan told me the airplane was heading back to Galveston that evening and said he'd try to get me a spot on board. He pulled some strings, I met the crew, and they did, in fact, have a seat available!

I scrapped all my Sunday evening plans, grabbed a still camera and hopped on board. I was given the opportunity to come up into the cockpit and fly this wonderful airplane for about 40 minutes during our flight. After being accustomed to flying smaller, newer, and more nimble planes, flying the four-engine B-17 seemed to take a lot more muscle and discipline. It seemed to me like I was sitting on a front porch, flying a house. It took a lot of concentration to keep the engines in sync and keep the course lined up while keeping the assigned altitude. It was a real workout.

On the flight I thought back to World War II, when pilots were very young and were trained to go into combat with nine or ten crew members on board and a huge bomb load. The young pilots of World War II—some of them only in their early twenties—were great, heroic people. Young men put into such a position needed the skill, dedication, and fearlessness to go into combat. I think back on some of those young pilots and I'm amazed that they were able to do it at their age—fly right into anti-aircraft batteries and deliver bombs on the enemy.

Long after *The War Lover* had been made (and I have watched it probably fifteen times) I finally got to be at the controls of a B-17 bomber. That to me was as exciting as just about any other aviation experience I've had. They're all different and they all have a special niche in my brain. But the B-17 is one I'll never forget.

Astronaut in Waiting

When NASA decided they would take a journalist up on one of the space shuttle flights, they held a nationwide competition among print, radio, and television news people to select the first journalist in space. About 2,400 journalists, including myself, entered the preliminary competition. We were all required to submit examples of our work, including essays and resumes, to NASA. The folks there then cut the entries down to a short list and turned the list over to journalism schools around the country, who then pared the list down even further.

We were required as applicants to demonstrate and try to explain why we should be the first journalist in space. There was some very tough competition. Obviously this would be a chance of a lifetime—to ride the space shuttle and report back on it, not only to your own particular station or newspaper, but to the world. And the world would be paying attention to how a journalist interpreted the trip and described the flight, from the thunderous sensation of liftoff to the awesome feeling of re-entry and everything in between.

NASA announced the semi-finalists—they had narrowed it down to an even 100. I was notified that, indeed, I was among the finalists! I was in seventh heaven. I figured I had a real, though slim, chance at this because of my personal flying experience and because I had covered many stories about commercial and private aviation in the news. I had a pretty good handle on aviation in general; I couldn't claim to be an expert, but I had a very strong background in different aspects of aviation. And besides, as a television news anchor, you often have to improvise on the air about a breaking news story—you're required to think on your feet and describe things as they happen. The NASA people wanted experience in all these areas too.

But then, as we all unfortunately remember too well, tragedy struck. On January 28, 1986, the space shuttle Challenger blew up. There was a teacher on board—Christa McAuliffe—and six other astronauts: Commander Francis R. Scobee; Pilot Michael J. Smith; Judith Resnik; Ronald E. McNair; Ellison S. Onizuka; and Gregory B. Jarvis. They all perished when the spacecraft blew up exactly seventy-four seconds after liftoff.

After the accident, the competition for journalists in space still continued, but I think NASA had already decided internally that it would not allow civilians to go up any more. And it never did. NASA finally publicly admitted that because of the Challenger tragedy, it would not allow journalists or other non-professional astronauts to be passengers.

Still, I was very honored to be in that final 100; in fact, Walter Cronkite was another finalist. The disappointment was very real for all the finalists when NASA said no one would go up into space. The chances of me actually going on the shuttle mission I'm sure were very slim because of the strong competition. But there was that glimmer of hope, that small chance that I perhaps could have been on the space shuttle, or maybe at least be selected as one of the backup astronaut journalists, and get to go through all the training. Unfortunately, it didn't happen. Now I must be content flying my own planes—never getting high enough to go into orbit.

Space Men

When I arrived to anchor at KHOU-TV, the CBS affiliate in Houston, I got a call from the person in charge of Houston's annual party honoring the foreign consulates who are stationed there. Houston has a very expansive international community and many foreign countries have representatives who work out of consulate offices. I was asked to emcee and introduce the various guests at this party, which included numerous high-ranking diplomats from around the world. It also included some dignitaries of our own, which I found to be as exciting as anyone at the party— NASA's astronauts.

Among those I met was the first American in space, Navy Commander Alan Shepard. I had followed the space program, and was a big fan of all the astronauts, so I was delighted to meet Alan, and we got along famously. He's a very engaging guy, very attentive to others around him. Now, remember, this is the only man in the world who has ever hit a golf ball on the moon. He smuggled up the head of a six-iron on the trip, affixed it to one of the moon tools, plunked down a couple of golf balls on the surface of the moon and whacked them into the lunar atmosphere. And in one-sixth the gravity of earth, of course, those golf balls just took off, probably about 450 to 500 yards. About a year after meeting Alan, I invited him to play in one of my charity golf tournaments—it wasn't the moon, but it was for a good cause! He was happy to help and drew a lot of attention.

Over the next couple of years in Houston, I also got to meet Alan Bean, the fourth man to set foot on the moon. He is now a very accomplished artist who paints moonscapes on exclusive commissions. Aside from being wonderfully talented, the man adds a very unique twist to his art work. After returning from the moon, NASA gave him the name tag and other odds and ends from his space suit. Alan discovered these items were covered with moon dust. He ground these items up, and sprinkles a bit on each of his original paintings. Of course, no one else in the world, no one else in the history of art, could sprinkle moon dust on a painting. So, I tip my hat to a really creative and nice guy, Alan Bean. He has also helped me out on a number of charity occasions and given of himself and his talent to help children with cancer and folks who are undergoing treatment at MD Anderson hospital.

I also got to meet Dan Brandenstein, who until recently, was the chief astronaut at NASA. He was the pilot on the first night launch of the space shuttle and also accomplished the first night landing. He, too, came out to a golf tournament of mine to raise money for the American Cancer Society in Houston. I had asked Dan if he could bring us a model of the space shuttle to auction off at the tournament. He told me NASA wouldn't allow that, but that he'd be glad to come himself. He couldn't give us anything from NASA, but he gave of himself and that helped make the tournament a success and it sure as heck made a big impression on me.

It has been a thrill to have these men of history, these aviators who have reached for the stars, help out and lend their names to charity events. When NASA picks their astronauts, they pick men and women who are amazingly qualified for their work in space. The best pilots tend to have their own special way of carrying themselves, and it comes from a well-disciplined life. Some are a little more flamboyant, some are more outspoken, but they're all individuals who certainly have the right stuff!

V

STAR
MOMENTS

13

Lights, Camera, Action!

ONE DAY LATE IN 1987, OUR NEWSROOM administrator at Channel 8, the late Sidney Benton, made sure that I saw a memo she had written earlier in the day. It seems she had gotten a call from the movie director Oliver Stone and he wanted me to audition for a part in his next movie. At first I thought it was a joke, somebody probably just pulling my leg, but Sydney assured me it wasn't.

So I called, but I knew there was no way News Director Marty Haag and Assistant News Director John Miller would approve of me being an actor in a film. And as flattered as I was, I had reservations about it myself: my job is as a newsman, not an actor in Hollywood. But when I talked to the folks with the production company, they said Oliver Stone really wanted to meet me, so I figured what the hell—it would be fun to meet the director and it would be something to tell my friends and family.

I went to visit him knowing in my heart that it would never work out, that I could never be in a movie. It sounded like a lot of fun and maybe even glamorous, but it didn't really bother me that it probably wasn't in my cards. After all, being "just" a TV newsman isn't so bad—I make a good living and my job has its perks! I was thinking about all of this as I pulled up to the Stoneleigh Hotel, which is where Oliver always sets up his movie crew when they do movies in Dallas. (Oliver loves Dallas, by the way—he says he loves the clear sky.)

I went into the meeting with Oliver Stone without any nervousness. After all, I had nothing to lose. I wasn't a starving actor and I didn't really need a part in this movie. I looked at the whole experience as a kind of lark. Most of the people who were walking into Oliver's room at the Stoneleigh were desperate for a part in his film. I had no career at stake in any of this.

Oliver had just won the Academy Award for best director for *Platoon*. So when I walked in and met him, I said, "Nice to meet you Oliver, but I was thinking. I saw *Platoon* the other night and you know, I think it needed more intensity." That really cracked him up and got everything off to a good start. He asked me how long it took me to come up with that line and I said as long as it took me to take the elevator up to his room. He also asked me if I had a resume, which of course I hadn't thought to bring along, and he just laughed at that, too.

From the start, Oliver and I had a very good relationship. I think it was because I really didn't need a job from him. He picked up on that and I think it took off a lot of the pressure. If I had been a starving artist type of guy or an out-of-work actor, I'd have been on bended knee in his office and our relationship would have had a very different balance to it. But I came in just kind of loose and without any preconceived notions.

```
FOR _____ Chip _____
DATE ____ 3/8 ___ TIME 1.50 AM PM
FROM ____ Carl Scalione ____
          or Ted Johnston
FIRM ____
PHONE 626-5656 Casting Dir
     AREA CODE      NUMBER      EXTENSION

TELEPHONED          | PLEASE CALL
RETURNED YOUR CALL  | WILL CALL AGAIN
CAME TO SEE YOU     | RUSH
WANTS TO SEE YOU    | SPECIAL ATTENTION
WAITING TO SEE YOU  | HOLDING LINE

MESSAGE Oliver Stone want
to audition you
Thurs: between
12:00 + 6:00 pm — what
time can you do it

SIGNED _____   TOPS FORM 4007
```

MESSAGE

As we talked, it became clear that Oliver thought I could handle the part he had in this movie, which was to be called *Talk Radio*. The movie is based on the real life and murder of Alan Berg, the controversial talk show host from Denver, Colorado. Oliver said the part called for me to just be myself—a regular news guy. The casting director came into Oliver's suite, and the three of us talked a little bit about the role in question.

The script called for me to play a half-time announcer at SMU's Moody Coliseum during an SMU basketball game and to introduce local radio talk show host Barry Champlain (the character based on Berg, played by actor Eric Bogosian), who is then booed by the spectators. Well, it was not a big deal for me to read aloud the three or four lines in the script. We played around with it a little bit, and then Oliver said they'd give me a call back. I left the hotel thinking, well, that was my little brush with Hollywood, and left it at that.

But two days later, I got another phone call from the casting director saying that Oliver wanted to see me again. I thought, oh my goodness, wait a second, maybe he really does want me in the movie! Maybe this isn't just a lark. I went to our news director, Marty Haag, to see if there would be a problem with me playing a newsman in a movie. I told him I'd basically be playing myself and that it might be some good publicity for Channel 8. Marty said sure, as long as I'd not be doing any kind of out-of-character thing, or some kind of weird acting job that reflect badly on me or WFAA, the station would have no problem. So suddenly here I was about to be in a movie.

A month or two later it was time for the cameras to roll. For my part I was told to wear what I would normally wear to work. On the appointed day I arrived at Moody Coliseum, where the scene was being shot, carrying a blue sport coat, white shirt, and red tie. When I got there, I wandered around amidst the hustle and bustle of the production—big trucks, a lot of people running around with lights and tape hanging off their shoulders—wondering where I should go to change. I walked up to a desk that looked official and asked for instructions. I figured they'd send me to the men's locker room or something.

But no, I was told I had my own trailer! That stopped me in my tracks. I tried to cover up my surprise and play it real cool. But you can be sure I was thinking to myself, "Oh man, a trailer!" So here I am holding my shirt, pants, and jacket and I wander back outside behind the auditorium. And lo and behold, there along one street are about eight trailers and as I walked along them, one of them had a star on it and the name "Chip Moody" emblazoned across it in Magic Marker. I thought that was overdoing it, but it was kind of funny. Here it was, my own trailer.

Once inside, I found the trailer had a bed, a makeup mirror, a shower, a bathtub and music was playing on the radio. Boy they really treat their movie people well! And here I was in the middle of it all. I was carrying a huge,

I got my own trailer while filming Talk Radio.

thick script of the movie with me and I felt like a real professional. My part, of course, was only about half a page. But I was taken in, I was caught up in this movie stuff and I probably wouldn't have cared if I was only saying one word.

I looked outside my trailer and saw there was a large crowd of people, mostly extras, waiting in line for their lunch. The line was snaking its way in front of my trailer, and I have to admit I played the role of movie star just a bit. I walked in and out of that trailer, looking at my script as if I was reading Shakespeare. Of course a couple of people in the line recognized me and I just kept up with this nonsense—going up and down the stairs of my trailer so all the extras who were in line for lunch could see me. I think about it now and have to laugh at myself because here I was pretending to read my script over, looking real intense, when basically I knew it was only a few words I would be saying!

About an hour after my acting debut in front of the trailer, somebody came over and told me it was time for my scene. I went into Moody Coliseum and there were about 2,000 extras on one side of the gymnasium. As I mentioned before, my role in *Talk Radio* was the announcer who comes up to a microphone during half-time and tells people what's going on in other basketball games and then introduces the star of the show, the talk radio host who is so controversial, who then gets booed and pelted with hot dogs and other stuff.

Well, I looked at my lines in the script, which actually read something like, "And now here's the man you love to hate, Barry Champlain..." Well, I went up to Oliver, who had his director's chair set up on the floor of the gymnasium, and I told him that if I were really announcing at a ball game, I would give some scores from around the conference and I would talk a little about football coming back to SMU and other local things to get the crowd excited and happy. Then when I introduced Champlain, the crowd would quickly turn on him and there would be a nice contrast on film. Oliver thought it sounded good and gave me the go-ahead.

I ad-libbed some lines about scores around the conference and then talked about how it was a great day for SMU and the fact that football was coming back and then I introduced the guy everyone loves to hate. Well, it worked great, even though we did about five takes. On the first take, about 400 hot dogs came flying down from the stands when I introduced the talk show host. That was too many, so Oliver told everyone to just boo for a while and maybe fifteen or twenty people could throw food out in our direction. In the end it worked, and I still get tickled when I watch the movie, thinking I'd actually come up with some of the ideas for the scene.

A year or two after the filming of *Talk Radio*, I was talking to my friend Kenny Bob Davis, who is a Hollywood entertainer, singer, and bit player in various movies. I explained to him how I gave Oliver the idea for the scene and I'll never forget him saying, "You told Oliver Stone how you thought the scene should go?" Well, yes, I did. But over the years, Oliver has always hired people who know their field of expertise, be it stockbrokers for *Wall Street* or soldiers who worked in *Platoon*. In my case, when I told him about the extra scores and all that stuff, he knew it would work. And I think it did.

About six months after shooting *Talk Radio*, I got a message at work that Oliver Stone was on the line and wanted to know if I would like to be in a motion picture with Tom Cruise. Oliver would be shooting the film in Dallas in the next couple of months. The movie was *Born on the Fourth of July*. Oliver said he needed an anchorman for the scene of a GOP national convention, and I said, "Piece of cake." I mean, that was the sort of thing we do all the time. I figured it would be a pretty easy acting gig. Like *Talk Radio*, this was not a movie in which my role would interfere with my real life as a newsman. I wasn't playing a country-western singer or a rodeo cowboy. I was just doing what I do every day.

My role was the anchorman in the skybox watching over the GOP nomination of Richard Nixon. Oliver filmed the Dallas Convention Center as if it were the Miami Convention Center for the convention of 1972. The movie uses old file tape of the national convention and blends it in with a scene where Tom Cruise comes out on the convention floor in a wheel chair to protest the treatment of Vietnam vets after the war. My job was to comment on the interruption on the floor as if I were live on the air. I did my scene in two takes, and Oliver was happy with it.

Although my part was very small, I am proud to be a part of the movie *Born on the Fourth of July*. It was up for best picture that year at the Academy Awards, and it deserved to be on the list. It is a very powerful movie that makes a bold statement about how poorly Vietnam vets were treated during and after the war.

I mentioned earlier that Oliver had asked for my resume at our first meeting. Well, when we met to discuss my role in *Born on the Fourth of July* I was prepared. I said, "By the way, Oliver. This time I brought my resume." I then proceeded to hand him a resume I had hastily typed up earlier in the day. Needless to say, Oliver got quite a laugh reading it. I think you will too!

RESUME OF CHIP MOODY

OCCUPATION: Anchorman, WFAA-TV, Dallas-Fort Worth, ABC affiliate
AGE: 43
FILM AND ACTING CREDITS: *Talk Radio*, directed by Oliver Stone.

Film critics across the county were quick to note Mr. Moody's film debut in the major motion picture *Talk Radio*, and their acclaim was unanimous: He's a natural!

Mr. Moody took what some might have considered a minor role (one scene), and transformed it into what became the pivotal moment in the movie. Showing an all-too-rare sense of timing and inflection, Mr. Moody successfully brought the crowd of Southern Methodist University football fans to a cheering crescendo in his ad-libbed remarks about college football.

Director Oliver Stone later confirmed that the spontaneous remarks came so naturally for Mr. Moody that it amplified and gave greater impact to the next scene by providing a sharp contrast to the public perception of the movie's lead character, Barry Champlain, played by actor Eric Bogosian.

Moody, smoothly portraying the half-time announcer, delicately shifted attention to Bogosian while still commanding the presence of the camera, even though he had moved to stage left. It was this subtle movement that gave the audience a sense that "something" was about to happen. It was Moody's ability to both dominate the screen, and at the same time deftly shift attention to Bogosian, that caught the eye of long-time Hollywood observers and critics.

Moody's effective use of hand gestures and his sincere, winning smile, gave him a believability that few actors possess, say critics. One critic called Moody "a natural." Another said "he was born for the camera."

Variety magazine has expressed an interest in scheduling an in-depth profile of this young man—who has the eyes of Paul Newman, the chiseled profile of Clint Eastwood, and the intensity of Robert DeNiro.

Contacted through his executive assistant in Hollywood, Mr. Stone confirmed that Moody is the leading candidate to play a network anchorman in Stone's upcoming *Born on the Fourth of July*, the true saga of a disabled Vietnam veteran to be played by actor Tom Cruise.

Stone said Moody's presence will not only lend credibility to the climactic scene at the 1972 GOP convention, but will also cement his position as a particularly strong presence in the motion picture industry.

With a laugh, Stone added that "it's not often a rookie can show me how a scene can be shot differently and more effectively than long-time screenwriters . . . but Moody did. I don't usually tolerate actors giving me their interpretations of a scene, but when that suggestion has true merit, and can be executed so precisely, you know you're working with someone special."

14

Star-Crossed: Celebrity Encounters

Power Lunch

BACK IN THE 1980S, NORTH TEXAS civic leader Lyda Hunt Hill approached me for lunch and some charity brainstorming. She is one of the heirs to the H.L. Hunt fortune. Her wealth means that she could comfortably "kick back" and have a good old time, but she doesn't relax: she works hard for others, the sick and less fortunate. Lyda embraces a number of charitable causes, among them MD Anderson in Houston. We were both members of the MD Anderson Board of Advisors, and she wanted us to come up with a new fundraising event that would be unique and enjoyable.

There were already a lot of charity golf tournaments going on at the time, my "Chip Moody/Benihana Celebrity Chefs for a Cure" dinners, and a number of charity balls in the evening I was involved in, so I told Lyda I was really about out of fresh ideas. But as we talked, we did come up with a new idea, what was to be "Conversations with Living Legends." This event would be a top-notch luncheon featuring a one-on-one interview with a well-known personality—a "living legend." Lyda turned to me to conduct the interview since I was the "news guy."

Obviously, our first order of business was to find a living legend for our first event. We called on Nolan Ryan, the Texas Rangers pitcher, who is headed for the Baseball Hall of Fame. Nolan and his family met with me and my family at a restaurant in Arlington to talk about this. I explained that what we were looking for was a light-hearted interview—it would not be what they call an "ambush interview" in the news media, with a lot of pointed and controversial questions. We were just going to enjoy ourselves with have a good lunch and a nice chat.

Nolan agreed to it, and we knew that, with him, we'd make a great first impression on the people attending the charity luncheon. Sure enough, a week later we held the first annual "A Conversation with a Living Legend Luncheon" and it was a great success. There were close to 1,000 people in attendance. After the main course, Nolan and I sat down in a facsimile of a dugout constructed on the stage and had a great chat. He was so relaxed that he almost slid off the bench. I asked him fun questions—after a day at the ballpark and throwing a two-hitter, did he still have to take out the trash? (Yep!) He tossed out some autographed baseballs after the interview, and he gave me his cap.

Lyda's idea was a hit. Our committee's hard work and a fun, relaxed interview spelled success, with MD Anderson as the beneficiary. We've done five interviews now—including ones with Nolan Ryan, Tom Landry, Walter Cronkite, Margaret Thatcher—and all of them have been just wonderful and enlightening.

One year we had Arnold Palmer as our living legend. The schedule called for a small reception during the morning at Dallas' Loews Anatole for some of the big contributors, where they could meet Arnie and have their picture taken with him. Then Arnie and I would sneak off to the main ballroom for our introduction before a crowd of more than a thousand.

Arnie and I made our entrance into the main ballroom riding a golf

Vikki, Tiffin, and I met Walter Cronkite in 1993.

cart—it was a cute idea and got a big hand. But, before we got to the stage, we had to kind of snake our way through back hallways and the kitchen. I was tickled because a number of the staff members in the kitchen recognized me and said hello. But they didn't recognize Arnold quite as quickly. I was flattered and smiled to myself, thinking how ironic it was that these people noticed me and not the legendary golfer walking next to me. As we waited for our cue to go on stage, I nudged Arnie and said, "Obviously that's not the golfing crowd in the kitchen." And he said, "No, but you obviously have your own following, your own army." It was kind of neat to feel like I was somewhat of a star in my own community—even though I was with a guy recognized around the world as one of the best-loved sports heroes ever.

During my chat with Arnie I think the biggest laugh came when I asked him what was his favorite snack. He looked at me for a second and said, "Cheese crackers and vodka." That really broke the ice, and the whole room cracked up.

As we wrapped up our talk, Arnie began to tell the audience that one reason why he donated his time for the luncheon was because one of his daughters was fighting breast cancer. The night before, at dinner, he told me of her fight, and it was good that he did, because there at the luncheon he choked up and started to cry a little while trying to explain it to the 1200 people there. I finished the story for him. Seeing him on the verge of tears because of his love for his daughter was a heart-rending moment for the audience and me.

It was a great interview; I found Arnie to be a very down-to-earth guy despite his fame, wealth, and notoriety. He was a very attentive listener and friendly and the event was a big hit.

In another "Conversation with a Living Legend" luncheon, we contacted Walter Cronkite's office and he agreed to be interviewed. I was in the hospital at the time and had to check out to go over to the Loews Anatole to meet Walter the evening before the luncheon. I checked out of the hospital, and went over to visit with Walter and talk about some of the areas I wanted to cover in our interview.

I had not met Walter before and wasn't sure what kind of a guy he was. I had heard he was very demanding as the managing editor and anchorman of the CBS Evening News and I wasn't sure what to expect. What I found was a very friendly, gracious, and talented man who was very down-to-earth. When I got to his room, he was getting ready for dinner with former Governor and Mrs. John B. Connally, who had been instrumental in getting Walter to accept this charity appearance.

Walter had a small bar set up on one side of the room, and asked me if I wanted a drink. Then he said he had been trying to get "60 Minutes" on, but couldn't figure out the television set. I fiddled around with it a bit, and got the set up and working, and that pretty much broke the ice. Walter told me just to hang out as he puttered around the room getting ready and we could talk about our discussion the next day.

Well, I sat on the side of the bed and, while we talked about his career and world events, he proceeded to undress, changing out of his casual clothes and into a suit while we chatted. Here I was, talking with Walter Cronkite—the world's most well-known and respected journalist—while he stood around in his socks and underwear. I went back to the hospital shaking my head and thinking I'd probably never see the likes of that again. And I haven't.

The luncheon the next day, of course, was a huge success. Our conversation ranged from his coverage of the Kennedy assassination and the Kennedy funeral to coverage of the first man on the moon. For several generations, Walter Cronkite has embodied the word "anchorman" and it was a real treat to be able to go over the high points of his career with him.

Spanky McFarland

While working at Channel 5 in the late 1970s, one of the items we did on the news one night was a reasonably quick story on Darla, one of the stars of the old kid's show "The Little Rascals." She had passed away, and I read a thirty-second story on her death, and we ran a still picture of her.

When I got back to the newsroom, I had a telephone call from someone who said, "Hi Chip, this is Spanky McFarland." He was, of course, another former Little Rascal—the leader of the gang. Spanky said he had just heard my announcement that Darla had died. She had been a close friend of his for many years and he was wondering if I knew any other details about her death that didn't make the air.

I was shocked and thrilled to get the call. I had grown up, like millions of kids, watching Our Gang and Little Rascal comedies, both at the theater and on television. I had no idea Spanky lived in the Dallas-Fort Worth area. He lived in north Fort Worth, and was a regular viewer.

For him to call me up, and call me by name as if we knew each other, and ask for details about Darla really floored me. I went back through the wire copy and found as many additional details as I could on her death and conveyed them to Spanky.

That started a long-term friendship between Spanky and me. We started running into each other at charity golf tournaments and other gatherings. I was so happy and privileged that Spanky and I could call each other friends.

In 1993, Spanky passed away suddenly. He had a heart attack as he was getting ready to go out to dinner. He died at home. As soon as I heard the news, I called his home and talked to his wife Doris to ask if there was anything I could do. I shared in her grief because Spanky was such a genuinely nice fellow with a good head on his shoulders.

A good friend and great guy, Spanky McFarland.

Well, Doris and Spanky's daughter Betsy called me back about an hour later and said there was something I could do for them—deliver the eulogy at Spanky's funeral. I considered this a high honor, to be able to speak for Spanky's many fans, friends, and family members at the service. Just to explain our friendship and my love for Spanky I'm going to include the text of my eulogy here, which I delivered at his service on July 3, 1993. I think it speaks for itself, and I want to share it with others in memory of Spanky.

❖ ❖ ❖ ❖ ❖

"What a guy. What a great guy . . . what a wonderful contribution he made to the lives of millions of people. What a deep, heartfelt loss this is for everyone of us here today and everyone who knew Spanky.

"The day Spanky died, I called Doris to offer my sympathy and support and while I was talking to her, something unusual happened. Tears came to my eyes and my voice started cracking. That's not supposed to happen to news guys . . . but it did.

"I had a great fondness for Spanky and I am deeply touched and honored that the family asked me to say a few words about our good buddy. As I went to bed Wednesday night, a number of memories and thoughts went through my head. I got to thinking about how many people saw Spanky and had their day brightened by watching and laughing during those early episodes of 'Our Gang' and 'The Little Rascals.'

"It occurred to me that some of the men who fought in the Civil War would still have been living when the series started, so Spanky touched generations dating back to the 1800s. His personality and talent spanned across individuals who were born more than 140 years apart, and that was just during his lifetime. Many more people will enjoy the reruns for generations to come.

"I first got to know Spanky about twenty years ago. I was doing a newscast, and relating the death of Darla, one of the 'Our Gang' stars. After the newscast, the phone rang in the newsroom and when I answered, the voice on the line said, 'Chip, this is Spanky McFarland, and I just saw your story on Darla dying, and I was wondering if you had any more details . . .'

"I had really only been in Dallas-Fort Worth for a short time, and didn't realize the McFarlands lived here. And here was Spanky himself watching me, and asking me for information. I was taken aback . . . after all, I had grown up watching Spanky and his pals on TV.

"From that telephone conversation we began a rich and caring friendship. His stardom in Hollywood did not make him a wealthy man by any means. I seem to remember him telling me that he was signed as a contract player for a flat fee of something like $75 a week. It didn't take long to shoot those twenty or thirty episodes. They could shoot one or two per week. It doesn't take a degree in math to figure out that didn't amount to much money. No bonus, no residuals.

"Later in life, there were moments of reflection for Spanky that would make him bitter. And rightfully so. He wasn't bitter so much for himself but for the way his success and stardom could have provided a little measure of security for his family . . . and peace of mind for himself.

"But despite all of this, Spanky never lost the warmth, the personality, the genuine friendliness that was his hallmark. This week, I was quoted in one of the papers as saying Spanky had a heart 'as big as Texas.' I think that all I was doing was expressing something that everyone here today already knows.

"Spanky didn't tolerate people with inflated egos. He had a knack for reading people pretty quickly. He had precious little time to waste with people who couldn't see past the mirror. But if you were a genuine person, he would count you as a friend, no matter what your station in life or your status in politics, show business or the business world.

"Whenever he and I would get together at a charity event or some gathering, I took tremendous pride in introducing him to my friends. It filled me with pride to be able to say 'so and so, I'd like you to meet my friend Spanky McFarland . . . yep, the guy from Little Rascals, and Spanky and Our Gang . . . he's one of my buddies.'

"A great test of Spanky's strength and faith came about six years ago, when his three-year-old granddaughter Lanay was diagnosed with leukemia. As we all know, cancer is an awfully tough opponent, and radiation, chemotherapy, and surgery are not taken lightly, especially for children. In my case, I told one of my nurses that it seems like they had to damn near kill me to get me better. The nurse said, 'That's right, you've got to be strong and lucky to survive.'

"The long-standing concern and love Spanky had for children, especially those facing serious, life-threatening or terminal illness, suddenly hit very close to home. The apple of his eye was facing a very real and very scary fight for life. He intensified his charity work and he crammed his schedule with as many celebrity appearances as he could . . . .golf tournaments, chili cookoffs, celebrity chef for a night. You name it, he did it. And with a smile. Lanay, we are happy to say, is now in remission and doing fine. She is with us today and I'd like her to stand up.

"I hope Spanky realized that his contributions to raise research funds helped not only Lanay survive, but thousands of other youngsters he would never know. Just for that alone, the good Lord has reserved a spot for Spanky in heaven.

"Spanky was one of the very first 'one-name' stars, leading the way for other stars known simply by their first name . . . like Bing, or Lucy or Elvis. I looked at the letters in Spanky's name and here is what they said to me. 'S' is for short, special, and sincere. 'P' is for personable and polite, almost to a fault. 'A' is for all-time, as in all-time great, all-time star, all-time good guy. 'N' is for nice. 'K' is for kind hearted. With a capital `K'. 'Y' is for yes . . . as in 'yes, I would be glad to help with your charity event,' 'yes I'd be glad to give you an autograph.'

"And yes, Spanky we love you and yes, we will miss you a lot.

"As I went to sleep Wednesday night, I imagined a scene being played out in heaven. As Spanky makes his way to the pearly gates, the Lord breaks into a big smile, and says: 'Welcome to heaven, you have done so many good things in your life on earth, we are so happy to have you with us. I know you will miss some of your friends back on earth, but Alfalfa, Darla, and Buckwheat have been up here in heaven for some time and they've all been eagerly awaiting your arrival. In fact, they told me to tell you they have a 'Little Rascals' talent show scheduled for this evening, and you are the emcee and magician.'

"Then the Lord paused and said, 'I've been wanting to ask you a question. How in the world did Alfalfa make his hair stand up like it did with that pointy end?' Spanky answers: 'Simple, we put a pipe cleaner in his head and wound his hair around it!'

"Then the Lord says: 'By the way, is there any way I could come visit you and the other little rascals in your clubhouse?' Spanky answers, 'Of course we'd love to have you, but remember the rules, no girls and you have to know the password. This week it's abracadabra.' And then Spanky adds, with a wink: 'In your case, though, if you forget the password, don't worry. Just show up with this special pin with my picture on it and that will get you into the clubhouse anytime.'

"One of the reasons I feel so honored to be able to share these personal thoughts and feelings with you today is that Spanky was much more than a star or celebrity. And he was much more than a nice guy.

"Spanky was, and is, a part of 'Americana,' part of what defines us as a nation. Spanky was as much a part of this country and its heritage as baseball and hot dogs, the Fourth of July, the Model T Ford, Coca-Cola, and Rock-n-Roll. I think Spanky has been, and is, part of the fabric of the American flag. Good-bye Spanky. And God Bless You."

Buckwheat

Shortly before Spanky passed away, ABC's "20/20" news program had a feature about old movie and television stars and where they were now living and working. The teaser for the show came on just before the program started, and it included video of a grocery store worker out west, I think it was in Arizona. It claimed that the worker was Buckwheat from "The Little Rascals" series of the 1930s and '40s. As "20/20" promoted the show, they showed Buckwheat sacking groceries and signing autographs at a supermarket.

I was watching the teaser as I prepared for the 10 p.m. newscast. Just as it ended, my telephone rang and it was Spanky, saying that ABC was making a huge error. Spanky said, "I knew Buckwheat, but he's dead. I went to his funeral in California ten years ago! That is not Buckwheat." He was adamant and he asked if there was anything I could do to help set the record straight. I said I'd give it a whirl and I called the ABC newsroom in New York.

I explained that I had it through an unimpeachable source that the story "20/20" was about to air was a sham, that the producers should put a disclaimer on the segment and not air it as fact. The person I talked with said the segment was already set to run and there was no way they could add anything to it or take it off the air. I told them the story would be in error and would probably come back to haunt ABC.

When I got off the telephone, I went to our 10 p.m. news producer, Holly Shannon, and told her of the problem. I told her we needed to trust Spanky and set the record straight for those viewers who would be watching "20/20" and counting on Channel 8 for the correct story. As his long-time friend, it was incumbent on me to try to do the right thing.

Shannon agreed that we should air Spanky's story. I scribbled some notes and we ran our story in the middle of the newscast. I explained to viewers that if they had seen the "20/20" program and the man purporting to be Buckwheat from "The Little Rascals," they should think twice before believing it. I reported that Spanky McFarland, who lived in Fort Worth, had tipped us off that actor Bill Thomas, who played Buckwheat, had died ten years earlier. The man sacking groceries and signing autographs on "20/20" was a fake.

A week later, the error did come back to haunt ABC. Hugh Downs and Barbara Walters had to apologize on air, saying that the field producer on the story had been duped and that the real Buckwheat had died a decade earlier. It's not often ABC makes a mistake, but reporters and producers are not infallible. I've made a few mistakes myself, but I don't think I've ever made a goof that big! I'm just sorry that when I called ABC and said we had Spanky McFarland's word on the story— that he was an unimpeachable source—the folks there didn't get the message . . .

Clint Eastwood

In 1971, Clint Eastwood had a movie out called *Play Misty For Me*, which was about a disc jockey who was harassed by a psychotic fan. As part of the pre-release publicity, the studio public relations folks sent out flyers to area anchors and movie critics to see if they'd like to see a sneak preview. I'd always been a Clint Eastwood fan and enjoyed his westerns, so I accepted the offer.

Unfortunately, however, the screening was on an evening I was doing the news, so I called the theater and asked if I could see the movie some time the next day. The manager invited Vikki and me to come to a private screening the next morning. There was no one else in the theater, so we were middle row, center. We had our popcorn and Cokes and settled in to watch the movie. We'd never had a private screening in a big theater in downtown Dallas, and I thought the whole experience was pretty great.

As the movie opened, for the first minute and a half I was in shock: One of the first images was a close-up of a dashboard and I recognized it

I learned about modesty and real class when I met Clint Eastwood in 1971.

immediately, because it was the dashboard of my car. . . an unusual car . . . a 1957 XK 150 Jaguar. I saw the dashboard first, and stood up—this was all during the credits still—and said, "Wait a minute! That's my dashboard." I guess it was a good thing no one was in the theater. Then the camera panned to a wideshot and I saw the car was the very same color as mine—a dark midnight blue, and a convertible, too. I was so excited, thinking here's Clint Eastwood driving a car just like mine. As I said, I was a big fan.

In any event, I enjoyed the movie and found out Clint would be in town that week to meet with movie critics and promote *Play Misty for Me*. Our Channel 5 movie critic Bobbie Wygant set up an appointment at the Fairmont Hotel, and I asked her if I could tag along and meet Clint. So Vikki and I went and we beat him to his suite and spent a few minutes waiting for him to arrive.

Then there was a knock on the door. I opened it up, and there was Clint Eastwood carrying two suitcases. He was very casually dressed in slacks, an open shirt, and jogging shoes. He's a tall fellow—about six-foot-four—as big in life as he looks on screen. I was startled because there was no entourage, no public relations people. He was just there all by himself—not even a bellman.

He came in, Bobbie did the interview, and she and the cameraman left. Well, I got to talking to Clint and told him I anchored the news at Channel 5, was a big fan, and had wanted to come by and meet him in person. Well, the thing that still startles me to this day is how casually he said that he didn't have any lunch plans and asked if Vikki and I would like to join him for the next hour or two. He'd have some food sent up

The barn at my farm in Unityville, South Dakota.

Mom and Dad with Star at Unityville.

Working on the farm.

The Moody Coat of Arms,
"Through Various Crises."

"R and R" at home in Arlington.

Ready for take-off in an Australian World War I "Tiger Moth," Oakgrove Airport, Fort Worth, Texas, in 1978.

Just after flying the World War II B-17 Bomber "Flying Fortress."

Aviation legend Chuck Yeager at a fund-raiser for Frontiers of Flight Aviation Museum at Dallas's Love Field.

After flying the F-16 Fighting Falcon.

Me and Dad in the Bahamas in 1991.

*Kelly (left) and Bruce (right) came along
for the Bahamas vacation.*

*The one that didn't get away—on our
Bahamas trip.*

The Elvis impersonator.

The pool hustler.

Munching on some Texas ribs.

The Marlboro Man.

Forced to wear a funny hat while touring the famous Mary of Puddin Hill, 1992.

With some very special friends at The Big Brothers and Big Sisters Golf Tournament in Arlington, 1992.

American Airlines CEO Bob Crandall helps with the cooking at the "Chip Moody Benihana Celebrity Chefs for a Cure" at Benihana Restaurant.

Instructing the Benihana chefs in the fine art of Japanese cooking (ha ha!).

Other Chip Moody Benihana Celebrity Chefs for a Cure:
Jimmy Dean and Santa Claus, 1990.

Cooking with Channel 8 coanchor Gloria Campos at the
Chip Moody Benihana celebrity chef dinner, 1991.

Visiting the home of Tom Landry.

*With Roger Staubach at a
charity fund-raiser.*

Introducing Cowboys quarterback Troy Aikman at a Fort Worth fund-raiser.

Cowboys owner Jerry Jones.

Vikki and me with golf legend Arnold Palmer.

*With Mancil "King of Aces" Davis, world record holder for the most holes in one.
I just beat his shot!*

Talking with a living legend, Nolan Ryan.

With actress and supermodel Christie
Brinkley at the Celebrity Cutting Horse
Competition at Will Rogers Coliseum,
1990.

Academy-Award-winning actress and dear friend Greer Garson
Fogelson welcomes me and my family to celebrate her birthday.

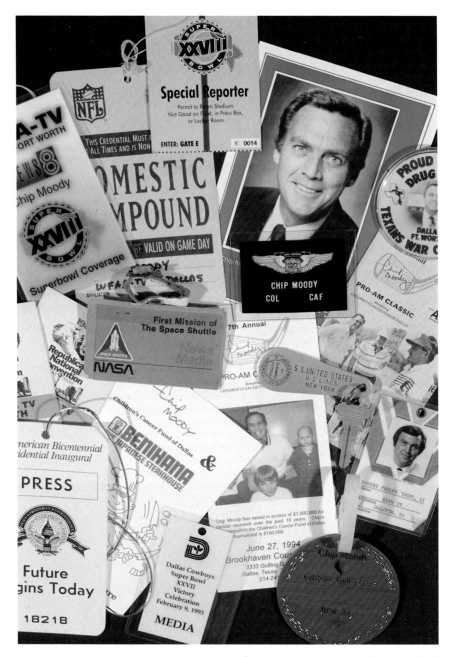

(Allan Beutler)

and we could sit around and talk. Needless to say, I was stunned and said no problem.

The hotel brought up some hors d'oeuvres, drinks, and pastries—I was still completely floored that Clint would take this time to visit with us. I had brought along pictures of my Jaguar to show him so we'd have that connection. We talked about the car, and he said he used to own one and thought it had a lot of character. He had since purchased a Maserati, but he said when he was younger he'd liked the XK 150. And when *Play Misty for Me* came around, he thought this particular character, a disc jockey, would look good driving around in a Jag.

Clint told me he was just finishing up shooting on another movie and to stay tuned. That turned out to be *Dirty Harry*, which of course was the start of his tremendously popular role as the maverick San Francisco cop Callahan, who later came out with the famous "Go ahead…make my day" line, which is now a part of our cultural lexicon.

Instead of me asking him a million questions and trying to be friendly, he was very interested in my job as a newsman. We talked about some of the stories I'd covered. He couldn't have been friendlier. I was left with an unusually high regard for him, a star of his stature who could be so friendly and down to earth. I learned a lesson from him: having a huge ego is of no benefit to anyone. And no matter who you are or what you do, if you are a friendly guy it sure makes one heck of a good impression. I have always tried to be as friendly to people who I meet, people young and old, who have watched me on TV and may have held me in some awe or put me on a small pedestal. I learned that lesson from Clint Eastwood. He is genuinely a nice guy with no preconceptions, and I would like to think I am too. I always get a chuckle when I see minor stars with a huge ego and the big limo. In my heart, I know the really big guys can be really nice guys, too.

The Lone Ranger

I can't imagine anyone between the ages of ten and eighty-five who isn't familiar with two of the most popular characters in American folklore—those heroes of the Old West, the Lone Ranger and his faithful companion Tonto. The early radio series proved to be such a hit that it evolved into a TV series that ran for many years, with a couple of motion pictures thrown in along the way.

I never did meet actor Jay Silverheels, who played Tonto and who popularized the phrase "kemo-sabe." Silverheels died perhaps a decade ago. But I did get to meet Clayton Moore, who had captured the imagination and hearts of millions of young Americans. It was a special moment for me because of the influence the Lone Ranger had on my life.

When I was in the third grade, one of the hottest items you could have was a Lone Ranger lunch box, which I had. The Lone Ranger was one among many stars in sports, movies, television, and radio during those postwar years who had a widespread and profoundly positive affect on the boys and girls—baby boomers. It's hard to forget Buffalo Bob, Ralph Cramden, Willie Mays, Mickey Mantle, Desi and Lucy, the Nelson family, Clarabell the Clown, Lassie, Rin-Tin-Tin, Captain Kangaroo, and The Mickey Mouse Club.

It's also hard to forget the pop singers who appeared on "American Bandstand"—Dinah Shore singing "see the USA in your Chevrolet," or Perry Como crooning some ballad, while young rock and rollers like Elvis, Jerry Lee Lewis, Buddy Holly, Sam Cooke, and so many others where shaking up the American culture of the late 1950s. Looking back on that time, it seemed so wholesome, so blemish-free, so much the way America should be.

We as young Americans had many heroes, and right up at the top was the Lone Ranger. For my age group, Gary Cooper, Clark Gable, Spencer Tracy, and Marilyn Monroe seemed to be just a bit distant, just out of reach. But I and many other American children could relate to the masked man. When the "William Tell Overture" signaled the beginning of the latest episode of "The Lone Ranger," we sat transfixed in front of those funny-looking contraptions that were early model TV sets.

In the late 1970s, I had volunteered to be a judge in one of the local chili-cooking contests. A quick aside: my longtime friend, former all-pro Dallas Cowboys center John Fitzgerald, and I always seemed to end up at these chili cookoffs because we both love chili and knew we could eat as much as we wanted! This particular cookoff took place just south of Dallas and we were judging the competition.

At one point, I went looking for a bathroom. When I found one, I noticed a fellow sitting down in front of a mirror, putting on a bit of makeup. It took only a second and then it hit me like a lightning bolt—the man sitting there was none other than The Lone Ranger . . . and he didn't have his mask on!

I may be wrong, but I think just about every member of my generation wondered what the Lone Ranger really looked like without his trademark mask or a beard covering his face as he portrayed one of the goofy prospectors or oddball transients who happened to wander into town about the time trouble was breaking out. So you can imagine my delight when I realized that, by gosh and by golly, there he was, Clayton Moore, the Lone Ranger, sitting next to me without his mask! Thankfully, I didn't start mumbling or acting star-struck (even though I was). I introduced myself, and Clayton told me he had been brought in as a surprise guest for the chili cookoff. He could not have been more gracious and polite.

Shortly after our meeting, Clayton Moore was forced to trade in his mask for sunglasses because of copyright infringements, so I feel lucky I was able to meet The Lone Ranger while the mystique of the mask still surrounded him! And I feel lucky that I was one of the young people influenced by the Lone Ranger. Clayton Moore won't go down in history as one of our great actors, but he was a strong, steady, positive influence on at least two generations of Americans. He inspired so many of us to be "good guys" rather than "bad guys." We don't seem to have as many such heroes for young people today, and that is sad.

That Great Pop Artist Harold Smith

In 1978 I was at Channel 5. One night I had a speaking engagement in Dallas, and because the studios are in Fort Worth, I had to head back there to do the news. It was about 8:30 or so, and the turnpike was operating at the time. When I came up to the toll plaza at the west end of the turnpike near the Oakland exit, there was a tremendous backup of cars waiting to go through the booths. I rolled down the window and I asked the passengers of the car next to me if they knew what was happening (I thought perhaps there had been a big accident just beyond the toll booths). They told me there was a fellow performing at the Tarrant County Convention Center, and they were all going down to see him. I said, oh . . . a concert . . . that explains it.

So I walked into the newsroom and told the folks there about the bumper-to-bumper traffic and said it seemed everyone was heading down to a concert by some guy named Harold Smith, who must be pretty popular and a pretty good artist since he was attracting so much attention. Right there I showed my age. Everyone in the newsroom, most of them at least five years younger than me, all started laughing. "No, Chip, it's not Harold Smith. It's Aerosmith." Obviously, I was a little out of touch with the hot bands of the time . . .

Mary Kay

I was attending the marriage of Clarice Tinsley, my co-anchor at the time, and her husband-to-be Steve. They had the reception at the

Mansion on Turtle Creek, and Mary Kay Ash, the Dallas doyenne of cosmetics and a friend of Clarice's, was there.

I was having a discussion with Mary Kay, and she was wearing a blouse tucked into a pleated skirt. As we were talking, her skirt fell off. It literally fell off. There was only one button in the back holding it together. Well, the button popped off, and her skirt fell down around her ankles. She and I never really even missed a beat—well, she didn't miss a beat. She kept talking and slowly bent down lower and lower, and I went down lower and lower, sort of like a limbo dance. She managed to get down low enough, pick up her skirt, stand back up, and hold her skirt around herself. I know it caught her by surprise. She had been wearing a slip, but there were a few people, despite Mary Kay's incredible grace under pressure, who began giggling and spilling champagne. But I must say, her handling of the situation was amazing—her aplomb, her suaveness, her total control of the situation was outstanding. She didn't blink an eye, she didn't miss a beat, and she didn't miss a word in her sentence.

It was one of those moments that has gone unreported until now. I'm happy to say both Clarice and Mary Kay Ash are both doing very well. (Although Mary Kay probably isn't wearing those one-button skirts these days.)

VI

CLOSING MOMENTS

15

When the Bleeding Wouldn't Stop

As MOST OF YOU MAY KNOW, AS OF THIS morning in June of 1995. . . I recently had an extremely close call.

In late April, I came as close as a guy can come to "signing off the air" permanently. I almost died. In fact, at one point in this medical emergency, I actually did stop breathing for a time, until they resuscitated me at Baylor Hospital with a respirator. This is the story of those days I spent on the edge of death.

❖ ❖ ❖ ❖ ❖

After I had finished brushing my teeth that Tuesday morning, April 25, I noticed a vaguely familiar, somewhat metallic-type taste in my throat. This had happened two years before while I was on vacation in Germany—apparently a bleeding ulcer. I stuck my finger down my throat to confirm what I had already pretty much determined: that I was bleeding internally. The natural gag reflex brought up a small amount of black fluid. This was blood, but since it was black and not red, it indicated that I was not actively bleeding. So I was somewhat relieved, although naturally concerned that my bleeding ulcer or ulcers had returned. I went on into work and had a routine day doing the 5 and 10 p.m. newscasts.

The next day, Wednesday, April 26, was almost an exact repeat; I again used the gag reflex to expel another quantity of black blood. But at work that evening, I passed a fair amount of black blood in the bathroom and noticed I was feeling a bit weak. But I hadn't had much of an appetite that day and figured that losing a pint of blood and not having much on my stomach combined to cause the fatigue.

It was what happened the next day, Thursday, that got my attention.

Again, the metallic taste and again, I stuck my finger down my throat, but this time I threw up a quart or more of blood, and it was red—bright red—and there were several large clots that resembled calves' livers.

I was lightheaded, and as I rinsed out the bathroom sink to get rid of the blood I thought I probably shouldn't drive myself to work. So I called Vikki and asked her if she could drive me to the station for the 5 p.m. newscast. I figured I could go over to Baylor Hospital to get checked out later. After all, the important May ratings were about to get underway, and we would want our full news staff on hand with everybody in their regular slots whether it be behind the camera, out in the field reporting, at the producers' desks, or behind the anchor desk.

I know it sounds kind of stupid to be worrying about a newscast when you're throwing up blood, but that was primarily because I *had* lost so much blood; I wasn't thinking very clearly. Fortunately, Vikki saw the remnants of the mess I had made in the sink and said I was nuts and that we weren't going to the TV station but right to the hospital emergency room.

Vikki alerted the hospital and my primary gastrointestinal physician, Dr. Bill Santangelo, and called John Miller to advise him of the situation. John was there at the hospital when we arrived, and at this point, I start forgetting what happened.

Thus began the most critical days of my life. Vikki, John, and my parents stayed at the hospital by my side almost around the clock for the next several days. I later learned from them and the doctors what happened over the next week and a half, none of which I clearly remember.

The last thing I do remember is that the emergency room personnel were having a real hard time getting a IV needle into a good vein in either arm. The chemotherapy from years earlier and heavy-duty drugs to clear up serious body-wide infections, help various abdominal and back pains, and a couple of kidney stones, all combined to render most of my veins quite scarred and in some cases clotted off or collapsed. When you put that together with a serious loss of blood quantity, the veins get very small indeed. With time being so critical, the IV specialist told me he had no other choice but to go into a seldom-used area— directly into my bicep muscle. He told me it was going to hurt and it did. Big time. I remember my back arching up off the emergency room table, but it gave the doctors what they needed most, an entry for starting a blood transfusion and a variety of drugs to knock me out. It also allowed them to start a battery of tests and start inserting tubes and such to keep me alive. After that, I remember nothing at all.

In the way of some background now . . . In 1991 I underwent major abdominal surgery when I had an intestinal blockage that prevented me from digesting any food. During that operation, Dr. Zack Lieberman and Dr. Butch Derrick at Baylor University Medical Center fashioned a new opening out of my stomach and routed it down perhaps a foot below my stomach to permit somewhat normal digestion. A new unblocked passageway was constructed so I could at the very minimum have a liquid diet.

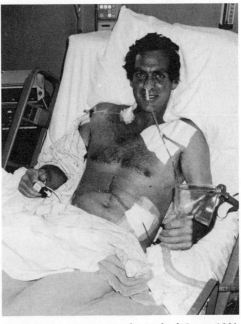

Keeping my spirits up at Baylor Medical Center, 1991.

During that operation, Dr. Lieberman discovered that I had been born with a divided pancreas, a birth defect affecting perhaps four or five percent of the population. What this meant was that in my case the organ that breaks down fats, alcohol, and greasy foods had been operating at only fifty percent for the first forty-four years of my life. Also, the chemotherapy used to treat my cancer did a tremendous amount of damage to my stomach. Both he and Dr. Santangelo told me that, among other things, I should never have another alcoholic drink or it would most certainly result in additional and quite serious medical problems. But I somehow thought deep in my heart they were exaggerating, that somehow I knew more, and I could not accept this message one hundred percent. In fact, a biopsy of my liver showed it to be completely normal and healthy. So I didn't abstain. Now, of course, I know better, because almost without a doubt, this latest problem was exacerbated by alcohol intake and undue demands on my pancreas. When you hear "doctor's orders," I would highly recommend you pay close attention to the men and women who work for so many hours a day to save lives. Sure, I'm going to miss a glass of wine or two with dinner out on the town or a margarita by the pool during the hot Texas summer, but that will be a small price to pay for continued life.

Anyway, now back to the hospital.

To find out more clearly what happened during these days and nights I don't remember, I listened to what Vikki and my parents had to say and "interviewed" John Miller this month to get an idea of what happened and when.

Through them, I can relate those critical hours and days.

As Vikki drove me to the hospital that Thursday mid-afternoon, I continued to bleed internally and slipped in and out of consciousness. After John had gotten the original call, he sensed that this was serious, knowing I would have to be quite ill to miss the first day of the important May ratings period. He beat us to the emergency room. He said when he first saw me wheeled into the hospital, his first thought was that I had lost virtually all my blood. I was literally as white as a sheet of writing paper. And although I was talking, my appearance was what doctors call "moribund." John said that was an understatement. (That was the word used by doctors to describe President John F. Kennedy when he arrived at Parkland Hospital on November 22, 1963.)

John said I was experiencing quite a bit of back pain while lying on the stainless steel emergency room table waiting for someone to start an IV and begin pain medication and a blood transfusion. He was there when the IV specialist poked his needle into my bicep. He saw me arch up in pain and said he was afraid I was going to fall off the table onto the floor. At this point, John decided to leave the emergency room. He wasn't very comfortable watching all this, and there wasn't anything he could really do anyway except perhaps throw up.

By 8 o'clock that evening, the doctors said my condition was stable, so John went home. Vikki and my parents stayed late into the night, keeping a vigil outside the intensive care unit.

By Friday evening, I had been given eight pints of blood and was conscious and talking. I knew I had bled a lot and had gotten a major transfusion. I was talking to John that night, asking about what was going on at the TV station. He said I was quite coherent and sensible, even though the doctors said I would never remember any of it.

On Saturday, however, my condition took a turn for the worse. At 4:30 p.m., Dr. Santangelo called the TV station, and our assignments desk tracked down John for a conference call. Dr. Santangelo told him that I had started bleeding again and had suffered a seizure or a stroke at midafternoon. They were having a lot of trouble controlling the bleeding. He said that he had called my family, and that I was being prepared for surgery that night. It appeared to the doctors that the only option they had was to remove my stomach and then start a race against the clock to tie off all the veins that had ruptured and reconnect some major blood vessels from below my stomach to some above it. He said it was doubtful that I would make it through the night. John and his wife immediately drove to the hospital.

That evening the hospital was assembling a surgical team for the expected operation. Shortly before 8 o'clock, I was wheeled out of ICU en route to have an arteriogram to show doctors which blood vessels were leaking and which ones might be reattached to keep me alive.

John said he saw me as I was put on a gurney and began the trip from the fourth floor down to a room on the first floor for the arteriogram and thought, "Well, this is the last time I'll see Chip alive." Our friendship of twenty-four years was coming to a sad and premature conclusion.

John called the station manager, Cathy Creany, plus my broadcast partners, Tracy Rowlett, Troy Dungan, Gloria Campos, and editor Ed Danko (who originally encouraged me to write this book and who became my literary advisor). John had the task of telling them just how bleak things looked and that Tracy and Ed should plan on meeting him at the station Sunday morning to start working on my obituary.

About 10:15 that Saturday night, Dr. Santangelo came out and advised my family and John that doctors could not find two veins good enough to even attempt the operation. For the time being, the surgery would be put off, and extra drugs were injected to help the blood coagulate and perhaps clot off the leak or leaks—about the only other thing anyone could do was cross their fingers and pray. Vikki and the kids stayed overnight at the hospital, hoping for the best but getting prepared for the worst.

Sunday morning John, Tracy, and Ed met at the station and began gathering biographical info, videotape, and old pictures to put into my TV obituary. John and Ed worked on the videotapes and pictures; Tracy started doing the writing. The local newspapers and other TV stations were notified, and everyone worked to get something together for the 10 p.m. news and the morning papers in case I didn't pull through.

Tracy's first version ran a whopping twelve minutes, but John and Ed said they didn't have enough video to cover what he had written, so it was trimmed back to eight minutes. Even in cases of personal closeness to a story some rules of broadcasting have to be followed!

But by eight o'clock that evening I was holding my own. And if I started to slip, the doctors would operate to make every attempt to save my life. Any such operation would last an expected eight to twelve hours. Even in a worst-case scenario, I would live past the ten o'clock news. So the obit was put on hold.

Monday morning brought the presence of neurologist Dr. J. Ted Phillips. John said Dr. Phillips told him that he had been watching me on TV for twenty years and it was so odd and uncomfortable to be standing over me in this situation. There was concern that I had suffered some brain damage because of the loss of blood, stroke, or seizure. I will have to meet Dr. Phillips soon and thank him for his expertise.

On Monday there was a surge of optimism when one of the experts said he had spotted something on the arteriogram that indicated a successful operation might be possible. A procedure was being contemplated that would involve inserting a tube into an artery in my neck, heading south to the critical area, and punching through to the lower abdominal area to reduce a difference in blood pressure which had the doctors worried. That pressure differential might have been contributing to my bleeding. Oddly enough, I had been briefed on the procedure, and for a time was alert enough to explain it to Vikki and John. John said he was really impressed with my medical knowledge. I would later explain that when you spend as much time in the hospital as I had over the years, you start talking like a doctor and get a pretty good pre-med education.

Unfortunately, the possible good vein spotted on the arteriogram turned out to be seventy-five percent blocked and not very good after all. And when they punched through to the lower abdomen, the pressure was found to be roughly equal. John said a depression set in among my friends and family. This had seemed to be my last chance, and it was gone.

On Tuesday my condition slipped badly. This was perhaps the lowest point for my family and friends. I stopped breathing, and fluid started building up in my lungs. They put me on a ventilator/respirator, and there was concern I was on the verge of getting a fatal case of pneumonia. This tube down my throat was uncomfortable and made me unable to talk. I started trying to pull it out along with various other tubes and IV lines. They gave me what is called a "paralytic" that allowed me to stay conscious but not be able to move any muscles very much. According to everyone staying with me, I was quite unhappy with all this.

The obit at the TV station was finished and ready for airing if needed. All this is terribly scary to reflect on now. Of course at the time, I was completely unaware of it or how close I really was to dying.

But I guess the good Lord had decided it just wasn't time for me to go.

On Wednesday I opened my eyes, and since I couldn't speak out loud, I mouthed a simple question to Vikki. Those silent words, "What happened?"

Vikki told John that she could tell by the look in "those big blue eyes" that I had made an unexplained, but miraculous, comeback.

It was miraculous all right—after losing sixteen pints of blood and being on death's doorstep for five days, the bleeding just stopped. The blood coagulants and my body teamed up for success. All I know is that something happened, and I'm still alive. My doctors said they had seen younger and stronger patients without my attendant ailments fail to survive similar episodes of uncontrolled bleeding, that nine out of ten such cases end in death. I am a very, very lucky guy. And I have to think that the thousands of prayers, get-well cards, and letters all combined to tip the scales in my favor.

Vikki and Tracy both told me about studies in which prayer was actually shown to make a difference. They said in one study, the names of patients were given to church and prayer groups while the names of another group of patients with similar ailments were not given to prayer groups. There was a substantially better recovery rate for those patients on the prayer lists, even though those doing the praying didn't know the individuals. I will never get the chance to thank so many of you in person, but I am convinced that the prayers from thousands of friends and viewers kept me alive. And I take this opportunity now to say, "Thank you from the bottom of my heart."

In a talk with John, Dr. Phillips said his tests showed I was better "one thousand percent neurologically."

On Thursday, the breathing tube came out, and I was moved out of intensive care into a regular hospital room and slowly began to make a conscious return to the world. My memory starts clicking in around Saturday, and I can remember a few things from that weekend. It had been ten days since I had first arrived at the hospital—the most critical days of my life.

A few days after I was out of ICU, I had the incredible experience of seeing my own obituary, the one that Tracy, John, and Ed put together. Words cannot describe what that was like. I can only tell you that my whole life flashed before my eyes right there on the TV set in my hospital room at Baylor. It was a frightening, yet somber moment. After viewing it, I immediately talked with Tracy, John, and Ed, apologizing to all of them for the difficult situation I had put them in. I know how extremely hard it must have been for them to work on their friend's obit. I also know how difficult it was on my family—at the same time my friends were working on my obit, my family was put in the terribly distressing position of trying to figure out funeral arrangements. Thankfully I pulled through.

In the post-crisis period, about a month later, a long search with a tiny TV camera (an endoscope) turned up an ulcer hiding in a fold of my stomach lining. It was cauterized, hopefully repairing the weakest part of the system. In time, with proper diet and medication, my digestive tract should become stronger and more immune to bleeding. That's the plan—the hope.

As I mention earlier in this book, I sometimes think of myself as a cat with nine lives, and I have wondered at times how many of those lives I have used up. I now know that I have probably used up eight of them. I need to be extra careful with the ninth one, and you can bet the farm I will be.

I would like to make a promise to my family and to all of you, my friends and supporters, that I will take much better care of myself in the future and do everything I can to stay healthy and out of the hospital. I'm a very lucky guy to say the least. I've got a lot going for me and quite a few things to live for. And through the grace of God, I've been given one more chance.

16

A Few Final Words about Cancer

WHEN YOU ARE SERIOUSLY ILL, YOU tend to block out the scary things until after you get better. I remember that during my hospitalization at MD Anderson, I was bombarded with various frightening tests. Once, I came down with an infection inside my chest cavity. There was a blood clot in one of the arteries near my chest and it became infected. A tremendous amount of fluid was sloshing around my lungs, stomach, and chest cavity. The only way doctors could get the fluid out was through a procedure called a thoracentesis.

As I sat on the side of a bed, the doctors put a very long needle through my back and into the chest cavity. I was then hooked up to a vacuum that sucked the fluid out into a bottle. The first time I had the procedure, more than a quart of fluid was sucked from my chest. Two days later, we did the same thing again and got more fluid. Well, the doctors finally got the infection cleared up, and it was only later that they showed me the length and the size of the needle they had used. They said there was no way they would have shown me the needle before they did it because if I'd have seen what they were sticking in me, it would have been pretty tough. I looked at the length of this needle and it was scary. At about eight inches in length, it looked more like something out of a horror movie than a doctor's office. Thankfully, my back had been to the doctors when the procedure was performed!

I think it is only natural that sick people don't ever want to remember the pain they endured after they get better. And I would say to cancer patients that they have to accept that they will undergo procedures—be it a thoracentesis, a bone marrow extraction, or surgery—that will hurt. But the thing to remember through it all is that the doctors are doing the best they can to give you a longer life. Right now, eight years after the thoracentesis, I remember it, but I don't dwell on it and it doesn't hurt me. Life is precious, and I'm very glad to be here to tell this story.

During my stay at MD Anderson, I came to realize that there is a tremendous psychological burden that the cancer patient has to bear. The treatments—chemotherapy, radiation, surgery—are tremendous physical demands on the body. But aside from that, there is a mental load that is very, very heavy. When friends or relatives come to visit you in the hospital, you try to be as positive and as upbeat as you can. You want to show this exuberance and show people that you believe the treatments will work, that you will survive.

You say to your visitors: "It's tough now, but by golly, I'm going to make it." And at the end of the day you are sometimes very weary of being so upbeat. All day long you have been trying to convince yourself and your friends that you and the doctors can win the battle. But it is a psychological roller coaster you're on. You're up one minute, and then, in the space of less than an hour, you're in deep despair. You feel sorry for yourself. You're wondering why it's all happening to you.

Then somebody comes to your room for a visit and you bounce back up and play the cheerleader again; you're strong again. But when the visitor leaves, you drift back into despair. It's a roller coaster that is very difficult for most patients to handle. You want to be positive, but at the same time, in your gut, you're scared to death. It all turns into a real exercise in handling your emotions.

The psychological battle against cancer is, I think, as important as the medical treatment. Some folks crack under it. They get so depressed that they won't let the treatments work. The doctors know that they're hitting you really hard with all their procedures. Nobody questions that and nobody tries to downplay the seriousness of your illness. But it gets difficult to bear the long days in the hospital. As a patient, I only lost my temper once that I can recall. I was brought some food but was feeling too sick to eat. I was so frustrated and so angry that day that I picked up a container of chocolate pudding from my meal tray and threw it against the wall. I'm not one to do that sort of thing very often, but I was just so damn mad. I thought, why am I here? I'm only thirty-nine years old and this shouldn't be happening to me.

But then reality set in, and I realized it really was happening and I would have to do my best to stay positive. I think what I could offer as advice for other patients who are going through this very scary period is for them to realize that many, many other people have gone before them and have undergone what they're going through in the way of treatment—the radiation, the chemotherapy. They have felt just as badly. They have also hurt, they have also been frustrated and angry. Thinking, "If I can get through the treatment, then the treatment will work and I'll be okay for the foreseeable future," is the key. And if you can to do that, just make it a goal to get through the treatment even week by week, then, God willing, you'll be okay.

You've got to try to remain positive and say, "I can win." If you give up mentally, then there's not much the doctors can do. It is so easy to think, "I'm going to die." And because the treatments are so debilitating, it's also easy to say, "Boy, I just can't handle much more of this." Believe that you *can* handle it. The human body is a miracle, and it can recover. The trick is to give it a chance and try to look at every day as another small hurdle to get over. You're going to feel better. You're going to win.

Sadly, a lot of people with a great attitude still won't make it, but I think those last days, weeks, or months will be much more fulfilling if you can keep that positive attitude and realize that the doctors are doing everything they can, your body is doing everything it can, and you are doing the best you can. Nobody can ask for anything more than that. And if the cancer is so widespread and so lethal, and the prognosis is so poor, you can still go out with your head held high and saying, "I met this challenge and did the best I could." That's all anybody can ask.

One thing I learned during my treatment as a cancer patient is that if you put your lip out and start feeling sorry for yourself, it just won't get you through. It's a very common, natural feeling to feel sorry for yourself at moments when you are in the midst of a tremendous, life-threatening challenge. But I found out that anytime, virtually anytime, you start to say, "Oh, woe is me," you're going to run into problems.

I remember a fellow I ran into in the halls at MD Anderson. He came up to me and said he recognized me from television. He said he was sorry to hear about the cancer. I shook his hand and asked him about his situation. He told me he also had cancer. And a heart problem. And AIDS. Suddenly I realized that this man—who was perhaps ten years younger than me—really had more devastating problems and a much bleaker future. My problems seemed insignificant in the face of his.

So I think I learned my lesson very early to not put my lip out and feel sorry for myself. Compared to some folks, I'm very, very, very lucky. I think that applies to 98% of the population. Try not to feel too much self-pity. Keeping that attitude up, day in and day out, is no easy matter. I know. But that should be the goal. You say to yourself, "I've had some bad luck, but I'm going to make it."

❖ ❖ ❖ ❖ ❖

My battle with cancer, the enemy within, wasn't fought alone, and I'll always treasure the support and soothing words brought by my family and friends. The cancer has been in remission for eight years now, after seven grueling months of surgery, chemotherapy, and radiation and another nine months of recovery and rehabilitation. As much as I count myself lucky to be free of it, cancer is still an ongoing issue in my life— one that propels me to raise money and consciousness throughout the state. Unfortunately, my family still battles cancer. . . .

The doctors were never able to explain it, but, just days after my final radiation treatment, Dad was diagnosed with a very similar cancer to mine—non-Hodgkin's lymphoma—and, like me, he had a tumor in his neck. Well, we knew right away which doctor we wanted, and Dr. Rich Hagemiester brought MD Anderson's aggressive treatment plan to Dad. But then, less than a week after Dad's diagnosis, doctors discovered that Mom had a cancerous tumor in her colon. All this less than two weeks after my final treatment.

I remember the three of us sitting in Dad's car—and shaking our heads, just dumbfounded by the whole mess.

At least I had been through a lot of testing and treatments, so I could offer them some insight and support. I took that support as far as I could: I got checked out to administer chemotherapy at home, so I could give Dad his treatments without the regular, arduous trips to the hospital. I went from patient to caregiver rather quickly.

Dr. Hagemiester did a great job with Dad, and some heavy radiation and a couple doses of chemotherapy got rid of Mom's tumor.

Then, about a year later, my sister Kate came down with a small tumor in her thyroid gland. But once again, chemotherapy saved the day. She's doing fine now. As hard as it was, we all tried to keep positive during the treatments, praying for an end to them. It's really been a blessing that we've all survived.

At this writing, however, doctors have discovered that cancer has reappeared in Mom, this time in a lung. She is yet again undergoing chemotherapy and is holding up as well as can be expected. She's always been a fighter, and she knows it is a real physical challenge to get through the treatments—and the roller coaster of emotions as well. We are all sending our prayers up for one more miracle. . . .

That's why, as lucky as I've been, I can never rest in the battle against cancer. I want to offer as much hope as I can to cancer patients now and hope that all of us can bring about an end to the enemy within.

APPENDIX

People Who Have Made a Difference

OVER THE YEARS, THERE HAVE BEEN SO many individuals who have made an impression, an impact, or an important contribution to my formative years, personal life, and professional career, that to write a story about each and every one in this book would be virtually impossible. Yet that is exactly what I wanted to do: write a story about each and every person.

However, my good friend and literary agent, Ed Danko, reminded me that to include everything I wanted to say about each of these treasured people would not only prove daunting but make this book so doggone thick no one could lift it to read! Ed suggested that I put together a list of these people, describing them briefly with one or two sentences. I thought that was a great idea, and so the following pages are devoted to them.

I have spent many hours on this part of the book, noting the special people in my life. The biggest challenge has been trying to keep each individual's "thumb sketch" down to a couple of sentences. And I know that I am somehow going to inadvertently miss mentioning someone. To you, I can only apologize, and emphasize that any omission is purely a regretful oversight on my part.

To most of the readers of this book, you'll recognize quite a few of the following names, and I hope you will enjoy reading how they have touched my life. For those who are actually named, I wish the accolades could be longer and in more detail.

With that said . . . here are many of the people who have made and continue to make a difference in my life.

Troy Aikman—At last! A young superstar with a level head on his shoulder, a gifted athlete who knows he has been blessed but understands the responsibility that goes along with his talent. A down-to-earth guy who acutely knows his celebrity status, but accepts that role in life and somehow handles his stature in the eyes of young and not-so-young fans. Troy is a caring guy who hasn't forgotten his roots.

Tom Alexander—He's one of those not-too-common individuals who consistently puts other people and their needs ahead of himself. He's an unsung, behind-the-scenes key player at WFAA Channel 8, who helps keep all of our complicated electronic gear up to snuff—that means a quality product for our viewers.

Dr. Mark Altgelt—You could say this guy put the smile on my face. He's been my dentist in Arlington since the 1970s. He's made the repairs when needed and even fashioned a couple of beautiful caps. An artist, he is.

Ward Andrews—The longtime anchorman at Channel 5 during the 1960s and 1970s, Ward used a fine artistic talent to enhance our daily newscast along with his crisp, clean writing. Ward enjoyed a few parts in Hollywood movies before turning his career to broadcast journalism in Wichita and Dallas-Fort Worth. He anchored through some of this nation's toughest years. We covered the civil rights clashes, assassinations, Vietnam and Watergate. He has earned a happy retirement.

Susie August—A fireball of a personality, she's one of the most engaging sales executives I've ever met in the television business. It's no wonder her daughter is a vivacious and outgoing college cheerleader!

Howard Ball—An all-around solid reporter at KWTX-TV in Waco, he showed me how to gather facts at the scene of the story, shoot a variety of 16mm newsreel scenes, and then condense everything into a sharp broadcast news story.

Ernie Banks—A baseball superstar who has a down-to-earth personality despite his Hall-of-Fame status and perhaps the most popular player ever for the Chicago Cubs. A native of Dallas who exemplifies good sportsmanship and compassion.

Ed Bark—As TV critic for *The Dallas Morning News*, Ed keeps us on our toes and won't accept sloppy work. Some TV reporters will tell you it doesn't matter what the critics write, but in my heart I think they are fibbing. Ed doesn't miss much.

Bev Bass—Now one of the senior female airline captains at American Airlines, Bev gave me my third flying lesson back in 1974 when she was an instructor at Fort Worth's Meacham Field. She made the history books by piloting American Airlines' first all-female flight crew on a flight out of Washington. Even today, though, Bev would confess that her landing on that training flight back in 1974 was pretty bad—we didn't scrape the tail, but we did some bouncing. But all is forgiven—and congratulations on a wonderful career.

Alan Bean—The fourth man on the moon, an accomplished artist in Houston who has donated his time and talent to some of my charity efforts. He's humble, funny, a great pilot and a sincerely nice fellow.

Craig Belknap—A Richfield High School cheerleader in Waco who almost lost his life when a land mine blew up next to him in Vietnam, Craig has suffered pain, disfigurement and crippling injuries. He also beat alcoholism and is a winner now.

Sidney Benton*—One of the most dedicated, loyal, and efficient newsroom people I have ever met. News directors who were her supervisors thought they were running the newsroom, but in so many respects, Sydney was the person who made everyone toe the line. We lost her far too early to cancer. She was a true legend in local broadcasting and she is held in high regard.

Rolando Blackman—Some people are blessed from birth with an honest caring for children, the less fortunate, and those in need. Rolando is one of those rare persons. He has excelled in the tough world of professional basketball, but he has never forgotten that he is an idol to youngsters and a competitor on the court who should be emulated. His smile is real, and his caring is genuine.

Russ Bloxom—One of the pioneer TV journalists, who first honed his skills on radio, and then transformed them to television news at Channel 5 in the 1970s, covering local politics and courthouse activities. He's a no-nonsense journalist.

Bob Bolen—Put a cheerleader, a smiling business executive, and a good ol' boy Texan together and you get the former Fort Worth Mayor, Bob Bolen. The city of Fort Worth owes much of its current boom status to the plans and vision laid out by Bob years ago. If you don't know where the West begins, just ask Bob.

Tom Bond—Tom was one of those classic men on campus at Richfield High School in Waco—one of the most popular student leaders, a football and track star, and one of those guys who always got great report cards. Tom has always had a real zest for life and a desire for excellence that has served him well

through college and into the world of law. A neat guy.

Buddy Bostick—He "signed off" and approved my hiring at KWTX-TV in Waco. As general manager, he explained and demonstrated the difference between talking from the throat and from the diaphragm in order to produce better clarity and projection with my voice.

Clint Bourland—As a writer and producer at WBAP-TV and KXAS-TV Channel 5, Clint demonstrated to me the skills and judgment in assembling a particular newscast, and how to write to the various pictures and video made available to us from local or national sources.

Pappy Boyington*—He was leader of the so-called "Black Sheep" fighter squadron of World War II in the Pacific. Pappy was an "in your face" pilot, drinker, and barroom brawler. He was nice to me during our television interview, but I have heard you could get roughed up pretty good if you got on his wrong side. The TV series "Baa Baa Black Sheep" was based on his life as a fighter pilot. I think it is safe to say that the phrase "Full Throttle" applied to Pappy and his whirlwind life.

Dan Brandenstein—As former chief astronaut at NASA, Dan showed me that no matter how important you are, it never hurts to put in a helping hand when there's a good charity event to support. Dan showed up at my first golf tournament in Houston and impressed every participant with his friendliness and humility. He was pilot for the first night launch of the space shuttle and made the first night space shuttle landing.

Frank and Debbie Branson—A self-made success in the rough and tumble world of lawyering, Frank is the definition of a successful attorney. He and

---

Debbie have shown their generosity year in and year out, making time to help out on charity events. Their Christmas open house on Turtle Creek is special.

Dr. Jack Brooks—A dedicated radiologist who can see the worst news one day for one patient and the best news for another patient the next day. It must take strength and understanding to deal with life and death issues on a daily basis. Thankfully, he enjoys a good game of blackjack or a day at the races to keep him levelheaded.

Bill Brown—As Channel 8's senior military reporter, Bill never fails to impress me with his award-winning documentation of the tragic, and sometimes triumphant, stories of war and the people who fight them. His reports are compelling without exception. Great work.

Doug Brown—A superb role model for me, he was an unusually talented broadcaster at KWTX -TV in Waco and KTRK-TV in Houston who was just as personable and friendly off camera as on.

Jack Brown—One of the most unique, original and entertaining broadcast journalists I have ever known. He has a wonderfully dry wit, with an uncanny ability to see subtleties in a news story that few other reporters can. He spent 22 years at Channel 5 and then moved to Channel 4 in Dallas.

Dr. George Buchanan—To lead a hospital's fight against cancer, with its daily defeats and victories, takes a very special kind of person. When the cancer patients are all children, the job is even tougher. Somehow, Dr. Buchanan finds a renewed determination when he loses a child to cancer at Children's Medical Center in Dallas—and along with that renewed determination there is a new commitment to try to prevent it from happening again. Thankfully, his victo-

ries are many and they are in large part due to his talent.

Norm Bulaich—A stand-out athlete and football star at Texas Christian University and in the National Football League, winning a Super Bowl ring that he wears with understandable pride. Few people I know can match his visionary discipline for regular and committed mental, spiritual and physical exercise. A bright-eyed example of how an athlete can remain in condition and take up a professional life after football.

Andy and Tan-Tan Bundgarrdt—This delightful couple served as captain and second mate on board Dallas millionaire Ray Miller's yacht *Alpha Centauri*. It was following a tough surgery that I spent time on the yacht, and the couple was not only gracious, but became as close as family members. We did a little fishing and flew in a seaplane—their warmth and generosity helped me get well more quickly than I could have imagined.

David Burroughs—Lawyers as a group seem to take a lot of heat these days, but those shoveling out the criticism don't know David Burroughs. David has long ignored his well-to-do background and represented those who are sometimes swept under the rug by the community. He is a champion to many.

George Bush—What a great example of how dogged determination after bitter defeat can eventually win exceedingly high honors. After losing a U.S. Senate battle to Lloyd Bentsen, I watched Mr. Bush work 18 hours a day for the GOP. It took a few years, but when his calling card read 1600 Pennsylvania Avenue, it was all worth it. No matter what your political philosophy, no one can deny his well-earned retirement. Give 'em hell, George!

Blake Byrne—As general manager of Channel 5, he was compassionate and understanding, with creative ideas and goals. He always had a strong personal relationship with his employees and a keen sense of business—something the corporate execs like, as well as the stockholders.

James Byron*—As the number-one executive at WBAP-TV Channel 5 in the early 1970s, he went out on a limb to promote me to weeknight anchorman at the age of 24. Mr. Byron forced me to try to achieve higher levels of broadcasting.

Sanders Campbell*—He was one of the visionary Dallas real estate developers. His premier development, the gold-plated twin towers on Central Expressway near Northwest Highway (The Campbell Center), is testimony to his business acumen. In private, Sanders was a generous benefactor for several charities, but always insisted he remain anonymous.

Gloria Campos—She's got it all—personality, beauty, intelligence, and commitment. As co-anchor with me over the years, Gloria has demonstrated much more than the broadcasting talents which are necessary in this market. She has shown a commitment to enhancing the lives and well-being of those who watch our broadcast. Her concern for Wednesday's Children is real.

Sharon Carr—There aren't too many people who can sing in the church choir with the voice of an angel, have the good looks to go along with the part, and the red hair to make them even extra special. But such is the case for Dallas travel agency owner Sharon Carr. Sharon has demonstrated to me the courage and the faith it takes to face losing a child to leukemia. A lesser person might have forsaken her faith in God, but for Sharon that faith was strengthened. Here is a hug for Sharon.

Jimmy Carter—I got him to chuckle when I threw him a curve during a reasonably serious interview: I simply asked him how he was enjoying his new job as president. He said the job was fun, but that it had a lot of ups and downs.

Paul Cato*—As former chairman of the Colonial National Invitational Golf Tournament, Paul worked tirelessly to make the N.I.T. one of the truly outstanding tournaments in professional golf. A quiet, soft-spoken and successful businessman with a stadium full of friends and fans, Paul waged a strong and courageous battle against cancer. The cancer won, and Fort Worth and the tournament are poorer for it. His memory, however, is rich and wonderful.

Art Chapman—An upbeat, honest TV critic for the *Fort Worth Star-Telegram*, Art has always had 20/20 eyesight when it comes to critiquing the news operations in Dallas and Fort Worth. I have never been misquoted or seen an error in his reporting.

Ron Chapman—The long-time guiding force and strength at KVIL radio, Ron has been voted most popular DJ in the country many times. I envy his energy—he's a legendary broadcaster for all the right reasons.

Eddie Chiles*—The pioneer Texas and Oklahoma oilman, who started from scratch and built an international oil company. He was a gutsy Texan who was not afraid to take a gamble and was as personable to his friends and employees as a father is to his children. A rare and wonderful Texan.

Carl Churchill*—My cadet commander at Baylor University, he was later killed in action when shot down flying an Air Force F-4 on a mission over North Vietnam. A sharp, intelligent young man of leadership.

Cynthia Clark—I am always amazed how we can learn things from each other all the way through life. I have a lot of respect for those people who make it part of their life to help others through volunteer and charity work. In the past few years, I have seen Cynthia grow and mature in her efforts for the American Cancer Society. Much to my surprise, she recently told me that she had always been too shy to step out and help at various fundraising events. To my even greater surprise, she said I was the one who inspired her to reach beyond herself. That to me is a terribly huge and humbling compliment. Cynthia, keep up the good work.

Casey Cohlmia—A long-time public relations executive in Dallas who came to me several years ago and offered me the opportunity to raise money for the Children's Cancer Fund of Dallas or any other charity of my choice, by hosting a celebrity chef dinner at the Benihana Steak House. The fun event has proved to be a huge success for five years—and if you haven't taken part, you should! It's usually every January.

Jan Collmer—He's cleared for take-off in aviation and business, as one of the biggest aviation enthusiasts and supporters in Texas and an air show pilot extraordinaire. The "Frontiers of Flight Museum" at Love Field is largely the result of his unceasing efforts for pilots and aviation history.

Tom and Carol Craft—Tom lost a leg to diabetes, almost lost his life to a heart attack, but has never lost his sense of humor or a deep-felt commitment to helping others. Carol has been a model of how a person can hold a family together through crises.

Bob Crandall—I honestly cannot imagine what it would be like to be the boss of 120,000 workers and also have to answer to an airline's board of directors and stockholders as well. Goodness, that has got to be a huge responsibility. Just a few years ago, I felt professionally respected when Bob agreed to be interviewed exclusively by me, one-on-one, on a touchy national labor issue with no pre-interview demands and guidelines. I was told by one of his top executives that, in addition to liking me personally, he respected my factual reporting. What a compliment!

Cathy Creany—She's a rare and understanding station manager. Too often, station managers have their eye on stock options, perks and Christmas bonuses. But with this lady that's not the case. She has championed a station-wide commitment to helping families of the '90s face and solve their problems. She's a top television executive who really cares about trying to use this medium to improve the lives of our viewers.

Rich Creehan—Maybe it's that Celtic background, but Rich and I enjoy a close rapport and share a team effort in writing news stories for the various newscasts throughout the day on Channel 8. It's nice to work with someone who is thinking along the same lines.

John Criswell—We have been competitors, but also friends. John has been a supporter of good causes in Dallas and Fort Worth over the years and has demonstrated that being on television carries with it an obligation to help the community wherever possible.

Walter Cronkite—The original TV anchorman and the "most trusted man in America," he wielded an incredible amount of influence over this country and was a tough and demanding journalist who scoffed at the idea that the anchorman was more important than the story. He showed me that those of us who are on television have a serious responsibility to communicate the news in a factual and unbiased way.

Jack Cunningham—a broadcast photojournalist at Channel 4 who learned his craft the hard way—in combat in Vietnam. A busted-up body and bad knees never kept him down—or away from a good story. And he never lost his great sense of humor.

Walt Cunningham—A former NASA astronaut who has led an aviation career most pilots would be envious of. He looks more at home in his flight jacket than I do in a coat and tie.

Floyd Dakil—He's a great friend to Dallas, and a natural-born entertainer who knows at least two lines of every song ever written. He continues to donate time and talent to Dallas charities, in particular the Salesmanship Club at the Byron Nelson Golf Tournament. He has never said no to any request of mine for charity help.

Ed Danko—Ed is the person who suggested I write a book, and is now my literary agent and executive producer for this book. He's a close, dear friend who's always there when I need him. His broadcast journalism and editing skills helps make WFAA-TV the very best local news operations in the country. Ed has also worked at NBC News and CBS News, with such pros as Dan Rather and Lesley Stahl.

Duane Dauphin—As the director of food and catering at Brookhaven Country Club, Duane has provided tremendous support and energy to the Chip Moody Pro-Am golf tournament. Although he coordinates more than 20 golf tournaments a year, he has joined our effort and the Chip Moody team in heart and soul. (Hey Duane, how about some shrimp for lunch at our next meeting?)

Alex and Lee Davis—When illness strikes, some strangers become loving caretakers and friends. Such was the case with this Florida couple, who took me under their wing and showed me a few fishing tricks aboard their boat *Sea-Sun Ticket* while I was recovering from surgery.

Brad Davis—When I think of Brad, the phrase "be true to yourself" comes to mind. One of the most energetic, talented and caring members of the Dallas Mavericks basketball team, Brad has always been a classic example of a team player and a guy who put others— teammates, fans, and kids—way above himself.

Kenny Bob Davis—Musician, singer, comedian and all-around nut, Kenny Bob lives in North Hollywood but calls Dallas home. He's a bigger ham than I am. Next time you see him, ask him to perform "Handsome Stuff."

Jody Dean—The single most creative radio personality I have ever met. He writes funny songs on current events, and has them sung and recorded. A super-nice guy who is smart as a whip.

Father Mark Deering—The long-time leader of the St. Louis Catholic Church in Waco. Anyone who knows Father Deering knows they have been blessed by meeting such a special person. He has compassion, understanding, and humor. He's not a bad poker player, either.

Bill Dietz—Movie legend Gary Cooper has always been described as the strong, silent type. That description fits Bill to a Texas T as well. He was the outstanding running back for the Richfield High School Rams in Waco and helped lead them to the 1965 Bi-District championship. Even though I was the new kid from Europe, Bill and I hit off a friendship that lasts to this day. He was the classic "football hero" but impressed me more with the humility with which he handled his fame and popularity. He hasn't changed a bit—just don't ask him to arm wrestle.

James Donaldson—In this day and age of superstar basketball players with supersized salaries and egos, this friendly giant for the Mavericks was the exception to the rule. With a smile as wide as the Trinity River and as bright as the lights he played under, James was forever reaching out his oversized hand to help the less fortunate. I remember he cooked for one of my charity dinners at the Benihana Steak House and was taller than the vent-a-hoods above the grills.

Kirk Dooley—A true Texan from his boots on up, Kirk has faithfully published books, articles and even a newspaper for homesick Texans. He's a great chronicler of this great State and the men and women who make it unique.

Bill Doerr—An outstanding broadcast journalist who works and plays hard. He has been in charge of numerous special live reports from the scene of a breaking story, and once traveled to war-ravaged Bosnia to make sure our reporter Bill Brown and his crew were able to get the story. Bill also helped coordinate our coverage of the Persian Gulf War.

Kirk Douglas—One of the first really big Hollywood movie stars who showed me that humility is a virtue. He shifted attention away from himself to his son Michael during a joint guest appearance on an afternoon talk show at Channel 5.

Ron Dowd—A soft-spoken professional floor manager and studio director at Channel 4, he's an unsung hero and good guy behind the scenes who made sure the anchors were alerted to story changes and aware of which camera to look at.

Troy Dungan—Reliable, knowledgeable, dependable, friendly and sincere. Those are just a few words that describe this long-time Channel 8 weatherman. Troy is usually the first member of the late shift to arrive at work. He's a professional who recognizes his responsibility to the community and to our news operation. Meteorology may be an imperfect science, but Troy does his best to make the forecast as accurate as humanly possible.

Harlan Durgin—He was a high school classmate who had more girlfriends than I did and was probably a better athlete. He went on to become a high-ranking Navy officer and pilot and a person I really admire.

Clint Eastwood—A role model for me, he showed me that humility is so much more valuable and endearing than carrying a chip on your shoulder and also that, no matter your station in life, you are never better than the next guy.

Bruce Eaton—He was a classmate and fellow athlete in Belgium. Bruce shared with me an intimate knowledge of Europe because of his extensive travel. We anchored on the front line of the International School of Brussels soccer team and formed a bond and friendship which has last more than 30 years.

Roy Eaton—Anchorman and nightside assignments editor at Channel 5 in the 1970s, he demanded that our 10 p.m. news not miss anything that would be on the front page of the next morning's paper. A friendly and outgoing guy who has his roots in Texas.

Mac Ellis—One of the unsung heroes at WFAA-TV, he is the floor director whose responsibility is to make those split-second decisions which can make or break a newscast. He's behind the scenes, but makes sure those of us on the anchor desk know what is going to happen next, when, and on which camera.

Lee Elsesser—He was a newsroom leader at Channel 5 in Dallas in the 1970s who set the pace for pushing the level of excellence for employees to a new high—a journalist who would not excuse poor performance in reporting.

Ivar* and Camilla Erikson—A pioneer South Dakota farmer who literally helped settle the state, the best horseshoe player in several counties, and perhaps the friendliest man I have ever known. Ivar's famous advice for horseshoes: "come from above." He is missed, remembered and loved. Camilla is my counterpart in rural South Dakota, writing a weekly news column for the *Unityville News*.

Cecil Ewell—Chief pilot for American Airlines (think about that!), and a heck of an F-4 fighter pilot. And he's a really nifty, nice guy to boot.

Louis Fadel—Louis was the all-star shortstop for our Richfield High School Rams in Waco, and owned perhaps the most classic American-made car in history: a red and white 1957 Chevy convertible. I was the new kid in school, and Louis took me under his wing and gave me good advice on the baseball field and which kids to stay away from in school. And he let me drive that Chevy. We spent many nights enjoying each other's collection of 45 RPM rock 'n' roll oldies. Some of the best guys I know are the ones who are good at what they do but don't brag about it—and he's one of them.

Frank Fallon—The legendary sports broadcaster based for many years at KWTX radio in Waco. He executed play-by-play football and basketball games across the Southwest as well as anyone and was the voice of the Baylor Bears. A pro to be emulated.

Carolyn Fessler—An unusually caring and thoughtful executive producer keenly aware of making sure that any story which airs on Channel 8 news is factually correct. She doesn't hesitate to double-check with any reporter or anchor to make sure the facts are straight.

Felder "Fats" Fitzgerald—You know that mammoth electric train set-up at Children's Hospital in Dallas? The one with the mountains and trestles, valleys and towns? Well, Felder is the "engineer" in charge, working five days a week to make sure the trains run smoothly and on time for the youngsters (and for their parents!) who are being treated at or are visiting Children's. Here's a guy who really loves his work—and the smiles it brings.

John Fitzgerald—A friendly and caring individual, John has one of the most generous personalities I have ever been honored to know. He is not at all hesitant to sacrifice time from his job to help raise money for charity causes. If there has ever been a guy who personifies the wonderful and uplifting "Irish spirit," it is John, and I'm proud to call him my friend.

Dr. Jack Flanders—The pastor who married Vikki and me, a professor of religion at Baylor University, pastor of the First Baptist Church of Waco, and a World War II combat pilot. He is a trusted friend who made religion understandable.

Betty Ford—A shining example of how the human spirit can overcome a weakness of the flesh. She has a delightful smile that matches her heart.

Terry Ford—He's a maverick TV management type, not afraid to take risks and tell you where you stand. He was a demanding boss at Channel 8 in Dallas and at Channel 11 in Houston.

Win Frankel—He gave me my first opportunity to dive into broadcasting full-time. As control room director at KWTX-TV and a broadcasting professor at Baylor University, he alerted me to a job opening at KWTX. He opened the door, and I walked through.

Dr. Lillian Fuller—She has been a pioneer in the field of cancer radiation treatments, who not only supervised my treatments at Houston's M.D. Anderson Cancer Center, but also cheered me up and gave me much-needed encouragement during some emotionally low periods.

Billy Gamble—As chief Boy Scout executive for North Texas, Billy has had a positive and lasting impact on thousands of young Texans. I have been honored to speak to some of the young men who achieved the lofty rank of Eagle Scout. One year, the Circle Ten Council put a lump in my throat when it named an entire class of 263 Eagle Scouts in my honor. I have a picture of the Chip Moody class proudly displayed on my office wall.

Greer Garson Fogelson—The first time I was hospitalized in Dallas I was surprised by a huge bouquet of striking Hawaiian flowers that came to me, much to my astonishment, from this Academy Award-winning actress. I had not yet met her, but later we formed a hugging friendship and she told me in her wonderful British accent, "Oh dear, I seem to have developed a crush on you." What a sweetheart.

John Gary—The classic Irish tenor with a twinkle in his eye. A worldwide recording artist who lives in Richardson, has fought and won his own battle with cancer and has made a substantial contribution to my charity golf tournament. His "Danny Boy" will make you cry.

Ronda Gibbons—Part of the new generation of TV broadcasters, she is energetic and committed to learning all she can as she helps write headlines and news updates for broadcast on Channel 8. Ronda, keep up the good work!

Frank Glieber*—A legendary sports broadcaster for CBS, KRLD Radio and Channel 5 in Dallas. He demonstrated to me the skills so many broadcasters covet—a quick mind, an unusual measure of confidence, and cordiality on the air. I miss him.

Alva Goodall—If you could have a caring aunt in your family—Alva is that person. She is concerned and caring about individuals and charity groups almost to a fault. Alva is one of those persons who is blessed with compassion and understanding.

Bob Gooding—Bob was the likable co-anchor at Channel 8 in the 1970s; a friendly guy who was part of the family.

Ray Green—World champion Bar-B-Q chef—no brag, ma'am, just fact. He's a big-hearted guy with a zest for life that matches his nationally recognized pork ribs. North Main Bar-B-Q in Euless is just this side of heaven.

John Gudjohnson—Dallas-Fort Worth has been blessed by the work of John over the years—he's an individual any university or professional broadcast department could use as an example of how to do things right and how to do them well. He spent quite a few years at Channel 5 before moving to Channel 8—an exceptional journalist.

Kurt and Jeanne Gustafson—He's a Scandinavian goodwill ambassador who calls Dallas home, and co-owns Mattito's Restaurant in Oak Lawn. Kurt's one of those special life-long friends who, thankfully, has a good woman to keep him on the straight and narrow. They are both generous to a fault.

Marty Haag—The individual who set the standard for broadcast journalism in

Texas and the Southwest, he's a visionary and almost scary broadcasting executive, because he sets such high standards and expectations for himself and his newsroom members. Few in the business are his equal.

Dr. Rick Hagemiester—As my primary cancer treatment doctor at M.D. Anderson Cancer Center in Houston, Rick was in large measure responsible for my successful fight with cancer. I probably owe him a steak dinner every month for the rest of my life. (Rick, don't hold me to that—I can't eat as much steak as I used to!)

Dr. Kent Hamilton—He literally knows me inside and out. Kent has put a medical TV camera down my throat and into my intestines more often than most people have lobster. He's also a great Civil War historian.

Dale Hansen—You love him or you hate him. Dale is truly one of the outstanding television personalities ever in Dallas-Fort Worth. He's a big guy with a sharp mind and a booming voice—and also a big heart that some people don't know about.

Glenn Hardwick*—When I returned from Europe, Glenn was a cheerleader and one of the most popular students at Richfield High School in Waco. It is hard for me to believe he has been gone for more than 20 years, lost to a car accident. Everyone who knew him still misses him.

Don Harris*—Don was a former Channel 8 anchorman and NBC correspondent who was killed while covering what would turn out to be the mass suicide in Jonestown, Guyana. Don was never shy or retiring. He turned in some excellent investigative reports and was also an affable host of a morning news program called "News 8, Etc."

Holly Hassman—As executive director of the Children's Medical Center, this hardworking redhead puts in long hours, long days, and long weeks to make sure as many children as possible benefit from charity funds. She also works to make sure that the public is aware of the importance of giving—because it makes you feel so good, but, more important, because it improves the quality of life for youngsters facing serious or critical health problems.

Bill Herring—National and world news editor, plus anchor at KWTX-TV in Waco, he demonstrated to me the value of surveying the major national and international news stories of the day and how to pick the top 9 or 10 to broadcast that night.

Lyda Hill—Although a wealthy member of the Hunt oil family, Lyda is down-to-earth and a hard-working, well-organized charity benefactor. She, Charles Simmons, and I came up with the concept of "A Conversation with a Living Legend" fundraising luncheon for M.D. Anderson Cancer Center in Houston. Now in it sixth year, this event has proved to be one of the most successful fundraising events in M.D. Anderson history. Lyda's vision made it possible. She also enjoys photo safaris and travel to exotic locales.

Charlie Hilliard Jr.—A former world aerobatic champion pilot, Charlie won the title over the Russian competitor with a last-day, never-before-seen aerobatics maneuver. He has a small job on the side selling cars to pay for his aviation gas as leader of the "Eagles" aerobatics team. Charlie, thanks for the many rides.

Bard Holbert—My brother-in-law, who has established his own company to provide temporary help for Dallas-area businesses. I think he could have been a successful pro golfer if he had foregone girls and dating in college. Even now he is a 1- or 2-handicap player—maybe even a scratch golfer. Great sense of humor!

Kate Moody Holbert—My sister, the most thoughtful of all the siblings. She is always sending cute notes in the mail, along with appropriate pictures cut out of magazines, or her own line of home-made greeting cards, featuring thought-provoking and beautifully composed portraits of life in rural South Dakota.

Bob Hoover—Air-show pilot extraordinaire is how I would describe Bob. He has flown more than 200 different types of airplanes in his stellar aviation career, and he has entertained millions and millions of people with his almost unparalleled skills in the cockpit.

Ward Huey—He has brains, compassion and high expectations. There are hundreds of top-level broadcasting executives in this country, but few have demonstrated to me the human and business acumen I have witnessed in Ward over the years. He is perhaps only second to Roone Arledge in demonstrating how a gifted individual can rise through the ranks of television jobs . . . starting as a studio cameraman and rising to head an incredibly widespread and diverse broadcast division for a major corporation.

Bobbie Irwin—One of those rare individuals who puts personal friendship and loyalty ahead of all else. She has been a constant and upbeat supporter of me and my parents, as all three of us fought serious medical illnesses. She has stood tall, straight and strong, and all of us thank her for it.

John "Jack" Jackson—A retired Dallas oilman, John has looked beyond the pump jacks of East and West Texas to share some of his wealth with a number of charities, including mine. A quiet supporter of worthwhile endeavors who supports his city, his friends, his alma mater, and his wonderful wife, Katie, with conviction.

Kenny and Arvella Jacobsen—One of the nicest and most caring couples I have ever known. Kenny is retired from farming in South Dakota now, but he showed me how hard work is a virtue. Arvella just might be the best cook in the state—her "sticky buns" just melt in your mouth. Their hearts are as big as the Midwest plains.

Bob Jeffery—How anybody could survive seven years as a POW in North Vietnam is hard to imagine. Bob, who now flies for American Airlines, not only survived, but has subsequently had a great flying career and is at peace with himself and his long ordeal.

Nick Jent—He was the first chairman/coordinator of the original Chip Moody Pro-Am golf tournament to benefit the Leukemia Society of America. He's one of those executives every company wants on their team. I'm glad he has used his time and talent to help in some very worthwhile charity causes.

Felicia Jeter—Co-anchor with me at KHOU-TV Channel 11 in Houston after a stint with CBS and a woman who demonstrated concern and care for victims of poverty or violence in the community, she has an engaging personality off the air, and a big heart.

Darcy Johansen—She was the first great love of my life, and was with me in Brussels, Belgium the night John Kennedy was assassinated. While at the Vietnam memorial, I touched the name of her brother on the wall and my heart broke for her and her mother.

Jim Johansen*—As the older brother of my first girlfriend and a helicopter pilot in the U.S. Army, Jim was one of the first people in my life I looked up to. He was shot down and killed in Vietnam. To me, his death exemplifies our wasted effort there.

Dennis Johnson—I sometimes wonder why the state medical association doesn't make Dennis an honorary doctor—his knowledge of medicine and medical procedures is truly impressive. I would trust him to take care of me if I were injured or sick. However, it's all those puns he comes up with that tell me he's got a couple crossed wires upstairs.

Janet Johnson—She's smart, decisive and she has the split-second decision-making talent that is so critical for a news producer. She weighs the value of any given story for the 6 p.m. news at Channel 8 and decides what stories are the most important for our early evening news viewers. It's a job that calls for cutting here, trimming there, adding this and subtracting that to make it all come together in the best possible information package.

Judy Jordan—The first lady of broadcast journalism in Dallas-Fort Worth, she co-anchored the news at Channel 4 in the early 1970s, carving out a place for women in what had been an all-male locker room.

Herb Kelleher—In my next life, I think it would be a hoot to be Herb Kelleher. This outgoing, friendly, and handsome man has made Southwest Airlines one of the real success stories in corporate America. Herb is probably the most personable, goofy and sincere boss in the world today. One Halloween, I was more than surprised when a giant pumpkin welcomed me at the door—everybody was in costume at the corporate headquarters.

Tom Landry—A person can easily run out of superlatives when talking about Coach. When I interviewed Tom for "Conversation with a Living Legend," Tom surprised everyone, except those who knew him, with his humor and engaging conversation. In a private conversation, he told me his faith continues not to be tested, but to get stronger, in the face of his daughter's battle with cancer. Our thoughts and prayers go out to him and his family now. One of his famous gray felt hats occupies a place of honor in my home.

Dave Lane*—The heart, soul and driving force at Channel 8 for many years, Dave was compassionate, understanding, patient and visionary. A president and general manager of WFAA-TV, he created the hugely successful and meaningful "Listening to Texas" campaign in which we travel to smaller north Texas communities, meet with citizens and air their hopes, concerns and suggestions for the problems facing families today. A cancerous brain tumor took him from us far too soon.

Dr. Charles LeMaistre—He likes to be called Mickey, but it just seems too informal for the man in charge of the entire University of Texas system. Yep . . . the whole system! He's a wonderful friend, a keen executive and the man who has shown me the rewards of awfully hard work.

D.D. Lewis—Since I have never been in the Dallas Cowboys' locker room, I really don't know how some football players demonstrate the leadership qualities and convey to their teammates the need and the willingness to endure injury and pain for the good of the group. But D.D. is one of those special athletes whose performance and attitude made the difference between a winner and an also-ran.

Jerry Lee Lewis—I met "Killer" during a low ebb in his career—he was playing a one-night stand at a VFW hall in Elm Mott, Texas, outside of Waco. Jerry Lee played "Great Balls of Fire" like it was still number one. He took the time to introduce himself to me, saying simply, "Hi, I'm Jerry Lee Lewis," as if I didn't know. Even to this day, if Jerry Lee is in the room, there is a whole lot of shaking going on.

Mike LiBassi—American Airlines' front man for charity event participation and sponsorship, I couldn't ask for a nicer and more generous airline executive. He makes me justify the major contributions that American Airlines donates to my various charity events. (I keep hoping that one of these days he'll give ME a free trip!)

Dr. Z.A. "Zack" Lieberman—He's perhaps the best abdominal surgeon in the Southwest, period. He's a talented humanitarian who has always put his patients and their well-being first—and he does so with a big heart and an engaging smile.

Bruce Lietzke—He's a pro golfer who really seems to have his priorities in line. He sets aside several months each year away from the PGA circuit in order to spend time with his family. You sure as heck don't see that too often.

Jerry Loftin—He's a crackerjack lawyer with a smile as big as Texas and a laugh to go along with it. Jerry has been a fun, positive, hardworking fixture on the Tarrant County law scene since the early 1970s.

Bill Mack—The legendary "Midnight Cowboy" of WBAP-AM, Bill is heard coast-to-coast after he opens with the "Orange Blossom Special." He has been voted most popular country DJ many times over. He has a strong grip, a quick smile, and a classic Texas drawl.

Joe Macko —Courage, goodwill and a wonderfully engaging personality are how I would describe Joe, the equipment manager for the Texas Rangers baseball club. He and his wife lost a son to cancer when he was in the prime of life. Joe has never carried that tremendous loss on his sleeve, but instead has volunteered and worked overtime to try to save other youngsters and their families the heartbreaking loss his family had to endure.

Debbie Macziewski—Debbie is one of those hard-working, behind-the-scenes, "don't mention me" people who make the difference between a so-so charity event and one that is really successful. She gives of herself unselfishly to help others, young and old, and has been a huge factor in the success of my golf tournament to benefit Children's Hospital. The epitome of a giving woman.

Harvey Martin—A football star with shoulders wide enough to carry a team. And he did. An ambassador of goodwill for not only the Dallas Cowboys, but the city of Dallas and the greater North Texas area as well. A caring and concerned individual who does not shirk from his responsibility as a role model.

Murphy Martin—A long-time anchorman for WFAA-TV and one of the early anchormen for ABC-TV, Murphy went with H. Ross Perot to help gain freedom for the American POWs in Vietnam. You can still hear his deep and resonant voice at Texas Stadium, calling the action for the Dallas Cowboys. A pro in every sense of the word.

Alfred and Anita Martinez—He is a downtown Dallas fixture, and has been for several generations. Founder of the El Fenix restaurant chain, he can be found at the main restaurant on McKinney every day except Tuesdays graciously seating new friends and old. Anita is the founder of the internationally acclaimed Anita Martinez Ballet Folklorico. Their contributions to Dallas are immeasurable.

Brenda Mauldin—As executive catering director for Baylor University Medical Center, Brenda has rubbed elbows with some of the most wealthy, powerful, and influential leaders of the Western world. From the Saudi Crown Prince to heads of state, Brenda has never failed to put Baylor and its Board of Trustees in the best light. Happily, I am able to report that Brenda and I have the same rare blood type, A-Negative, and that she is a regular blood donor at Baylor. Considering that I just received 16 pints of the blood, surely one or two of those came from lovely Brenda.

John McCaa—When John joined Tracy and me in the 10 p.m. anchor rotation at Channel 8, he brought years of experience, diversity, and solid reporting to our broadcast. John looks serious a lot, and he is. But just ask him to play a set on the drums, and his eyes light up and he gets a big grin on his face.

Kevin McCarthy—You wouldn't know it by looking at him, but Kevin has been in the radio business for 62 years. Just kidding, but I can't figure out why he still looks 26 when he's been working in Dallas radio at least that long. We are good friends, but why in the world did he nickname me "Noodles"? He's fun, relaxed and a real pro. (Noodles?)

John McCrory—The primary decision-maker at the *Dallas Times Herald* and Channel 4 in the '70s and '80s, who decided to hire me away from Channel 5 in 1980. It worked out well for him, for me, and for Channel 4.

Tom* and Marilyn McDonald—Tom was an honest-to-goodness broadcasting pioneer at what was then called WBAP-TV Channel 5, in Fort Worth. He voiced over the legendary newscast called "The Texas News," the first newscast in Texas. Over the years, Tom not only demonstrated excellence in every phase of broadcasting—from writing to producing to editing—he taught two generations of journalists "how to do it right." We were all stunned when this active and healthy man was unexpectedly stricken with Lou Gehrig's disease. When I bought my first house in the Meadowbrook Hills section of Fort Worth, it was no small coincidence and good luck that Tom and Marilyn were my next door neighbors. Our families grew up together and we were sadly helpless as Tom lost his valiant struggle against this incurable disease. They brought up their children well. In fact, one of their daughters married the son of Lieutenant Governor Bill Hobby.

Spanky McFarland*—If you read the chapter in the book about Spanky you know how deeply I admired and cared for this man. He was, in my opinion, a part of the fabric of the American flag. Three cheers for Spanky.

George McGovern—A longtime family friend who also just happened to run for president after a long career in the U.S. Senate. He and Mom used to date in college. George has always stood up for what he believed in. In the decades following the Vietnam War, some people say they now know they voted for the wrong man when the White House was up for grabs.

Buster McGregor*—A longtime assignments editor at Channel 4, Buster had a keen eye for what makes a story interesting. He was tragically killed in a news helicopter crash while helping cover a story in West Texas.

John McKay—He is one of the finest television general managers I have ever had the pleasure of working for. While at KDFW-TV Channel 4, John led a personality-driven newsroom into a head-on, "in your face" competition with the staid and solid journalism broadcast on

Channel 8. John had a magic personality—I could go into his office with six or seven gripes and come out 30 minutes later smiling, even though I hadn't won a single case. He's now owner of Channel 27.

Lisa McRee—Now anchoring the news in Los Angeles, Lisa came to Channel 8 news in 1989 or 1990. She was paired up with me to co-anchor the 5 p.m. news. I will never forget her first words when I met this lovely young woman about to be my partner on the air. I said, "Hi, I'm Chip Moody." She said, "Oh, I know. I grew up watching you on TV!" Indeed, she was a teenager in Fort Worth while I was anchoring at Channel 5. Yipes, the years fly by, don't they?

Rodger Meier, Sr.—To some people, Rodger may be only the name on the back of a Cadillac. But to people who know Dallas, what makes it tick and who pulls the strings, Rodger is the man in charge. I am surprised that at some point during his distinguished and noteworthy civic career he didn't change his name to Dallas. He has always cared so much for the city and its citizens—if you look up the expression "Pillar of the Community" in the dictionary, you're likely to find his picture.

Mike Miler—Mike has worked hard and diligently to help Circle Ten Boy Scouts across North Texas form a successful blueprint for life.

John Miller—An outstanding example of the second generation of broadcast journalists—high standards and no excuses. He is also quiet and thoughtful, and right about broadcast decisions 99.9 percent of the time. He's a journalist of many skills who started at Channel 5, and, as news director at WFAA-TV Channel 8, today, he continues to set the goals and the high standards Channel 8 demands.

Ray Miller—The unexpected generosity of some people never ceases to amaze me. After I had gone through an especially debilitating operation, I got a call out of the blue from a man I had never met. It was Dallas entrepreneur and millionaire Ray Miller on the line. He was offering me a stay on his yacht based in Freeport, the Bahamas, as part of my rehabilitation. This 110-foot ship would sleep 20 people. It didn't take long to respond with a yes! The sun, fishing and being allowed to bring my parents, brothers and family on board was truly a once-in-a-lifetime experience.

Terri Buchanan Miller—When I returned from Europe in 1964 and started my senior year at Richfield High School in Waco, this tall, attractive brunette caught my eye and captured my heart. I was glad to be of some comfort that year when her father passed away. Terri went on to become a Tyler Junior College Apache Belle, and for some reason fell in love with someone else. But, the strength she showed through her father's illness has always impressed me, and we still share a very special, close bond.

Megan Mills—Megan's mom said she was sunshine. This little girl was not only that to me, but, as a brave young cancer victim who didn't make it to her tenth birthday, she was also my inspiration.

Mike Moncrief—He's a community leader who never allowed his family fortune to spoil his sense of values. Mike has worked hard to serve the community at large, especially those less-fortunate. He's a heck of a nice guy and a dedicated state senator.

Christy Montgomery—A dedicated employee who cheerfully keeps track of each and every piece of videotape that airs on Channel 8. Despite a debilitating disease, she has a cheerful smile, bright eyes, and a devotion to doing her job the best way possible—that sets her at the top of her contemporaries.

Kelly Moody—My younger brother, who has become quite a successful professional artist in Columbus, Ohio. He teaches French at a private boys school, and has coached state-ranked soccer teams. He composes songs, sings them, and plays the guitar—a wonderfully creative and talented individual.

Bruce Moody—My youngest brother, who is now taller than me! He's an up-and-coming architect in Columbus, Ohio, and has a real gift for playing the guitar and singing. He's also the doting father of two young boys. I think Bruce has somehow gotten the very best qualities of all his brothers and sister.

Paul and Marilyn Mortensen—Paul speaks seven languages but none better than the language of true friendship. As a former airline executive, Paul has been around the world more times than most of us have even boarded a plane. Marilyn somehow keeps up with him and always has a hug and a smile.

Scott Murray—Talk about energy, community service, and goodwill, not to mention a heck of a sportscaster at Channel 5, that's Scott. He finds true enjoyment giving of his time and talents to a host of charity endeavors all year round. He's a genuinely nice and caring guy with a real smile and a real heart.

Bruce Neal—The longtime public relations director at Six Flags Over Texas, Bruce has been a friend of more than 25 years and a generous sponsor for the Chip Moody Pro-Am. He's been known to call himself the world's greatest PR man, but only after I've identified myself as the world's greatest anchorman!

Giff Nielsen—A former Houston Oiler quarterback who joined Channel 11 in Houston, and began to learn the broadcasting business on the front lines. He's a straight shooter, a delightful person, and more righteous than your grandmother.

Jayne Noble—A bright young writer for *The Dallas Morning News* who cheerfully took on the not-so-easy task of helping me write this book. My thanks to her for a great job.

Lyndon Olsen—Even though a double amputee, Lyndon has always demonstrated humor, compassion, understanding and was an unselfish and meticulous trainer for the Richfield High School athletic teams in Waco. He went on to become State Insurance Commissioner. Two thumbs up to a great individual.

Oliver Omanson—This ordained minister and World War II POW is much like the traveling preacher of long ago: He travels South Dakota conducting Sunday church services for a host of rural churches and their congregations. He's always been there with a smile, laugh, or shoulder to cry on.

George Osborne—He was my high school classmate who showed me the true meaning of a dedicated and gifted athlete. George did it all and did it so very well. He gave up a career in the FBI to be a school teacher and coach. I called him "the Oz" and he definitely earned his star status at Arizona State University.

Arnold Palmer—You'd think that the man who made professional golf the success it is today would carry an ego the size of a Cadillac on his shoulder. But not so. He's a gifted athlete who showed me that to be a real success, you have to put your ego in your back pocket.

Alan Parcell—Newsroom administrator in Dallas and Houston and now with CBS, he's a man with a quiet but strong work ethic. He sets goals, and pushes a department to meet or exceed those goals.

Dick Pearson—He is one of the "young lions" of South Dakota. Few people I know work harder and have more talent for just about any job—be it in the house or on the farm. Dick is a member of a new generation of successful South Dakota businessmen, plus he has a wonderful gift for woodworking.

Drew Pearson—He's a really fun guy who went from walk-on tryout player for the Dallas Cowboys to superstar status on the field and in the community. He's a tireless worker for children and a man with a keen feel for business. He overcame personal tragedy in the death of his brother and rose to the top in Dallas business and social circles.

Boone Powell—When I was first hospitalized at Baylor University Medial Center in Dallas, I was lying in bed in my room and a kindly old gentleman in a cute little electric transport cart wound his way into the room and asked how I was doing. I was pleased to tell him I was improving daily and expected to go home soon. His face broke into a wide grin, and he said that made him happy. I had just met the legendary Boone Powell, Sr., past president and longtime driving force at Baylor. He isn't able to use his little get-around cart as often these days, but his heart is surely wandering each and every hallway.

Boone Powell, Jr.—Boone Jr. has had some mighty big shoes to fill, but he has filled them and has pushed Baylor University Medical Center to prominence on an international scale. Smart as a whip in business, he's never too busy to hold the elevator door for a patient.

Jim and Barbara Pratt—Jim is a shining example of the American entrepreneur, building a small fortune by buying companies in financial difficulties and turning them around. An insightful businessman who has generously supported my various charity fund-raisers. Barb was a huge help on my golf tournament committee in 1994 and 1995. Jim and Barb—don't move away!

Elvis Presley—Never met him.

Charlie Pride—Boy howdy! Talk about a great ambassador of goodwill, not only for the city of Dallas, but for all of Texas and the burgeoning country music industry around the world—that's Charlie. Behind all the talent, Charlie has an unusual gift for astrology. No kidding, nine times out of ten he can walk up to a person and tell them their correct astrological sign. He did it to me after we had talked for only a few minutes. The next time I saw him in person—six or seven years later—his first words were "Hi Chip—Aries, right?" Charlie has a talent the size of Texas and a heart to go with it.

John Pronk—You know the guy at the State Fair who can play eleven instruments at the same time? No, that's not John, but I bet he could do it! John is a one-man band for Channel 8 News, roaming to find the most unusual people and topics in the state. A great guy who shoots, writes, edits, and narrates those priceless "Texas Tales."

Jethro Pugh—Jethro is one of the kindest major athletes anyone could ever hope to know—a big guy with an even bigger heart.

Frank and Marie Putt—If you were to look up the word "gentleman" in the dictionary, you would probably find a picture of Frank. And if I could pick someone to be my uncle, it would be Frank, a successful businessman who loves kids, golf, and enjoying life. Marie is his outgoing wife. Her wisdom and big heart have helped several generations of Putts.

Anthony Quinn—A nifty and talented actor, who showed me that you can have a career, do well, and enjoy yourself all at the same time. An actor whose soul carried over not only to the screen, but to his family and his millions of fans.

Tom Rafferty—Most professional athletes seem to disappear after they have had their day in the spotlight. But this former Dallas Cowboy keeps on giving, and giving with a smile.

Bonnie "Bunny" Mallow Raines—Yes, this was the Queen Cool of the infamous Cool Club in Brussels, Belgium. She captured my eighth-grade heart—the first girl I went steady with. She wore my ring around her neck.

Dan Rather—A prime example of how hard work and determination can pay big dividends. A dogged reporter at KHOU-TV Channel 11 in Houston who went on to an outstanding career at CBS. He once told me, "I hope KHOU-TV is as good to you as it was to me."

Jim Read—Some of us are fortunate to have jobs we really love, and Jim is one of those people. His love has always been flying, and as chief test pilot for LTV, Jim was like a kid in a candy store. No wonder he was always smiling. One rare occasion he let me fly LTV's newest jet trainer, and I was honored that he had the confidence in me to let me fly this prototype. Thanks Jim—it was a great lesson in flying and personal professionalism.

Ann Richards—She put a refreshing and unique stamp on the office of the Governor of Texas. Humor, understanding, drive and a good vision for the Lone Star State made her unique. She gave me a clearer picture of the varied talents and credentials one must have to rule Texas.

Robert Riggs—Talk about investigative reporters! Robert has worked very hard to come up with some superb examples of strong and effective investigative reports—some of which resulted in changes in state law. A terrific journalist.

Norm Robbins, Jr.—Sometimes a bond of friendship can be formed through telephone calls, letters and a sincere respect for the other person's professional achievements. Norm labored long and hard in helping develop and promote the world famous F-16 jet fighter. My charity work for General Dynamics and The United Way paid off in a neat way when Norm offered me the chance to fly what is regarded as the best light-weight jet fighter in the world. I will never forget the thrill of being in control for an hour and twenty minutes, doing every aerobatics maneuver I could possibly execute. My enthusiasm for the flight was second only to his, and only later did I realize he had never even had a chance to take the controls. He always put others before himself.

Tracy Rowlett—Journalist, colleague, friend and confident. Few people in my life have earned the respect I have for Tracy. Some personal tragedies and setbacks he has endured have only enhanced my opinion of this hard-working, talented and award-winning TV broadcaster. The daily challenges are always there, and he meets those in fine form. At the same time, he looks ahead for ways to improve our news product and gives our viewers the very best.

Nolan Ryan—He showed me that you can be one of the most outstanding people in your given profession and at the same time keep your feet on the ground and keep a level head, despite the public acclaim or the riches that accompany your success.

Scott Sams—An unusually smooth TV talent, Scott can really do it all. He's a young man who has cracked me up on more than one occasion.

Dr. William "Bill" Santangelo—Dr. Santangelo is the Baylor physician who has saved my life on several occasions. He is one of the youngest, fully accredited, board certified and internationally recognized gastro-intestinal specialists in the Southwest. I have never failed to be impressed by the long hours he spends at the hospital with his many patients. I think he is trying to set some kind of record. He's a stern and demanding doctor, but one with a sense of humor.

Clara Sayles—You could say that Clara is part of the glue that holds the Channel 8 newsroom together. Soft-spoken, always has a cheery smile, unbelievably organized—you would never know she has fought cancer and continues to battle other serious health problems. Her optimism has been an inspiration to me. She can use my desk to watch the noon soap operas anytime she wants.

Penny Scott—As Channel 8 News Director John Miller's administrative assistant, Penny has an almost incomprehensibly difficult job. She's so organized it's scary. At some point in time, I wouldn't be surprised if Penny ends up running heaven.

Alden and Dolores Skoglund—Think of the American farmer on his John Deere in the middle of a sweeping field of corn stalks and you'll think of Alden, a South Dakota farmer. I can remember back 40 years ago and seeing Dolores separating fresh milk in the little room off their farm's kitchen.

Charles "Chuck" Skoglund—Charles and I were born about the same time and he showed me at an early age how much responsibility a young man on an American farm must shoulder, raising cattle, wheat, corn and soybeans. He's also a heck of a mechanic who helped me rebuild an Austin-Healy engine while in college.

Brad Sham—What a talent in the radio booth! Brad has been, and continues to be, the man who sets the standard in Texas for football play-by-play announcing. And he's doing the same for baseball. He can handle any sport and just about any situation—a broadcaster's broadcaster.

Holly Shannon—As producer of our 10 p.m. "News 8 Update," Holly holds my career in her hands. She is a consummate journalist who is charged with deciding which stories will air on any given night and how much time we will devote to each. She has a wonderfully keen and unbiased eye for what news is important, interesting and critical to our viewers. She makes the tough calls every night of the week.

Mike Shapiro*—The legendary Dallas broadcaster who led WFAA-TV through the Kennedy assassination and into the 1970s. His program "Let Me Speak to the Manager" was a huge rating success and provided a good and interesting public service.

Wayne Shattuck—As nice a guy as you will ever meet. A wonderful talent with a comfortable on-air presence that gave viewers not only the weather, but a reassurance that no matter how bad the weather, it was bound to improve. A close friend and a caring guy.

Charles Simmons—A self-made Texas oilman, Charles, Lyda Hill and I kicked off the hugely successful "A Conversation with a Living Legend" fundraising luncheon series for M.D. Anderson Cancer Center in Houston. There is no rule that a millionaire is required to contribute time and energy to charity, but Charles does so in grand Texas fashion. One of these days he'll cut me in on an oil well...I hope!

Dr. Neal Sklaver—Neal is the man who allowed me a second chance at life by making an early diagnosis of my cancer. He's a true friend whose gift of life to me I can never repay.

Bland Smith—Now, if I were to tell you that the chief test pilot for the F-16 jet fighter built in Fort Worth by General Dynamics and then Lockheed was named Bland Smith, you wouldn't believe me. Well, it may not be a Hollywood name, but Bland is indeed the top F-16 test pilot in these parts. I got the rare opportunity to show off some of my flying skills to him during a flight over West Texas. Bland showed me that being calm, cool and collected and having exceptional piloting skills mean a lot more and go a lot further than a loud voice and hot dog stories at the Officer's Club bar.

Major D.L. Smith*—Leader of the USAF Thunderbirds aerobatics demonstration team, I got the rare opportunity to fly cross-country with the Thunderbirds under the leadership of Major Smith. I remember us at low altitude screaming over Camp Bowie Boulevard, heading north to Carswell Air Force Base at close to 500 m.p.h. What a thrill it was to not only fly with these guys, but to join them in singing Air Force songs at 43,000 feet on our closed circuit radio intercom. Tragically, Major Smith was killed less than a year later when his parachute failed to open after his T-38 jet struck a flock of birds and burst into flames on a take-off from Cleveland.

Steve Smith—A strong and steady TV anchorman at KHOU-TV Channel 11 in Houston, he somehow survived the suicide death of a teenage son, and always demonstrates accuracy and compassion in covering the news.

Steve Smith—As a TV critic for the *Fort Worth Star-Telegram*, Steve is good about asking the right questions of the right people. It is so refreshing to know your quote will be right.

Dave South—A solid radio sports broadcaster at KWTX in Waco in 1968. He recommended I drop my name and go with something more conservative or traditional—like Robert or Bob. I hung in with Chip, and I'm glad I did.

Carol Sprinkle—She's a real live, honest-to-goodness spark plug and organizer who has put in hundreds and hundreds of hours behind the scenes to make the Chip Moody Pro-Am charity golf tournament the continuing success it is. I may get the headlines, but she has been one of the truly important people who have helped raise almost $500,000 for the Children's Cancer Fund of Dallas. She's a true friend.

Archie "L.L." Staccone*—One of the really neat and unique characters I have ever met and worked with in broadcasting. He was a salesman at KWTX-TV and radio in Waco. Archie could charm you right out of your socks...and your shoes...and make you feel good about it.

Roger Staubach—He's a leader and role model, a man who has demonstrated his devotion to family and church. He's an overachiever who is an ambassador of goodwill for Dallas, Texas, and all of the country.

Oliver Stone—Although strangers when he asked me to be in one of his movies, Oliver and I had one of those sudden and unexpected friendships. He provided me with my brush with Hollywood in *Talk Radio* and *Born on the Fourth of July*, and we also shared quite a few laughs and stories away from the movie sets. He's a fun guy who really knows how to make motion pictures. When I told him I thought his Oscar-winning movie *Platoon* needed more intensity, he could only laugh.

Dave Strait—Dave has been bitten by the flying bug. As president of the Sierra Hotel Company (which has nothing to do with hotels), he rebuilds, flies and sells exotic military jet fighters... from Migs to the monstrous F-100 Thunderchief. Dave... you are cleared for takeoff!

Jim Sundberg—He's remembered for his talent behind the plate as a catcher for the Texas Rangers, but what some people don't know is his care and concern for youngsters. One of the nicest guys I have ever met.

Harold Taft*—Truly one of the great broadcasting pioneers, Harold's word on the weather was something akin to a chapter in the Bible. Forty years in the business, he took his job at Channel 5 and WBAP radio more seriously than he took himself. A sweetheart of a man.

Dick Terrell—A retired Xerox executive who has been one of the driving forces behind the Chip Moody Pro-Am golf tournament, raising money for the Children's Cancer Fund of Dallas and the Children's Medical Center foundation. He's a tireless worker who is far more organized than I could ever hope to be ...and a really nice guy to boot.

Margaret Thatcher—She demonstrated to me that standing your ground is a personal and professional attribute that some people fail to recognize. You must believe what you carry in your heart, and be willing to stand up for it to not only be true to yourself, but true to those who know, support, and believe in you.

B. J. Thomas—He's the gospel, country, rock singer who has shown personal courage and strength in overcoming drug abuse. He's an example of how life can be re-gained.

Wayne Thomas—He was one of the key men involved in my move from Channel 5 to Channel 4 in 1980. As the news director at Channel 4 in the late '70s and early '80s, he had the vision to see the value in an anchor team with four distinct and appealing personalities.

Jackie Thornton—A tireless worker who has been an incredible help in my charity work, she has helped with my golf tournaments and celebrity-chef dinners. Thanks Jackie!

Russ Thornton—The person who hired me at Channel 5 WBAP-TV in Dallas-Fort Worth in 1971. As news director, he pushed me to try to improve as a broadcaster, and had faith in me that I would learn and improve as time went on.

Clarice Tinsley—A wonderful personality and good friend who co-anchored with me at Channel 4 and adapted well to her adopted home state of Texas. She brought sparkle and enthusiasm to the station and is a caring and concerned individual.

Bill Tippitt—What a character! A cameraman and photographer at Channel 5 who knows the business, and how to build contacts and get the full story, he's a guy who enjoys his work, fishing and life itself. You would be hard-pressed to find a harder-working TV cameraman.

Jerre Todd—For this man, public relations and Fort Worth go together like strawberries and cream. His silver shock of hair, ruddy complexion and constant smile have represented the Colonial NIT golf tournament and many other events around Fort Worth and Dallas. There's never been a field producer he didn't like.

Frank X. Tolbert*—One of those legendary Texans who helped define what the Lone Star State is really about, Frank was a longtime newspaper columnist who gained widespread fame as a storyteller and perhaps the original Texas "Chili-head." His book *A Bowl of Red* is the story of the legendary Texas dish that was his passion and his love. If you didn't like his chili, why, you might as well go back to New York.

Tom* and Helen Toler—"Big Tom" gave me my first aviation honor by sponsoring me and securing my membership as a colonel in the Confederate Air Force. He died too soon, but died doing the thing he loved (besides flying)—sailing the Caribbean. Helen has always been a dear friend and supporter.

Tom and Donna Toler, Jr.—Tom is now a "four striper" (captain) with American Airlines although he is several years my junior. It was in 1974 that Tom taught me how to fly and opened to me the wonderful world of aviation. He and Donna have stood by me through my life's crises.

John Tower*—Few U.S. senators have been as well spoken as this Texan. Always an impeccable dresser who smoked only a particular brand of cigarette from England. He had a wonderful sense of humor, even if a bit bawdy at times. Texas was well served by this longtime public servant.

Roy and Mary Trout—As founder of Atlas Enterprises Fireworks, Roy is far and away the godfather of Texas pyrotechnics, and has put on 4th of July shows across the country, including in Manhattan's harbor, with the Statue of Liberty as backdrop. Just like me, he's a big kid who never outgrew his love of fireworks. Roy and Mary have donated thousands and thousands of dollars worth of fireworks for my golf tournament, the Children's Cancer Center, and the Children's Medical Foundation.

Royce Trout—As Roy and Mary's son, Royce is doing a bang-up job enriching the Atlas heritage and is not afraid to say "I Love Texas" with multi-colored fireworks. He's my kind of guy (and his

mom's chocolate cake is as glorious as the family's fireworks displays).

Vernon Vest—An audio-visual expert with AT&T in Dallas, he's a young man who has demonstrated to me how some people volunteer their time, talent and energy to good causes with no expectation of reward or public recognition. A super guy.

Doyle Vinson*—He was my day-to-day mentor during my early broadcast years at WBAP-TV and KXAS-TV in Fort Worth. He encouraged me to set new levels of achievement for myself and others.

Falke Wahlstrom*—He was very much like an uncle to me growing up. He was a hired man on my grandfather's farm in South Dakota and, later, helped out on my farm. He showed ingenuity and a steady work ethic through blizzards and all sorts of rough weather.

Lanny Wadkins—One of the most talented stars on the professional golf circuit, but a star who always takes time out of his day to visit with kids, fans, and amateur golfers trying to pick up some tips. A sincerely nice guy who represents Dallas with a smile, a twinkle in his eye, and a firm handshake.

Bob Welch—An award-winning photojournalist, he showed me the importance of getting the facts straight—and conveying those facts to the viewing public. He gave up a network job to work in Dallas-Fort Worth at Channel 5.

Jim Willett—Nobody can really appreciate what a television newsroom assignments editor must do. Jim has always been superb at keeping track of police calls, developing breaking stories and then dispatching crews to cover them. I could not attempt to perform this high-pressure, minute-to-minute job that Jim does day in and day out.

Chuck Williams—As sports director of KWTX-TV in Waco, he showed me a good sense of humor and demonstrated to me the value of "pacing" certain newscast items, and the need to change the pace in any given broadcast to make it more interesting for the viewer.

Dave and Susie Winningham—Dave is one of those Texas "originals" and one of the first sheriffs out at Six Flags Over Texas. A straight-shooting businessman who enjoyed several lines of work and has always looked better having Susie at his side. They're now enjoying life in Granbury.

Greg Wooldridge—The epitome of a US Navy Blue Angel commander. They call him "the Boss," and he led the Blues for a domestic two-year tour, the first Blue Angel tour across Europe, and the first-ever U.S. military flying team demonstration in Moscow. Greg is an individual and a pilot to be emulated.

Jim Wright—I remember it was always so difficult to do a short interview with the honorable U.S. House Speaker Jim Wright. He had a way of talking and answering questions that never gave you, the reporter, a good place to interrupt and ask another question. Jim deservedly rose to the powerful post of U.S. House Speaker and, in my opinion, was somewhat undeservedly chased from office by what most consider a very minor book-selling scandal. Throat cancer has slowed his speech, but his mind is as quick as ever.

Bobbie Wygant—Goodness, I think Bobbie was the original "Entertainment Tonight," Siskel and Ebert, and Leonard Maltin all wrapped up into one person. Bobbie signed on the air at Channel 5 about the same time the station went on the air. She is THE active broadcast pioneer in this market ... and how come she doesn't seem to get any older? She ought to write a book about all the movie stars she has met over the past 50 years —I'd read it.

Chuck Yeager—The first man through the sound barrier and the crusty epitome of a hotshot test pilot, Chuck is engaging to a fault. But he doesn't stop talking long enough for us mere mortals to brag on our own flying. He wears his star as a retired Air Force General with well-deserved pride.

Walt Zwirko—A long-time friend who now knows more about computers and the Channel 8 news computer network (because he created it) than anyone else. A soft-spoken pro who enjoys his job and does it better than anyone else.

And finally, a special thanks to all of the viewers and friends who have written me cards and letters over the years. They have been a tremendous boost to me. Your encouragement and concern has been humbling and overwhelming.